The Strategic Manager

Strategy is something with which managers regularly engage throughout their working lives, yet it is often written and researched as though periodic box-ticking exercises are the only show in town. This textbook provides students and professionals with a solid understanding of the strategic management theories, along with the tools needed to apply them and contribute toward successful organizations.

The author starts from how strategy is realized in the business world and applies the key theories to provide a rounded understanding. Contemporary case studies are provided to help readers visualize the application of strategic thinking. By including the various stakeholders, organizational politics and culture, the author opens a window to the real world of strategic management.

Primarily aimed at postgraduate students and those in executive education, this textbook will also be useful as a handbook for managers looking to get their heads around this easily confused subject.

Harry Sminia is Professor of Strategic Management at the University of Strathclyde, UK.

This refreshing text puts managers and their processes at the heart of strategy theory. It will be interesting for MBA and other strategy students and help them generate effective practical insights into making strategy.

Paula Jarzabkowski, *Professor, Cass Business School, City University London, UK*

This important and useful book examines six different ways of doing strategic management. It focuses on how strategy is actually practiced and provides a repertoire of models and illustrations for engaging in these practices.

Andrew H. Van de Ven, *Professor, Carlson School of Management, University of Minnesota, U.S.A.*

Informed by different theoretical lenses, this is essentially a practical book about how to turn the performance and process logics of strategic management into effective thought and action. As such, *The Strategic Manager* can be a very effective educational tool for the making of strategy.

Andrew M. Pettigrew, *Professor, Saïd Business School, University of Oxford, UK*

The Strategic Manager provides a useful bridge between theory and practice through a range of real-life case studies. This approach is not just helpful for MBA students, but also for any business executive involved in developing and applying growth strategies in a commercial environment.

Kevin Thomas, *CEO, Support Services Division, Babcock International Group plc.*

The Strategic Manager

Harry Sminia

Routledge
Taylor & Francis Group

LONDON AND NEW YORK

First published 2014
by Routledge
2 Park Square, Milton Park, Abingdon, Oxon OX14 4RN

and by Routledge
711 Third Avenue, New York, NY 10017

Routledge is an imprint of the Taylor & Francis Group, an informa business

British Library Cataloguing in Publication Data
A catalogue record for this book is available from the British Library

Library of Congress Cataloging in Publication Data
Sminia, Harry, 1963–
   The strategic manager / Harry Sminia. — First Edition.
      pages cm
   Includes bibliographical references and index.
   1. Strategic planning.   I. Title.
   HD30.28.S5587   2014
   658.4'012—dc23

                                         2014010279

ISBN: 978-1-138-77881-8 (hbk)
ISBN: 978-1-138-77882-5 (pbk)
ISBN: 978-1-315-77163-2 (ebk)

Typeset in Times New Roman
by Keystroke, Station Road, Codsall, Wolverhampton

Contents

Figures

Tables

Illustrations

Strategy practices

Exhibits

Preface

This book has been written out of frustration. I have found what is available in strategic management textbooks to be less and less relevant. Over the years, my teaching had moved away from presenting strategic management as an exercise of strategy formulation and strategy implementation because research into strategy process, strategy-as-practice and my own experiences told me that this is not how strategy gets realized. Despite many firms, organizations and managers devoting considerable time and energy to strategy formulation, the realized strategy at best only partly reflects what had been originally intended. Yet the textbook orthodoxy continues to present it in this overly ordered fashion, with chapters devoted to establishing the firm's objectives, doing an external analysis, doing an internal analysis, formulating a competitive strategy, all to finish with a chapter on how then to implement it. Subsequent editions of some textbooks have grown to contain hundreds of pages but they all follow this basic template.

I was frustrated with this for two reasons: First, this is not how strategy and performance are realized. Instead it only helps to perpetuate this myth that strategic management should be this ordered process and that if you are unable to live up to these expectations, you are doing it wrong. Second, by grouping everything that has to do with the environment in one chapter and everything that has to do with the firm in another chapter, and so on, it prevents students from seeing how these ingredients of strategic thinking can be brought to bear upon each other. Since strategic management established itself as a distinctive management activity and field of study, various different approaches have been put forward, but this is barely recognizable in most of the existing textbooks. The integrity of each distinguishable theoretical approach gets lost. As a consequence, students and managers are not shown how to put an argument together. What tends to happen is that, when a strategic analysis is done, it is nothing more than a collection of separate tools, often without any attempt being made to explain how it all fits together and leads to an overall conclusion. If an attempt is made, the reasoning tends to be disjointed and fragmented. Furthermore, it hides the richness of the field in that different approaches offer different ways in which a firm's situation can be appreciated.

So I found myself in my teaching more and more at odds with what was available in the strategy textbooks. To remedy this, I started to write down what I was lecturing about. And fortunately, Routledge saw sufficient merit to offer me the opportunity to publish. This book takes emergent strategy as its point of departure and fits elements of strategy formulation and implementation within it. In that sense, the strategy textbook orthodoxy is turned on its head. It presents strategic management as a real time and continuous activity. Strategy needs to be the subject of ongoing debate. The world changes continuously. Consequently, a firm's strategic management has to constantly question what is going on and how it affects a firm's performance and future potential to perform. Strategic management requires managers to always be critical and self-reflective about how they go about and understand what is going on. To help achieve this, the book explicitly presents six different strategy theories, emphasizing their dissimilarity to fuel the debate. It is the quality of the debate that I believe is pivotal for whether a firm will remain viable.

This book reflects the experience of over 20 years in the field. During this time, students and colleagues have had to endure my attempts at designing strategy courses and classes that reflect how strategies actually get realized. More specifically, the students at the Sheffield University Management School and lately at the University of Strathclyde Business School have been on the receiving end, as I tried out various versions of this text. Their comments – negative and positive – helped to shape this book into what it is. There have also been numerous colleagues over the years, too many to mention, who I have worked with and from whom I have learned how strategic management can be taught. Frits Haselhoff set me on my way so many years ago and his teaching is still present in what I do now. There are also a number of strategy practitioners who have shared their experience with me. Their insights not only have been invaluable but also have been the inspiration to write this text. Terry Clague, Sinead Waldron and undoubtedly various others at Routledge have been very helpful in getting this book out. Finally, there is one person who deserves a special mention. Monique has been there for me for the best part of my life.

Harry Sminia
Seamill, West Kilbride, Ayrshire, Scotland

1   Strategic management basics

Strategic management is about making a firm or an organization perform and about maintaining the organization's or the firm's ability to perform (Sminia and de Rond 2012). This book explains how to use strategy theory to evaluate whether the firm or organization will be performing, whether the firm or organization will maintain the ability to perform and what a strategist can do about it.

Real time strategic management

Mintzberg (1987), very conveniently, came up with the five Ps of strategy. These Ps refer to the most commonly found definitions or usages of the term 'strategy' within management and organization speak. Strategy very often is seen as a plan: "some sort of consciously intended course of action" (p 11). In some instances, strategy refers to a ploy: "a specific 'manoeuvre' intended to outwit an opponent or competitor" (p 12). Describing what the strategic plan is about, strategy is also seen as a position: "a means of locating an organization in what organization theorists like to call an 'environment'" (p 15). On occasion, the actual content of a plan reflects a particular and favoured way in which the organization's circumstances are interpreted rather than an impartial assessment of the situation. Others have advocated that the way forward should be expressed in terms of a vision. In either case, strategy has taken on the meaning of a perspective: "an ingrained way of perceiving the world" (p 16). Other meanings refer to strategy as a 'Panacea', a solution to everything. To get you out of a problematic situation, you need a strategy. All of these definitions have in common that they look at strategy as just an intention; effectively downplaying the actuality that a strategy should be realized to generate performance.

Practising strategists very often see intentions never being realized. Most of what firms and organizations eventually perform is due to things that have emerged, despite carefully formulated plans, as illustrated in figure 1.1. This book therefore focuses on strategy as a pattern "in a stream of actions" and as "consistency in behaviour, whether or not intended" (Mintzberg 1987: 12; Mintzberg and Waters 1985). The emphasis is less on doing the strategic analysis to formulate a plan or an intended strategy and then implement it. This is a stylized representation of the strategy process – found in many contemporary strategic management textbooks. It has some but limited relevance for the actual practice of strategic management. Instead, the focus is more on realizing strategy and how to understand and manage the process by which this takes place. The starting point is how strategy is being practised. How it actually is being done. It is about creating performance as well as maintaining the ability to perform. In the real world things happen constantly. Realizing performance as well as maintaining the ability to perform can be hampered or enhanced by

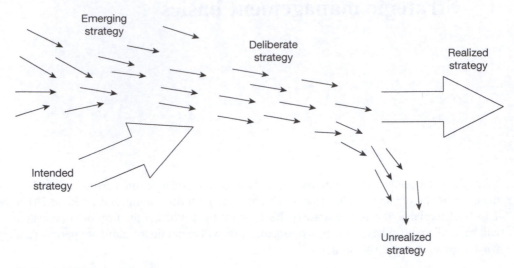

Figure 1.1 The strategy process

Adapted from Mintzberg and Waters (1985)

what emerges all the time. Strategic management requires to be done in a real time fashion. It requires instant evaluation about what is going on and the consequences this might have on the performance and viability of the firm or organization. It requires strategists to do things to move the firm or organization along. You often cannot afford to sit down and carefully write down your strategic plan. This book explains how these instant judgments can be made using currently available strategy theories and what strategists can do to affect the course of the process by which performance is realized.

It does not mean that formulating an intended strategy is meaningless. It means that this should be seen as part of a larger process by which a strategy – as this pattern in a stream of activities – is realized.

The essence of strategy theory

"Nothing is so practical as a good theory" (Lewin 1945, cited in Van de Ven 1989: 486). Strategy theory provides two things. First, it supplies a vocabulary to describe what is going on. Secondly, it offers explanatory logics by which to evaluate what is going on. A vocabulary to describe what is going on is useful because it provides a means to make sense of situations. Making sense of a situation by describing it in terms of a specific strategy theory is the first step in doing a strategic analysis. Strategy scholars have formulated theory to distinguish the wheat from the chaff; to see the wood for the trees; to focus on those things that need focusing on.

Anyone who provides a description of a situation essentially engages in theorizing. Sense is made of a situation by abstracting from all the day-to-day experiences and observations and focusing on those parts that are seen as essential, maybe simplifying it into a short concise statement (Weick 1989). Such a description is an interpretation of a situation and the words chosen to communicate this interpretation are an act of abstraction, focus and simplification. At the outset, anyone's interpretation can be just as valid as anybody else's.

Strategy practice 1.1: What makes a SWOT analysis useful?

The SWOT analysis is arguably the most used and most popular analytical tool in the strategy field (Hodgkinson, Whittington, Johnson and Schwarz 2006). It is meant to provide an assessment of the environment in terms of opportunities and threats as well as an appreciation of the strengths and weaknesses of the firm. Its origin is credited to Albert Humphrey, who devised this 4x4 matrix while working for the Stanford Research Institute in the 1960s. But on its own, it can be very misleading.

The problem is this. By itself there is little indication of when and why something needs to be qualified as a threat or an opportunity, or as a weakness or a strength. Assigning something to either of these categories is purely arbitrary, unless . . .

The 'unless' is where additional theory has to come in. This should be theory allowing for an evaluation of the situation; telling the analyst when something has to be qualified as a threat, opportunity, weakness or strength. It is only with the aid of additional theory that employs a performance logic that a meaningful and sound SWOT analysis can be done. The theoretical approaches featuring in this book can serve as such an additional theory.

Strategy scholars engage in research to find out what theories might be the most worthwhile. These theories allow a strategist to construct an alternative interpretation that is bound to be different from the more intuitive first impression that everybody can come up with. In that way strategy theory provides alternative points of view from what strategists might come up with based on their own instincts and presuppositions.

A description is not an evaluation yet. For this you need a reasoning by which a conclusion can be attached to the described situation. Some – not all – theories allow the strategist to draw conclusions. This is the case when theory not only describes but also explains. Strategy theory is strategy theory because it attempts to explain performance. An explanation of performance indicates how a strategist can intervene in the course of events by which performance is realized. Two explanatory logics are common to all strategy theories. One of these logics is the process logic. It provides a particular take on how firms and organizations function in the wider environment and suggests what strategists can do to affect this. The other logic is the performance logic. It takes firm or organization performance as the dependent variable (that is the variable that needs to be explained) to suggest independent variables that explain this success or failure.

The process logic

A functioning firm or organization is a process. The way in which strategy theories understand this process allows us to distinguish between three process spheres (see Figure 1.2).

The sphere in which all other spheres are embedded is the 'environmental survival process'. This refers to what takes place in the environment. The organization or firm takes part in this sphere to function and survive. In a manner of speaking, you can zoom into the process and focus on this smaller sphere that is the organization itself. The 'organizational strategy process' then comes into view. It is the process within the firm or organization that generates strategic intentions, deals with emerging issues and realizes performance. What happens in this sphere determines how well a firm or organization is capable of dealing with

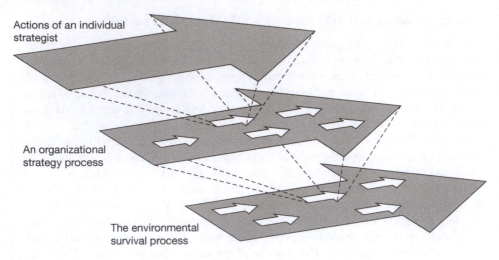

Actions of an individual
strategist

An organizational
strategy process

The environmental
survival process

Figure 1.2 The process logic: three zoom levels

what the environment throws at it. A strategist, in turn, has to function within this organizational strategy process. The 'actions of the individual strategist' refer to the individuals within the firm or organization and more specifically to the things they do. This in turn affects how capable a firm or organization is and whether the firm or organization realizes its potential. Zooming into this third reveals the detailed activities of the individual strategists taking part in the organizational strategy process.

Every strategy theory has a specific take on who these strategists are and what they are expected to do. Ideally, whatever a strategist does, should contribute to an organizational strategy process by which the firm or organization becomes a viable entity that can take part in the environmental survival process. You could say that the process logic refers to the management part in strategic management.

The earliest strategy theorists advocated an organizational strategy process that became known as strategic planning. The first strategy textbook portrayed the strategy process as consisting of two stages (Learned, Christensen, Andrews and Guth 1965). First you formulate a strategy, and then you implement it. This quickly evolved into the idea that an organization should do strategic planning. Strategic planning simply is an organizational procedure that follows this formulation-implementation process logic. It is a framework by which a whole firm can engage in a basic strategic analysis. It is often set out as a carefully managed method by which a firm has to go through a number of successive steps. Ansoff (1965) was probably the first to develop a strategic planning methodology (see Figure 1.3). Many have followed in his footsteps, the vast majority of strategy textbooks are written around it and they all incorporate the same basic template.

It starts with top management deciding on a set of broad goals or objectives for the firm. These are cast in terms of the kind of business the firm is in and explicate which performance levels are expected. This is followed by an internal appraisal and an external appraisal – others would refer to this as the internal analysis and the external analysis. These appraisals intend to assess what the firm is capable of and what the environment looks like. Findings in one step will inform the other two. For instance, the business definition can be derived from the markets the firm intends to operate in. All this information feeds into

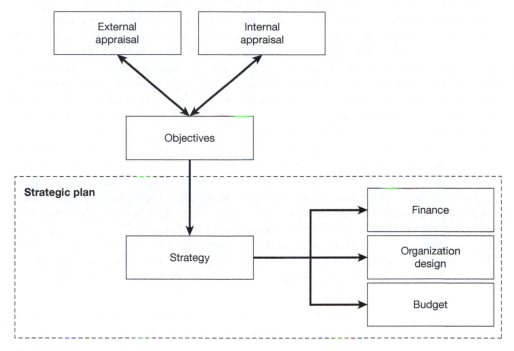

Figure 1.3 Strategic planning
Derived from Ansoff (1965)

a strategic plan. The plan is formulated by stating what strategy the firm is going to pursue. It is also supposed to contain detailed statements about how resources will be allocated – normally by deciding on budgets, how the execution of the plan will be financed and how everything will be organized. As soon as this is decided upon, it needs to be communicated to those who have to implement it. Many firms do this regularly. Larger firms tend to have departments devoted to generate such a plan on an annual basis.

Strategic planning has its uses but its universal applicability is heavily disputed. For instance, Mintzberg and Ansoff entered into an intense debate about whether strategic planning has anything to do with strategic management at all (Ansoff 1991, 1994; Mintzberg 1990, 1991, 1994a, 1994b). As can be expected, Ansoff sees it as the cornerstone of strategic management. To Mintzberg, strategic planning is an oxymoron – a term that denies itself – because the flexibility inherent in strategy as dealing with an unknown future contradicts with the inflexibility of mapping the future out in a plan. This book sides more with Mintzberg than with Ansoff. Strategic planning has its uses but its limitations need to be acknowledged as well. The real time nature of strategic management means that more often than not, a firm or organization cannot afford the luxury of limiting its strategic management to going through an extensive strategic planning procedure.

Nevertheless, the expectation that strategic management should incorporate rational decision-making remains. Many strategy theories are based on this notion. Consequently, these theories portray the strategist as a rational decision-maker. A strategist is seen as an information processor. The strategy theories that are built around rational decision-making are predominantly derived from economics (e.g. Barney 1991; Porter 1980). These specific strategy theories aim to explain firm performance. The explanations provide a means to assess situations and to rationally pick a strategy that promises to yield the best results.

Some strategy theorists investigated how strategies are actually realized and they drew a different picture (e.g. Johnson 1987; Pettigrew 1985; Quinn 1980; Sminia 1994). They overwhelmingly came across organizational strategy processes featuring continuous negotiating, people exercising power and struggles with the prevailing organizational culture. Instead of taking their cue from economics, their strategy theories are derived from sociology and psychology. They put question marks with the strategist as a rational decision-maker and emphasize other qualities that the strategist should have.

Albeit, all strategy theories – explicitly or implicitly – share this basic idea that strategic management is the one process in which you can zoom in and out of these three process spheres. They all incorporate a specific take on how a firm or organization survives and is successful in the environment, how the strategy process inside the organization takes place and what contributions an individual strategist makes. There are differences, however, with regard to how they think these process spheres are to be understood. This we can use to our advantage because the different takes on the same phenomenon provide us with a much more sophisticated understanding of what is going on. This book presents six different theoretical approaches that all understand the strategy process in their own specific way.

Illustration 1.1: Honda's deliberate or emergent strategy?

In the early 1970s, the then British Government commissioned strategy consultants BCG to write a report on the British motorcycling industry. It pinpointed the various reasons why a group of once proud and world leading motorcycle manufacturers had gone into decline. The authors put particular emphasis on Honda and the way in which they conquered the US market at the expense of the British. "The basic philosophy of the Japanese manufacturers is that high volumes per model provide the potential for high productivity as a result of using capital intensive and highly automated techniques" (BCG report quoted in Pascale 1984). It reveals how the consultants' account focuses on explaining the Japanese mechanism of success. This mechanism allows you to become very efficient and simultaneously to drown out the competition and become the market leader. Of course this does require a considerable investment up front in these 'capital intensive and highly automated techniques'. But if you have the money and the patience, this is how you do it. The report and subsequent cases used for teaching strategic management in many of the leading business schools in the world assumed that this was Honda's intended strategy. It was assumed that the people at Honda had worked this out and that they had been implementing this recipe for success.

Pascale (1984) went after the Honda executives concerned and asked them how they did it. They came with a completely different story. Their inroad in the US started in 1958. They went on a reconnaissance mission and found out several things about the US motorcycle market. People in the US drive big cars. Motorcycles are bought by a small leather clad subset of the US population. They are bought from a total of 3000 dealers who were motorcycle enthusiasts first and business people second. Annual unit sales were 450,000, with 60,000 imported from Europe. On that basis, they decided without much analysis that it would be reasonable to go after 10 per cent of the imported cycles. To compete with the Europeans, Honda would have to offer the 250cc and 350cc models.

They came back in 1959 but started only small and set up base in Southern California. Because of all kind of restrictions imposed by the Japanese government, they could only bring a limited number of cycles with them. They were able to convince 40 dealers to stock Hondas and registered a few sales. Almost immediately disaster struck and many of the bikes were returned leaking oil and with failed clutches. Apparently motorcyclists in the US ride their bikes much further and faster than in Japan. While Honda technicians were frantically trying to resolve this, they were contacted by a Sears buyer. He had noticed the small 50cc Honda Supercubs they had been riding around on in Los Angeles to do errands. The Honda people had brought a few with them but had not attempted to offer them for sale. They reckoned there would not be a market for them in the US, where everything was big and powerful. They first turned down the Sears buyer's requests. What would a 50cc moped do for the Honda brand while the market was in big bikes for macho motorcyclists? But with the big bikes breaking down and in desperation, they gave in. To their astonishment, there was a demand for motorcycles, not through motorcycle dealers but through sporting goods retailers. This gave them their first foothold.

Honda subsequently moved the US motorcycle market away from the macho 'black leather jacket' customer on the back of the 'You Meet the Nicest People on a Honda' advertising campaign. The most junior Honda executive in the US pushed this through at the time, against the wishes of his superiors. Motorcycles became more of a leisure item and less of a mode of transport. By 1964, Honda's market share in the US in lightweight motorcycles was 63 per cent, compared with 4 per cent for Harley-Davison and 11 per cent for British manufacturers (as cited from a teaching case by Pascale 1984).

So if such a successful outcome is a matter of events that emerge and just happen, even against the initial judgment of those who were part of this process, what is the use of intended strategy? In a debate between four strategy scholars, Henry Mintzberg used the Honda case to make his point that strategic planning does more harm than good (Mintzberg, Pascale, Goold and Rumelt 1996). Instead, strategic management should embrace emergence and the process should be one of trial and error; of learning while you go along. Michael Goold (who was one of the authors of the BCG report and by then had moved on to become an academic at Ashridge Management Centre) argued there was still a place for planning, analysis and rational decision-making. To him, learning and emergent strategy do not preclude the possibility that there are explanations of firm performance like the one cited from the BCG report above. His point is that such insights are worthwhile considering if you are interested in advising top management what to do (for a more extensive discussion also see Mair 1999).

The performance logic

The performance logic refers to the strategy part in strategic management. It underpins all considerations with regard to strategy content. As was indicated earlier, an important part of strategy research tries to establish and validate what explains performance. Once you know about what can explain success or failure of an organization or firm, you can describe the situation that you want to analyse in terms of this particular theory. Depending on your findings with regard to the state of the independent variables explaining performance, you

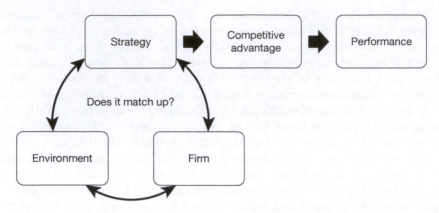

Figure 1.4 Performance logic for business firms in particular

can draw conclusions with regard to whether the firm or organization is destined for failure or success.

Most strategy theories are derived from economics. The most common explanation of success amongst strategy theorists is therefore competitive advantage (see Figure 1.4). To many strategy scholars, competitiveness is at the heart of strategy content (Porter 1980; Rumelt, Schendel and Teece 1994). Competitive advantage means that the firm is somehow better than its competitors. The majority of strategy theory tends to focus on the business firm and assesses performance in terms of one or more financial parameters. The assumption is that firms have to compete to remain viable and survive. The purpose of the firm is seen as generating a profit. In short, firm performance tends to be about the ability to outperform the competition.

Competitive advantage, in turn, is seen to be the consequence of the three main ingredients of strategic thinking. These three ingredients are: the environment, the firm and the strategy the firm pursues. Furthermore, these three ingredients need to match up in some way for the firm to be competitive and successful. Yet it is with regard to these three ingredients that, again, there are profound differences between the various strategy theories currently in existence. This book will provide an in-depth look at four theoretical approaches developed to explain firm performance through competitive advantage. They are 'marketing inspired strategic thinking', the 'industrial organization approach', the 'resource-based view' and 'agency theory and shareholder value'. These four approaches share a performance logic centring on competitive advantage. They differ with regard to how they describe the environment, the firm itself and the strategies the firm can pursue.

It is difficult to deny that strategy theory is somewhat biased towards the business firm. There is, however, some strategy theory that has relevance for both business firms as well as non-profit and public sector organizations. Many organizations are less bothered about competition but need to be concerned about their performance and about their continued ability to perform. Two of these theoretical approaches will be featured in this book. They are the 'stakeholder approach' and 'institutional theory'. Both approaches also have their specific take on the environment, the organization itself, and the strategies the organization can pursue. Instead of centring on competitive advantage, these two approaches focus on legitimacy as the explanation of performance (see Figure 1.5). An organization's activities are legitimate if these activities are considered to be desirable, proper and appropriate within

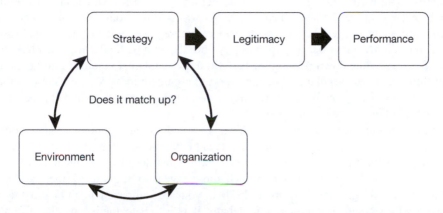

Figure 1.5 Performance logic for organizations in general

a system of norms, values, beliefs and definitions of the situation (Suchman 1995). These two approaches also allow for a description of performance in other terms than merely financial parameters.

This does not necessarily mean that strategy theory centred on competitive advantage is useless for non-profit and public organizations. There are many occasions where these organizations find themselves competing for something. Most of the time, this is about securing scarce funds and resources. In these instances, the more business-like theories centring on competitive advantage are useful.

Each one of the six theoretical approaches provides a means to evaluate situations instantly, which is a requirement for real time strategic management. Yet the way they reason can lead to conclusions that are profoundly different from each other.

Strategic management as continuous debate

There are very few certainties in strategic management. One of the few is that there will never be a definitive answer or an infallible judgment on a situation. There are a couple of reasons for this. The first obvious one is that different strategy theories will provide different

---

Strategy practice 1.2: How useful is a PEST analysis?

Almost every strategy textbook features the PEST analysis. It is normally the first thing in the chapter on the environment. Many management and business students never seem to progress beyond the PEST analysis. The assignments that they hand in tend to devote many pages to filling out this analytical tool. This is a shame because a PEST analysis has a very limited usefulness. It provides nothing more than a categorization. It tells a strategist to look at the environment and to decide whether something that is observed can be labelled as political, economic, social or technological. That is it. It does not tell the strategist anything beyond that. It does not give any indication of what to do or what is implied if something has been categorized as political, economic, social or technological. No further conclusions of any significance can be drawn. How useful is that?

conclusions about a situation. There is no way definitely to assess which one will be the better one. This is inherent in what theory does. As was said previously, its advantage is in abstracting, focusing and getting to the essence of a situation, to be able to draw a conclusion. This is also its disadvantage because each theory does this in a particular way, emphasizing one set of aspects while down-playing the rest. Strategy scholars do their best to get at the relevant things and each scholar has an equally valid argument to back up the choices they make in their abstracting and focusing. Yet they have to make assumptions and consequently they reason in different ways.

These assumptions are necessary to provide a basis under their arguments. The nature of these assumptions is such that their validity cannot be investigated nor tested because they touch upon the very nature of empirical reality (ontology), upon what constitutes knowledge (epistemology), and upon how such knowledge is to be gathered (methodology) (see Burrell and Morgan 1979; Morgan 1980 if you are interested in this). So this is one reason why strategy is a continuous debate. It is a debate fuelled by the different assumptions underlying the various theoretical approaches. The final chapter will come back to this to provide a little more insight how the various theories compare.

Another reason is that the world moves on. Things happen all the time and this urges the strategist to constantly re-assess the situation. In fact, firms and organizations failing to see change as a permanent fixture of their existence will find that they are eventually overtaken by the course of events. This often leads to the demise of the firm or organization (Johnson 1987; Pettigrew and Whipp 1991). This is another scarce certainty of strategic management: there will always be change. It means that there is a constant need to revisit previous conclusions in the light of changing circumstances.

Firms and organizations and their top management do not like to appear to be continuously reassessing their strategy. Yet this questioning and inherent doubt tends to define the nature of the managerial job (Mintzberg 1973; Watson 1994). The chapter on institutional theory will explain that there is an expectation in society for firms and organizations to have a strategy or at least some idea of why they exist and where they are going, not because it is necessarily useful but because it is seen as right and proper (DiMaggio and Powell 1983; Meyer and Rowan 1977). Their top management teams are expected to be all knowing, rational and in control, even if experience tells them that this is impossible. For that reason, the official line of many firms and organizations is that they have decided on a strategy – about which they are in no doubt and which they are implementing without fail. Portraying themselves in that way is part of the requirement of legitimacy. Nevertheless, the actual experience at the top often does not reflect this ideal. On the contrary, those firms and organizations trying to live up to these expectations and organizing their strategic management for rationality and control often end up stifling the debate and lose touch with many things that are going on (Johnson 1988; Pettigrew 1985). Real time strategic management recognizes this continuous debate as part and parcel of life at the top.

If you are cynically inclined, you may argue that not being able to provide definitive answers and questioning and debating everything makes strategic management a pretty useless affair. If you are unable to draw definitive conclusions, why bother? The counter argument is that any assessment of the situation and its conclusions provide an educated guess that is preferable over sheer ignorance. There is merit in being informed by analysis and in debating partial and temporary truths. This is preferable to not knowing anything at all. Utilization of strategy theory will enhance the quality of the debate. Helping to improve the quality of the debate is the primary purpose of this book.

Doing real time strategic management

So how do you do it? There are two types of activities that a strategist should to be able to do. A strategist should be able to act and make such contributions to the organizational strategy process that the firm or organization is able to function in the wider environmental survival process. And a strategist should be able to think and assess the situation so that the actions are well considered and have a chance of making the necessary contributions. This can be summed up as being able to answer two basic questions.

1 Are there any issues that might affect the future success and survival of the firm or organization?
2 If there are, what can you do about them?

Answering question 1: strategic analysis

Strategic thinking is about analysis. It is about answering the first question. Here the performance logic comes in. And to utilize this performance logic, two ingredients should be combined. One ingredient is the strategy theory and the basic explanation of performance that it offers. The other ingredient is the empirical evidence – or data/information – about the firm or organization and the situation it is in. A strategic analysis needs to start with the theory and then bring in empirical evidence to describe the situation in terms of the theory. More specifically, the theory is used to generate specific questions so that data can be gathered to answer them.

Strategic analysis is not a matter of following a small number of easy steps, which automatically leads to a conclusion. It is more of a puzzle and its solution depends on the pieces that are available. Yet to do it in real time for a firm or organization that you are responsible for, you should already know about the environment the firm or organization is operating in, you should know about the firm or organization itself and you should know about the strategy the firm or organization is trying to pursue. You should be able to describe the situation you are in, in terms of the performance logics of the various available theoretical approaches. Every firm or organization effectively has a strategy, whether it is articulated and consistent or not. There is an environment. The firm or organization is what it is. If you do not know about this, you cannot do real time strategic management.

Real time strategic management is about dealing with a situation when it happens, or when you become aware that something might happen, or when you are wondering what will happen if you embark upon some initiative yourself. You basically try to assess how any of this will affect the firm's competitive advantage or the organization's legitimacy. Answering question 1 above is actually answering the very basic question whether the match between the strategy, the organization/firm, and the environment is or will be affected. If you find this is the case, there is an issue. Strategic analysis is about asking questions and this is the question to start with. If you know nothing about these three basic ingredients and whether they currently match up or not, it is impossible to think about how issues might affect its future success, let alone doing something about them. If you know nothing, you need to get up to speed first.

Getting up to speed

You get up to speed when you become knowledgeable about the firm's or organization's environment, the firm or organization itself and the strategy it is trying to pursue. Explaining how to do this at this stage will probably appear rather abstract, dull and meaningless. It will become much clearer further down the line when this is explained again in the context of a particular theoretical approach.

As was said above, a theory provides two things: a vocabulary to describe the situation, and an explanatory logic that allows the strategist to evaluate the situation and draw a conclusion. At this stage, the explanatory logic to work with would be the performance logic. The theoretical vocabulary – the specific words, constructs and variables that are part of the theory – indicate what questions there are to ask. Taking your cue from these questions, you can then look for data or empirical evidence to provide answers. In this way you end up with a description of the situation for the investigated firm or organization in these specific theoretical terms. Each theory defines and describes the environment, the firm or organization, and the strategies in a very specific way.

You can then draw your conclusion by answering the question whether the three ingredients of firm/organization, environment, and strategy match up. If they do, everything is fine (for the moment). If they do not, you have got an issue and something should be done about it. It is simply a matter of finding out how the firm or organization fares in terms of a particular theory.

Such a very basic analysis can be the purpose of periodic strategy workshops or strategy evaluation exercises a top management team may engage in. This also covers much of the work of strategy consultants as they are often commissioned to help firms or organizations to assess the situation. There will always be a problem of insufficient data. Only so much empirical evidence can be made available – even if a consultancy company is hired to do much of the legwork. This makes the puzzle such a challenge: working and drawing relevant conclusions within the existing data limitations.

Going real time: debating strategy

A strategist in charge of a firm or organization is actually supposed to know the situation the firm or organization is in. Managers are supposed to know the extent of the match or mismatch between the environment, the firm or organization, and its strategy. And they are expected to have ideas about how these three elements should be matched up. Simultaneously, the world moves on. The influence of governments and supragovernmental bodies varies over time. Local, regional, national and global economies experience upturns and downturns. Societies change. Fashion changes. New technologies are developed and others become obsolete. The availability of natural resources fluctuates. Natural disasters happen. Governments introduce new legislation all the time. And many more things happen and can be expected to happen.

Additionally, all kinds of individuals, organizations and firms take initiatives to develop and change things. The firm or organization itself can become entrepreneurial by developing a new product or service, move into a new market or country, work on new technology, acquire or merge with another firm, or find a new way to do the same thing more effectively and efficiently. Evaluating how this may affect the firm or organization while all this is going on requires real time strategic management. It is also the reason for continuous strategy debate.

The purpose of going real time is to find out whether anything that crosses the path of a focal firm or organization, or any initiative the firm or organization may want to take, affects the competitive advantage or legitimacy of the firm or organization, either positively or negatively. It is about continuously asking the question whether things still match up. Real time strategic management is about debating what is going on, whether it will affect the firm's performance levels and potential to perform, and whether something needs to be done about it. Real time strategic management should find out about possible changes to the three elements, to then trace their effects through possible changes in the way in which these three ingredients match up and affect competitive advantage or legitimacy, and eventually performance. Again, each theoretical approach provides a specific vocabulary to trace changes. It provides the language to formulate questions and find answers. This is what it is all about.

Answering question 2: taking action

Strategic management is also about taking action. Or maybe about doing nothing and letting things develop naturally. Any action in essence is an intervention in a process that is taking place. A strategy will be realized with the associated performance levels, whether a strategist does something or not, as is depicted in figure 1.1. An intervention is necessary if an issue is seen to lead to an unwanted realized strategy, probably with the wrong or too low performance outcomes. There is a 'what' and a 'how' question here. What can you do and how do you do it?

With regard to the 'what' question, the performance logic points the way. Each one of the six strategy theories provides the strategists with a range of options. These options can be found with regard to all three elements. In principle, a strategist can change the firm's or organization's strategy, change things about the firm or organization itself, or can even attempt to change (aspects of) the environment. Yet each one of the theoretical approaches is built on a specific understanding of what these three ingredients look like. Consequently, each approach puts forward particular recommendations to what there is to change, and consequently what options exist and what recommendations can be made. Nevertheless, all options need to be scrutinized with regard to how well they address the issue that has been identified. This is also part of the debate.

The 'how' question should be part of the deliberations as well. This is where the process logic comes into play. How to intervene and create a result depends on what process sphere you are talking about. But all three need to be considered. An intervention in the environmental survival process is about the firm manoeuvring in the world at large. An intervention in the organizational strategy process is about the strategist contributing to the strategy debate and the functioning of the organization or firm. An intervention at the level of the strategist is about you yourself and reflecting on your own thoughts, understandings and actions. Again, each of the six strategy theories has elaborated the strategy process in a particular way. This means that each approach has specific answers to the 'how' question with regard to all three of the process spheres.

Nevertheless, there is one commonality. A process by which a strategy gets realized and by which performance actually is created is nothing more than a sequence of events (Pettigrew 1990; Van de Ven and Poole 1995). This means that any action or contribution made at all three levels adds events to the course of the process (Van de Ven and Sminia 2012). The implication is that any answer to the 'how' question takes on the general form of specifying what events to add to the sequence in the expectation that it changes the course of the process.

Strategy practice 1.3: Can you implement a strategy?

A common understanding in many strategy textbooks and also among many managers is that the 'what' and 'how' questions are a matter of strategy formulation and strategy implementation. You first decide on the 'what' by formulating your strategy. Once that is clear, you implement it and reap the results. But can you expect that there is a fail-safe method out there by which you can execute a strategy? Is it a matter of learning to apply an implementation tool?

Hrebiniak (2006) reports that implementation goes wrong for six reasons. A strategy does not happen when top management fails to overcome resistance, the formulated strategy is too vague, top management is not working according to an implementation guideline or model, there is poor communication, the strategy goes against the existing power structure, or when there is a lack of clarity about authority and responsibility. His remedy is to offer an implementation model that tells top management to derive local objectives from the overall strategy, communicate these to middle managers, accompanied by a clear structure of incentives and controls to make sure that people are doing what they are supposed to do.

Balogun and Johnson (2005) arrive at a different conclusion. They find that different parts of the organization interpret what might be intended as clear strategy, objectives, incentives and controls, in all kind of different ways, depending on how things are understood locally. Nobody at the top of any organization has enough local understanding to 'translate' anything formulated at the top in such a way that everybody everywhere in the organization understands it unequivocally. The local interpretations create their own dynamic and people down in the organization adapt whatever is coming at them in a way that makes sense to them. The unintended outcomes that are thus generated are not necessarily worse than what was intended at the top; they are just different.

Business level strategy and corporate level strategy

For the sake of argument, strategy scholars have invented the notion of the strategic business unit (SBU). Most theories imagine that a business produces one single product or service, which it tries to sell on a specific market. This is also often referred to as a product/market combination. The SBU is the unit of analysis that has to have competitive advantage to perform well. Talking about strategy with regard to the SBU or business level is referred to as either competitive strategy or business level strategy. The focus of any strategy theory dealing with the competitive strategy or business level strategy problem is on finding ways in which the SBU can compete better. How can it outperform the competition?

Most of the time, real firms offer more than one product or service. Strategy scholars then talk about multi-business firms. This is obvious for the large multi-national with a presence in many countries, offering a wide range of products and services, and consisting of various divisions and subsidiaries. It is also often the case for smaller firms, which have branched out over time into adjacent products but are organized along functional lines. The multi-business firm creates an additional strategy problem. By definition, two or more businesses have been put together and are part of one firm but each business has to compete in its own arena. The question then is whether a SBU would be a better competitor as part of the larger organization of which it is part, or on its own? Corporate strategy is about this.

Recognizable here again is the bias in strategy theory toward for-profit businesses, operating in an essentially competitive environment. However, the same distinction can be made for not-for-profit and public sector organizations. These types of organizations provide a specific public service or focus on a particular cause and business level strategy deals with the legitimacy of this public service or particular cause. This is the business level strategy problem. Often, non-profit and public sector organizations find themselves engaged with more than one public service or cause. The question then becomes whether this public service is better provided as part of an organization that provides many services or whether this public service would benefit more from a single specialized organization? The same question can be asked with regard to championing a specific cause. Is this better done as part of a multi-cause organization or would a single-cause organization create better results?

Strategy theory will not make much sense without understanding the meaning of the notion of the strategic business unit.

How to work the book?

This book aims to provide the reader with sufficient insight to 'practise' strategic management. One of the 'mantras' of strategic management is that there never is a 'right' answer. However, the expectation of many students is that there is. Most strategy textbooks are put together as if there is a single recipe – predominantly derived from a strategic planning approach – by which you arrive at the appropriate strategy. This book's premise is to emphasize that there are profoundly different ways of doing strategic management, which when applied lead to different answers. The reader is introduced to six different theoretical approaches. Each theoretical approach has its own chapter devoted to it. As was said earlier, these theoretical approaches are marketing-inspired strategic thinking (Chapter 2), the industrial organization approach (Chapter 3), the resource-based view (Chapter 4), agency theory and shareholder value (Chapter 5), the stakeholder approach and organizational politics (Chapter 6) and institutional theory and organizational culture (Chapter 7). Every chapter explains how an approach can be utilized to draw conclusions whether the firm or organization will perform, whether it will maintain the ability to perform, and what contributions a strategist can make.

Each chapter has the same structure. First, the process logic of the theoretical approach is explained. This is followed by an explanation of the performance logic. Each chapter then has a section devoted to some additional features that come with each particular theoretical approach. These are further elaborations within the same basic argument that either have gained some prominence in the strategy field by themselves or provide a further understanding of what is typical about the approach. Some theories have more of these features than others. By this time, the specific theoretical vocabulary that characterizes this approach has been introduced.

The chapter then moves on and explains how a strategist can apply this approach in a real time fashion. This leads to sets of questions by which a strategic analysis and a strategy debate can be done. The next subsection is on taking action, making use of the process logic of the theoretical approach to discuss the various options that a theoretical approach throws up. A final section draws things together and extends some of the criticisms but also offers some thoughts on how to work with the differences that exist.

This final section on further questions and unresolved issues is maybe the most important when it comes to the strategy debate. It introduces the limitations of each theoretical approach, in a way setting the boundaries around an approach's usability. However, some of these limitations exist because of some very basic assumptions that have to be made. There are two aspects to these basic assumptions. First, these basic assumptions define the nature and type of theoretical approach. They are linked to core philosophical debates that can never be resolved. Secondly, these assumptions apply to all strategists as well. Often involuntarily each individual manager adopts a basic stance and attitude towards management and the world in general in terms of these basic assumptions. These assumptions should be at the heart of any manager's self-reflection.

A short final chapter wraps things up, dwells on some of the similarities and key differences between each strategy theory, and provides some comments on the questions that remain unanswered. Moreover, this final chapter deals with the problem of abundance in strategic management: is there a way to use these many and often contradicting theoretical approaches alongside each other or not?

Every chapter also features little interludes about specific strategic practices, like the ones on PEST analysis and doing a SWOT earlier in this chapter. Strategic practices are ways of doing things that strategists draw on when they do strategic management (Whittington 2006). Some are derived from and therefor specific for a particular theoretical approach.

Illustration 1.2: SKF has a strategic issue

SKF appears to have been confronted by an issue.* One of their larger US-based clients wants to organize a reverse auction. This client has asked its suppliers to bid for its custom, with the lowest bidder getting the order.

SKF is one of the largest manufacturers of ball bearings in the world. Over a 100 years old and originally from Sweden, it now has a worldwide market share of about 20 per cent. It has organized itself into three divisions: industrial, automotive and service. The SKF Service Division serves this US-based client. The Service Division represents one-third of SKF sales. It provides replacement ball bearings and aftermarket services to manufacturing firms that operate machinery that contain ball bearings. A ball bearing is made up of small steel balls that are inserted into a bearing so that one object can rotate within another object. Every piece of machinery that has moving parts typically contains sets of ball bearings. SKF's strategy is based on providing durable solutions. It offers high quality replacements and services but typically charges higher prices. Their argument is that the quality of their hard-wearing ball bearings are worth the extra money because it makes machinery more efficient and reliable. Being asked now to compete on price is not something they are inclined to do. The question, of course, is: what should they do? Should they abandon their strategy and put in their lowest bid possible, or should they step away from it, accept that they will lose a big client but stay true to their strategy?

This issue will be examined in all subsequent chapters, examining the problem and making a recommendation utilizing the language and logic of each of the strategy theories.

* Value Selling at SKF Service, IMD-5-0751, 2009.

Others are less specific but take on particular meaning within a theoretical approach. All strategic practice can be used and abused. Additionally, there are a number of illustrations like the one on SKF above: stories based on real events that aim to make the abstract theoretical terminology more tangible and concrete.

Finally, every chapter ends with a case. The case allows the reader to go through the sets of questions identified earlier in a chapter to effectively interrogate the situation and enter into debate. The information provided in the case description is relatively raw. Part of the exercise is to find out what the case tells us and then to draw and debate conclusions and recommendations.

2   Marketing-inspired strategic thinking

The marketing concept provided a first rationale for doing strategic management. It directed strategists towards seeing the environment as filled with customers whose wants and needs should be fulfilled. They should then design a firm that is capable of pursuing a strategy aimed at fulfilling these wants and needs.

The process logic of marketing-inspired strategic thinking

The marketing concept has not only spawned a distinct management function and the accompanying field of research, it also inspired a particular way of thinking within strategic management. Most of the earliest ideas about strategy and what a firm should do to remain viable have a distinctive marketing flavour. Marketing as a concept is defined by Kotler (1976: 14) as "a management orientation that holds that the key task of the organization is to determine the needs, wants, and values of a target market and to adapt the organization to delivering the desired satisfactions more effectively and efficiently than its competitors". The idea that firms can only be successful if they are able to fulfil customer needs has developed a specific vocabulary as well as process and performance logics to do strategic management with (Biggadike 1981; Hunt and Lambe 2000).

From a marketing point of view, the environment thus consists of customers with wants and needs. These customers are taken to assemble into product markets on the basis of their specific demands. These can then be satisfied by the supply of a product that fulfils these demands. Firms compete with each other to offer goods and services, which customers value enough that they want to buy them. Firms then have to ask the highest price that customers want to pay for them. The environmental survival process, therefore, is understood to be a process of competition in product markets (see Figure 2.1).

To deal effectively with customer wants and needs and to be ahead of the competition, firms are urged to assess what these wants and needs are and formulate a strategy that tells the firm how to fulfil the customer demands. This firm should then be designed in such a way that it is capable of delivering the appropriate goods and services. The strategic management task – in this classic approach – is seen as making planning and execution decisions to secure a highly performing firm (Christensen, Andrews and Bower 1973). The internal strategy process is very much associated with the highest echelons of the firm. Top managers take the strategic decisions and it is up to the people lower down in the hierarchy to act on them. These decisions should be about the firm's goals and objectives in terms of what product markets to serve, as well as the plans to attain them.

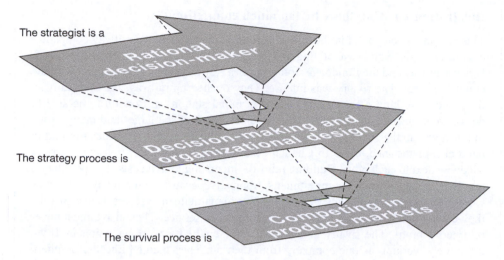

The strategist is a   **Rational decision-maker**

The strategy process is   **Decision-making and organizational design**

The survival process is   **Competing in product markets**

Figure 2.1 The process logic for marketing-inspired strategic thinking

Only after these decisions are taken and a strategy is formulated, can they be implemented. Such implementation, in turn, requires managers to design an organizational structure and procedures that allow the firm to operate in the desired manner, to allocate resources to give people the means to do what they should do, to secure the necessary finances for the firm to function, as well as putting in place a system of management control for top managers to check whether the firm remains on track. Ansoff (1965) developed this into an extensive organizational procedure and labelled this as 'strategic planning'.

From a real time strategic management perspective, extensive planning exercises are less called for. What remains is the expectation that the firm's strategy process is about decision-making and organization design, about gathering and processing information on customers and product markets, and about redesigning organization structures and procedures that allow the firm to deliver on its strategy.

According to this process logic, there are only a limited number of strategists and they are located at the very top of the firm. Top managers take the strategic decisions. Managers lower down in the hierarchy are there to act on them. However, middle managers can become part of strategic decision-making activities when they are asked to provide input or elaborate on operational consequences detailing how the objectives and strategic responses formulated at the top should be implemented. Middle managers are also often asked to report on their progress as part of periodic management control procedures. The strategists at the very top of an organization are expected to process information, weigh various alternative ways forward against each other and choose the one they see as the most appropriate. They are expected to act as rational decision-makers. Once they have made their decisions, they communicate them down into the organization so that middle managers and employees know how they should do their jobs.

To sum up, a strategist's contribution to the eventual success of a firm is processing information in order to make rational strategic choices as part of an organizational process of decision-making and organizational design. The purpose is to compete with other firms by fulfilling customer wants and needs better. If the strategist gets it wrong, according to this process logic, the firm will fail.

Illustration 2.1: Can there be too much competition?

This is some time ago but in the late 19th century, there were two railway companies operating in the Southeast of England (Bagwell 1955). The London, Chatham & Dover Railway and the London & South Eastern Railway connected London with the county of Kent. The rivalry was intense. They opened up railway line after railway line. They also built a succession of new terminal stations in London to be able to deliver passengers ever closer to the city centre. Most of the larger and many of the minor towns in the southeast ended up with two stations with many lines running in parallel. For instance, close to Chatham there were two bridges crossing the river Medway next to each other. Building railways incurs high fixed costs. The population numbers did not warrant the investments. Ironically, because both railway companies were so strapped for cash, they were barely able to maintain themselves. Consequently, they came to be known for their high fares and poor service. They also almost never returned a profit. The rivalry ended when they entered a working union in 1899, effectively working as one company from then on. They merged into the Southern Railway in 1923.

The performance logic of marketing-inspired strategic thinking

To make the right decisions, strategists should understand and utilize the particular performance logic of marketing-inspired strategic thinking. As was said, firm performance ultimately is explained by the extent to which a firm is capable of fulfilling customer wants and needs better than the competition. In other words, product market demand should be matched with the appropriate supply of products (Levitt 1960). Marketing scholars also found that most product markets can be subdivided into market segments on the basis of more subtle differences with regard to what customers expect from a product. Firms consequently have to take this segmentation into account if they want to be successful (Biggadike 1981).

Deciding which product markets or market segments to target is referred to as positioning. This is the way in which strategies tend to be formulated (Biggadike 1981). An example here is strategic positioning as a trade-off (Faulkner and Bowman 1992) (see Figure 2.2). Any strategy here is a compromise between perceived customer value and price. A firm positions itself on a product market by offering a product that has some specific attributes that a customer values, for a price that they expect this customer is actually willing to pay. If a firm offers a simple product that only offers basic value to the customer at a low price, this firm effectively operates a 'no-frills' strategy. A firm employs a differentiation strategy when it offers something more specific and special, and asks the customer to pay a premium price for it. Any firm should avoid offering a product that nobody wants or asking a price that does not match what customers want to pay.

A firm's ability to fulfil customer needs is expressed in terms of key success factors (e.g. Hofer and Schendel 1978) or critical success factors (e.g. Rockart 1979). From a marketing point of view, success factors are those characteristics of the firm that enable it to pursue a competitive strategy in a product market. It is therefore at the heart of competitive advantage. These success factors can be many and potentially refer to every activity that a firm can be engrossed in. A factor is 'key' or 'critical' for firm success when

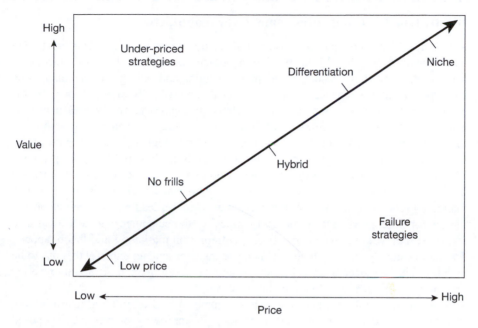

Figure 2.2 Strategic positioning as a trade-off

Derived from Faulknes and Bowman (1992)

it is essential for offering a product with the right customer value at a cost that allows for a sufficiently high margin.

Based on the marketing concept, Abell (1980) argued that a business should be defined in terms of the customer needs that are being satisfied, the customer groups that are served, and the technologies that are utilized to serve these customer groups. This came to be known as the three-dimensional business definition. It also defines a firm's opportunity space in terms of customer wants and needs, and of the specific ways in which these can be met. Furthermore, this model is utilized to assess how competitors compare by finding out which needs and wants they serve and what technologies they use.

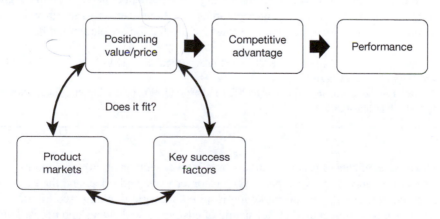

Figure 2.3 Marketing-inspired strategic thinking

Illustration 2.2: Competition among car manufacturers

Allegedly, Henry Ford said 'that you can have any colour, as long as it is black'. He was referring to the Model T, the first car manufactured in large quantities. Since then, car manufacturers have become so adept in designing and selling cars that many now have specific models for each segment they can distinguish. US drivers favour comfort and the cars manufactured for the US market have automatic gears and soft suspensions. European drivers like the frugality of diesel engines and prefer manual gearshifts to the extent that in many countries diesel cars warrant a higher price than petrol cars. Looking at what can be observed on the streets, US car buyers like pick-up trucks, SUVs and MPVs. Chinese buyers prefer saloon cars. Europe favours intermediate hatchbacks, while Brazil is a country for small hatchbacks. Within segments, manufacturers try to distinguish themselves even more, leading to specific success factors for different brands. Some try to appeal to the customer who sees a car as a status symbol, with the manufacturer concentrating on marketing and 'snob' appeal. To other customers, a car is merely a mode of transport and an expense that has to be endured. The key success factor here is less about marketing but more about low price and the most efficient way to build and sell a car.

Segmentation in the market for cars has become so well-established that it is even included in European Union decision-making in approving or rejecting proposed mergers. The document* that indicates approval for the merger between KIA and Hyundai refers to no less than nine segments, referred to them with the letters A to F, S, M and J. For instance, the B segment is small cars, the C segment is medium cars, the D segment is large cars, the M segment is MPVs and the J segment is SUVs. This categorization is commonly used throughout Europe.

A McKinsey** report on the future of the worldwide automotive industry distinguishes between a premium segment (10 per cent of the market, highest prices and margins), a value segment (mid-price and 70 per cent of the market), and an entry segment (least expensive and 20 per cent of the market). They reckon that it will become more difficult to differentiate premium cars from value cars, but that, if this has to happen, it will have to be through car design features. They expect the value segment to become even more competitive and efficiencies through scale are key, with globally operating volume firms having the best chances here. The entry segment is mostly relevant for emerging economies and their rise will fuel growth in this segment. Yet low price and therefore low cost production are paramount here.

* Case No COMP/M.1406 – HYUNDAI/KIA, Regulation (EEC) No 4064/89, Merger procedure (17–03–1999).
** McKinsey & Company 'The road to 2020 and beyond: What's driving the global automotive industry?' (August 2013).

The three elements of product markets (and market segmentation), positioning strategies in terms of a trade-off between perceived customer value and price, and the key or critical success factors, are all part of marketing-inspired strategic thinking (see Figure 2.2). The environment is a product market, consisting of customers with wants and needs. The firm is appreciated in terms of success factors that allow it to satisfy these wants and needs by way of a strategy that can be formulated as a trade-off between perceived customer value and price. Moreover, all three elements should fit together. A firm needs to have success factors that allow it to pursue such a positioning strategy that satisfies customer's wants and needs. If any of these three elements does not contribute to this fit, the firm is in trouble. At the heart of every decision that strategists may make on the basis of marketing-inspired strategic thinking, they need to address this question of 'fit'.

Additional features

Understanding the environment as a 'product market' lies beneath a number of early strategy concepts. This has led to specific rationales that have found their use in strategy formulation. 'Economies of scale', the 'experience curve', the 'product life cycle', the 'Ansoff matrix' and the 'growth-share matrix' deserve a mention.

The concept of 'economies of scale' refers to an insight from the field of microeconomics. It is based on the observation that the cost per unit is related to the production volume. Every production organization has a particular level of production at which it operates at its highest efficiency. This insight is particularly useful for manufacturing plants with enormous fixed costs. These can be spread out over large production volumes so that their relative contribution to the overall costs per unit becomes minimized. Low costs contribute to key success factors in that they allow the firm to compete on price. A strategic lesson derived from this is that a firm, especially when it has high fixed costs, should be the largest producer in a product market. This would make it the most efficient producer, as the competitors very likely use similar production facilities and have high fixed costs as well. Hence the recommendation is that a strategy should aim for market leadership. That is the firm with the largest market share and therefore the largest production volume.

The 'experience curve' is a similar concept. It refers to another apparent insight from microeconomics that the longer a product is in production, the lower the cost per unit will be. In the course of time, firms tend to become more competent in what they are doing. Bruce Henderson, founder of the Boston Consulting Group (BCG), realized that this effect offers possibilities for some strategic reasoning (Henderson 1984). It means that firms that become market leaders will have gained the most experience and therefore will have the lowest costs. The market leader, by definition, has sold and therefore produced the most products. For that reason, it has gone faster down the experience curve and is consequently the most efficient (see Figure 2.4). It is easy to conclude that here too a firm's strategy should be directed at becoming the market leader to be able to outcompete any competitor.

The 'product-life cycle' builds on a more general idea that everything goes through a process of birth, growth, maturity and eventual decline. More specifically this means that a product and its associated product market goes through these phases as well. Each phase should be managed in a specific manner (see Figure 2.5). Theodore Levitt (1965) was first to coin this life cycle idea. It has since gained considerable traction (e.g. Day 1981; Hofer 1975).

The basic suggestion is that every stage creates its own specific form of competition. When a product is first introduced, the situation is very uncertain and it is just a matter of sticking with it in the hope that the product will take off. The growth stage is expected to be a race for market share – cue the experience curve and economies of scale – with the market leader emerging as the winner. This phase also creates opportunities for differentiation, as both the product as well as customer demand tend to become more sophisticated. During the maturity phase, everything settles down and the competition moves to price, facilitated by decreasing cost bases of those few firms who have established themselves as the largest

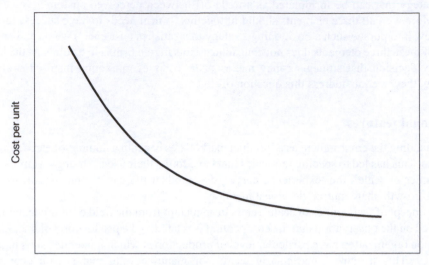

Figure 2.4 The experience curve

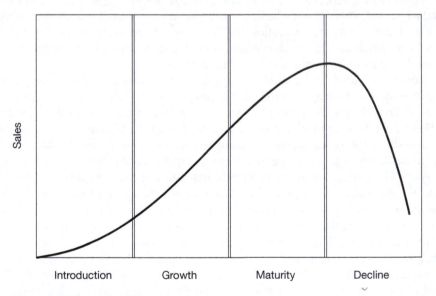

Figure 2.5 The product life cycle

players. This also tends to open up possibilities for niche players who can serve segments that the big players find difficult to satisfy. The eventual decline means the end for most firms (unless they have developed a new product and can take part in another life cycle) with a few who are able to hang on serving limited demand that may continue to exist

Apart from thinking about how to compete in a product market, marketing-inspired strategic thinking also leads to a vocabulary to describe the various ways in which a firm can develop itself either within a specific product market or across a range of product markets.

Igor Ansoff (1965) came up with the 'Ansoff matrix', summarizing the ways in which a firm can seek to grow its business in terms of just four growth vectors. Market penetration means that a firm seeks to gain market share with its existing product in the product market it already serves. Market development means that it takes its existing product to a new product market to create additional turnover. Product development means that the firm creates a new product for the market it already serves to grow in that way. Diversification means that the firm branches out by creating a new product for a new market. These four growth vectors are purely descriptive and do not indicate by themselves what the most sensible course of action would be.

Corporate strategy and the multi-business firm

These growth vectors suggest as well that firms can end up serving more than one product market. If this is the case, we are talking about a multi-business firm. It means that the strategic management of this firm not only has to deal with the business level or competitive strategy question of how it is going to compete in every single product market. The multi-business firm also has to think about how it is going to be able to keep it all together. The corporate strategy question needs to be answered too. Does keeping all of these businesses together in one firm make each separate business a better competitor or are they getting in each other's way?

From a marketing perspective, there are two ways to justify the multi-business firm. One way refers to sharing; the other way makes use of portfolio thinking. A multi-business firm is justified when some sharing is taking place allowing for lower costs or for utilizing the same success factors to serve more than one market. Ansoff (1965) labelled the advantages that come with sharing as synergy. Making two different products, each for its own distinct product market, in the same production facility can create synergy, if it contributes to economies of scale or experience, or if the second product utilizes spare capacity. Similarly, using existing marketing channels for additional products can also create synergy. It spreads fixed costs over additional volumes. However, it will create extra coordination costs.

Portfolio thinking imagines the multi-business firm as a portfolio of activities. The most famous portfolio based theoretical tool is the BCG 'growth share matrix' (Henderson, 1984). These tools follow a similar logic of categorizing business on the basis of various marketing-based variables to make an assessment of the portfolio as a whole. The BCG 'growth share matrix' uses two variables – market growth and relative market share – to characterize each business in a multi business firm as a 'question mark', a 'star', a 'cash cow' or a 'dog' (see Figure 2.6).

There are suggestions at competitive strategy level with regard to treating each one of these types of businesses differently. Yet its most important usage is at the corporate strategy level. What you are looking for is balance in the portfolio. You want that each type of business is represented, especially when you take the product life cycle into account (Barksdale and Harris 1982). Every business is expected to go through this cycle, effectively starting as a 'question mark' to subsequently develop into a 'star', a 'cash cow', and finally ending up as a 'dog'. You need the cash cows to generate the money that you require to grow the market for a question mark and to increase market share for a star. A dog can be maintained as long as it generates cash and helps to prop up the stars and question marks. An unbalanced portfolio will mean that this little motor of successive businesses eventually will stall.

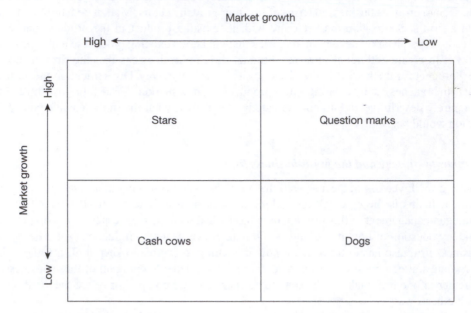

Figure 2.6 The BCG matrix
Derived from Henderson (1984)

Illustration 2.3: IKEA in Sweden, the UK and China

IKEA sells furniture in 37 countries. The firm is often perceived to be a global retailer, offering the same concept – flat-packed furniture at a reasonable price, which the customer has to put together himself – in the same way – big out of town stores where you drive to in your car to get the flat-packed furniture you want out of the warehouse yourself. However, IKEA operates more as a multi-business firm with adaptations to their concept tailored to the demands of different countries. There are differences in the way they operate in Sweden, the UK and China (Burt, Johansson and Thelander 2011).

In all three countries, IKEA operates under the same brand name. Across the world 95 per cent of the product range is the same. This is where synergy can be found. However, in Sweden, IKEA is a mature brand, the company having been founded there in 1958. The typical IKEA customer is a 20–49 years old woman with children, but increasingly the 55+ age group becomes attracted to the stores. IKEA is known for low prices and delivering value for money. Swedes are accustomed to 'do-it-yourself' (DIY) work in and around the house. They have fully accepted that IKEA's low price means that you have to assemble the furniture yourself. Because IKEA is long established and very well known, with almost every Swedish home having a piece of IKEA furniture inside it, it is relaunching itself and trying to make itself new and exciting again.

IKEA has been present in the UK since 1987. The typical UK customer is a 25–45 year old middle-class woman with her family. The British do not mind DIY and are therefore not averse to home assembly. They also realize that the low price point has to come with certain compromises. IKEA markets itself as being different – i.e. not British – to the British customer, as that is what is valued the most about their offerings.

IKEA entered China in 1998. Typical Chinese customers are 25–35 years old. They live in urban environments and typically do not drive a car. IKEA stores therefore tend to be located close to public transport facilities. The Chinese are also alien to DIY. Combined with IKEA's brand perception as an exclusive Western retailer for the Chinese upper middle class, and with a price level that is relatively high for Chinese standards, their way of operating does not naturally fit with the Chinese market. Chinese customers do not understand why you have to put this relatively expensive furniture together yourself. Instead of a low-price furniture retailer, IKEA presents itself more in terms of interior design, offering smart solutions for the relatively small apartments in Chinese cities. On the one hand, they are trying to educate Chinese customers on the merits of self-assembly. On the other hand, in some stores, IKEA has also started to offer a delivery and assembly service that is included in the price.

In terms of the product life cycle, you could argue that, in Sweden, IKEA is edging between maturity and decline. In the UK, IKEA has matured, while in China, its offering is maybe on the brink of the growth phase.

Doing marketing-inspired strategic management

From a real time perspective, the question that continuously should be asked is whether there still is a fit between the strategy (in terms of the trade-off between price and value) and product market demand, i.e. the wants and needs of the customers, and whether the firm's success factors are still in place. Anything that happens that disturbs this fit should be qualified as a strategic issue and action should be taken. Therefore, from a marketing point of view, the two questions to ask and answer are:

1   Are there any issues that jeopardize the fit between the product market (market segment) the firm serves, the positioning strategy it realizes and the success factors the firm has?
2   If there are, what can you do about them?

Answering question 1: strategic analysis

The purpose of a strategic analysis is to find out whether something that is happening or which is about to happen will jeopardize the fit. Doing a strategic analysis is about asking the right questions and finding answers. The things that trigger the need to analyse can come from everywhere. There might be something happening in the environment: a move from a competitor, an innovation, new legislation, a takeover threat, an economic upturn or downturn, or something else. The need to do an analysis can also come from internal reasons: the idea to make a competitive move, an innovation the firm is working on, the opportunity to do an acquisition or a merger, or something else. A strategic analysis' purpose is to assess what is going on, to decide whether it warrants an action. To be able to do this, the strategist needs to know about the firm's current success factors, the customer wants and needs, and what strategy the firm is realizing. If this knowledge is lacking, you need to get up to speed first.

Getting up to speed

If for some reason the strategist does not know about the firm's strategy, its success factors, or the customer wants and needs, then the performance logic tells what information should be gathered and how all this information should be evaluated. There is a very specific set of questions to answer. Exhibits 2.1, 2.2 and 2.3 provide the key questions for the external and the internal appraisal, and about the positioning strategy the firm is realizing.

The core question for any marketing-inspired strategic analysis refers to what the relevant product market is. Any answer should be based on customer wants and needs. A very common pitfall is to define the market in terms of a product: the market for product A or service B. The wants and needs that characterize a distinguishable group of customers should be assessed. The market should then be defined in terms of these wants and needs. Another common pitfall is to describe the market or a market segment in terms of customer characteristics or 'demographics': the demand from young people or old people or the market for people who buy groceries at supermarkets. These demographics and characteristics are just indicators for distinct product markets or market segments. They can be used as indicators because they coincide with specific wants and needs. Knowing that someone is old by itself does not tell you what that person's needs and wants are. Knowing that specific wants and needs coincide with the age of the customers that display these wants and needs allows you to describe them on the basis of these or other demographics.

Whether the firm is a multi-business firm or a single business firm should also be considered. The questions in exhibits 2.1, 2.2 and 2.3 refer to the single business firm competing in one market or market segment. It is about competitive strategy. If the firm consists of more than one business, we should think corporate strategy. This means two things. First, the competitive strategy analysis has to be performed for every SBU that can

---

Exhibit 2.1: Marketing-inspired external appraisal questions

- Who are the customers and what wants and needs do they have?
  - This defines the product market the firm wants to serve.
- Are there any market segments in this product market?
  - This tells us what segments there are to target.
- Who are the competitors, what is their strategy, how well are they able to compete?
  - This tells us how we compare.
- What stage in the product life cycle are we in?
  - This tells us to expect market growth or decline and what competition to expect.

Exhibit 2.2: Marketing-inspired internal appraisal questions

- What are the products that we have on offer?
- How are these products produced?
- What is it about the way they are produced that creates products that are valued by our customers?
  - These three questions tell us about our success factors.
- How efficient are we in making our products?
- Is there an experience curve effect?
- Are there economies of scale?
  - These three questions tell us about our margin.

Exhibit 2.3: Marketing-inspired positioning questions

- What are the qualities of our products and service?
- Are these qualities perceived by the customer as providing value?
- At what price level do we offer our products and services for sale?
  - These three questions tell us where we are with the positioning strategy in terms of the trade-off between value and price.

be distinguished. Second, an additional analysis at the level of corporate strategy should be performed as well. This corporate level strategy has to engage with questions with regard to synergy between the SBUs as well as whether there is a balance in the BCG matrix (see Exhibit 2.4).

Exhibit 2.4: Marketing-inspired corporate strategy questions

- Do different SBUs share facilities so that they become better competitors?
- Do different SBUs benefit from economies of scale?
  - These two questions tell us about synergy.
- What is the level of market growth for each SBU?
- What is the market share of each SBU?
- How much cash flow does each SBU generate?
  - These three questions allow us to fill out the BCG matrix and tell us about the balance in the portfolio.

Strategy practice 2.1: A marketing-inspired SWOT analysis

The purpose of a SWOT analysis is to find out about threats and opportunities in the environment and about strengths and weaknesses with regard to the firm. But what makes an opportunity an opportunity, a threat a threat, a strength a strength, and a weakness a weakness? Marketing-inspired strategic thinking may be of help here.

The environment is about product markets. Opportunities are product markets or market segments that are untapped and where the firm's success factors are particular promising for meeting this existing but as yet unsatisfied demand. These success factors obviously represent a firm's strength.

If a competitor can wade in on the firm's market and can do that because it is better equipped to cater for the customers' demands, this obviously is a threat. The apparent not-so-success factors of the focal firm have become a weakness. Anything that can happen to a firm that has an effect with regard to the 'fit' between a firm's success factors, product markets and segments, and positioning strategy, either positively or negatively, can be described as having consequences in terms of the firm's strengths and weaknesses and opportunities and threats in the environment.

At the level of corporate strategy, a similar argument can be developed. However, this has to concentrate on questions of 'synergy' and 'balance' in the portfolio.

Getting up to speed's main purpose is to get ready for a strategic analysis that fuels the strategy debate. However, it does happen that it uncovers issues by itself when a lack of fit, synergy, or balance becomes apparent. This, of course, requires that action have to be taken.

Going real time: debating strategy

For real time marketing-inspired strategic analysis, the strategist should have a comprehensive understanding of the firm's strategic position. On the basis of this, the strategist knows what customers want and need. The strategist knows what product markets and market segments are out there, about the various ways in which customer satisfaction can be created, and whether the firm is able to do this better or worse than the competition. The strategist also knows what strategy the firm is realizing. Also, if this concerns a multi-business firm, the strategist is supposed to know about the synergy that may exist and whether there is balance in the portfolio.

Exhibit 2.5 lists a range of questions by which impending developments can be traced. By searching for answers, the strategist is able to analyse and evaluate whether something that happens may endanger a firm's competitive advantage and associated performance. It does if it threatens to mess up the 'fit' between the strategy, the environment and the firm. This fit can become unstuck in all kinds of ways, depending on what it is that is happening. Or, in corporate strategy terms, the synergy between SBUs or the balance in the portfolio may be threatened.

Exhibit 2.5: Marketing-inspired questions to debate

Competitive strategy:

- Is there change to who the customers are and what wants and needs they have?
- Is there change to how the product market is segmented?
- Is there change to who the competitors are, what their realized strategy is, or how well they are able to compete?
- Has the product life cycle moved on a stage?
- Is there change in what it is about these products and the way they are produced, which is especially valued by our customers?
- Is there change in the price level at which we offer our products for sale?
- Is there change in how efficient we are in making our products?

Does any of this mean that the 'fit' between the chosen strategy, the state of the product market, and the firm's success factors is affected?

Corporate strategy:

- Is there change in the synergy between the SBUs?
- Is there change in the balance in the portfolio?

Does any of this means that the SBUs are better competitors if they operate on their own and not as part of a multi-business firm?

These questions cover changes to the circumstances under which the firm is operating. The strategy debate should concentrate on whether the changes that are happening or could happen are severe enough that it warrants a reaction. If it does not, the firm can continue to function as it currently does. If change could mean that this 'fit' between the strategy, the environment and the firm itself is in danger of disappearing, the firm is about to lose its competitive advantage and is in danger of underperforming. Such an assessment calls for an intervention. Action needs to be taken to pre-empt what will happen and to restore fit. At the corporate strategy level, the debate needs to focus on the questions of synergy and balance in the portfolio. It does not necessarily have to be bad news. Change might also strengthen the fit, the synergy or the balance, adding to the firm's competitive advantage; promising increased performance.

Answering question 2: taking action

Taking action utilizes the process logic (see Figure 2.1). Options need to be considered about 'what' to do and 'how' to do it. The first process sphere to consider is what to change about the way in which the firm competes in the product market(s). At the level of competitive strategy, the options what to do can be derived from all three elements of the firm's strategy, the environment in which it competes and the characteristics of the firm itself. With regard to the strategy, a firm can move up and down the trade-off between price and value and decide to reposition anywhere along it. With regard to the success factors, the decision can be made to develop them further. The firm can be reorganized or redesigned to lower costs or to improve the delivery of the value proposition of the products and services that are on offer. With regard to the environment, the firm can abandon its current product market and

---

Strategy practice 2.2: A marketing-inspired strategy workshop

Top management teams periodically book themselves into a nice retreat over a weekend to discuss how they or the firm are doing. This is an ideal opportunity to do some deliberate strategy debate. Quite often, an external consultant facilitates the workshop. He is asked to design a programme for the workshop and to suggest topics for discussion.

Marketing-inspired strategic thinking is very much suited to inform a consultant about how the workshop may be put together. He can have the management team discuss the product markets that the firm is targeting, what the status of the success factors is and whether the firm's positioning strategy is still suitable. Overall, he can have the top management team spending the weekend evaluating the question of 'fit'. Or, if they are responsible for a multi-business firm, they can focus on the questions of 'synergy' and 'balance' in the portfolio.

Alternatively, the reason why the workshop is organized may be because something alarming has happened recently and the top management team need to put their heads together to think about how to respond. Again, marketing-inspired strategic thinking can inform the content and nature of the discussion. The question of 'fit' and the effect this alarming incident might have can be the focus of the debate. The response should be aimed at restoring fit if this is found to be threatened.

Strategy practice 2.3: Internationalization from a marketing-inspired viewpoint

The idea that the world is globalizing has gained much traction over the last couple of years, which in turn is seen to have had a considerable impact on business. From a marketing-inspired point of view, Levitt (1983) has argued that customer wants and needs are converging around the world. This means that successful firms have to have a 'global' strategy, targeting customers around the world in the same way and benefiting from the economies of scale and the experience curve that comes with being the worldwide market leader. A global firm effectively is a worldwide operating single business.

To Bartlett and Ghoshal (1992) there are at least three more ways of operating strategically across a number of countries. The 'international strategy' is also highly centralized but operates as a multi-business firm. Instead of offering everybody everywhere the same product or service while concentrating on cost efficiency as the key success factor, the aim is to maximize synergy among the various businesses across countries to offer differentiated products or services. The 'multi-national strategy' is a highly decentralized multi-business firm that is highly adaptive to local markets' wants and needs. The 'transnational strategy' is a combination of the last two. The aim is to benefit from synergies while being adaptive to local circumstances.

---

position itself in another market. Yet every option needs to be assessed in terms of its potential to restore fit.

The Ansoff (1965) matrix describes four ways of developing a firm's competitive position (see Figure 2.6). Market penetration means staying in the current market but improving the firm's value proposition to gain market share. If there are economies of scale and the experience curve to benefit from, market leadership is the outcome to aim for. Product development is the other means by which a firm can improve its position in its current market. By concentrating on improving what is on offer, a firm can advance its value proposition in this way. Market development is entering a new market with the current product. This can mean going into markets where the firm's product happens to satisfy a different set of customer wants and needs. It could also mean going into new geographical areas, which includes going abroad to internationalize. Diversification is a combination of entering new markets with newly developed products.

Market development and diversification will change the firm from single business into multi-business. If the firm is already active on a range of product markets and there are issues with synergy or balance in the portfolio, regaining synergy or rebalancing the portfolio is what should be aimed for. Adding or losing business units through mergers, acquisitions and divestments can do this (Schoenberg, 2003). A merger or an acquisition is a way to enter a new market and to diversify. These, together with divestment, can change the shape and the size of a portfolio and can therefore rebalance it. Synergy is also a motive for mergers and acquisitions to take place. A lack of synergy is a reason to divide multi-business firms up into independently operating business units.

In the organizational strategy process sphere, what is supposed to take place is an ordered discussion among the top managers of the firm – maybe with the help of specialized staff members or external consultants – to assess the situation and to weigh the various alternative

---

Strategy practice 2.4: Formulating a strategic business plan using marketing-inspired strategic thinking

There are many occasions when a strategy needs to be formulated from scratch. This is what the early strategy scholars concentrated on and marketing-inspired strategic thinking, which they adopted, is therefore highly suited to do the job. What is advocated is to do an environmental analysis first. Find out about the wants and needs of customers in the market that you want to target. Then pick a strategy in terms of value and price that fits best with market demand. When this choice has been made, the firm needs to be kitted out. List the various activities, technologies, human resource necessities and the financial and capital needs that are required to have the firm up and running and delivering on its competitive strategy. Finally, do the sums. Check if the expected sales volumes and turnover allow for a sufficient margin, bearing in mind the running costs as well as a sufficient return on the initial investment need to be covered. If the sums do not add up, start again or abandon the plan.

---

options. Some have argued that the whole organization should become customer-driven or market-driven, with every decision made aimed at satisfying customer needs (Day 1994). The quality of the strategy process in this approach is primarily determined by the accuracy by which data/information is gathered and scrutinized. The expectation is that the content of the information will tell the decision-makers what the best option is. Individual strategists are assumed to act as rational decision-makers. The strategy debate is expected to take on the form of top managers checking on each other in order to collectively make the right decisions for the firm.

Criticisms and generating further questions

There is an emphasis in marketing-inspired strategic management on analysis and intended strategy at the expense of actually realizing the strategy. The theories and tools aim to help a strategist to formulate a strategy, but tell little about how to realize what is formulated. Consequently, there is a tendency to remain stuck in the formulation phase. The expression of 'paralysis by analysis' (Lenz and Lyles 1985) is one way of criticizing this mode of strategizing.

Realizing a strategy is seen as a matter of strategy implementation. Implementation is a subject that has seen far less interest from marketing-inspired strategy scholars. It is seen as simply executing the plan: a matter for operations management to get on with. When a new plan requires that something about the firm should be changed, another plan should be drawn up by which the reorganization will be accomplished. However, planned organizational change is something that is seen as falling more within the realm of the field of organizational behaviour and therefore not something strategy scholars should be too concerned about.

Furthermore, the notion of rational decision-making as a representation of managerial work has been heavily criticized. The basic thought behind emphasizing decisions as the focus for strategic management is that you have to think before you act. The most prominent result from putting this into practice is that many strategic decisions never get implemented (Kiechel III 1982, 1984). One reason for this to happen is that there is simply too much going on (Mintzberg, Raisinghani and Théorêt 1976). By the time a decision is

Illustration 2.4: SKF from a marketing point of view

Should SKF* compete on price and put in the lowest bid possible to retain a big US-based client, or should they step away and persist with their high-quality strategy?

The US-based client is a customer with wants and needs. Apparently their need is cheap ball bearings. Stepping back, the first thing to consider is what market and market segments there are that can be served with replacement ball bearings and services. The problem suggests that there are at least two segments: one group of customers want reliability and do not mind paying for it. Another segment is less bothered about reliability and does not need over-specified expensive ball bearings. SKF Services* positioning strategy is one of differentiation. SKF targets the high quality segment. To serve these more demanding customers, they not only fabricate high quality bearings, they have also equipped their sales force with a computer-based sales tool with which they can quantify and demonstrate the value that their products bring to the customer. This piece of software allows sales representatives to demonstrate how using more reliable and hard-wearing ball bearings in the long run will save clients money. This combination of marketing ploy and product quality has been SKF's success factor. Their main competitors in the US are American-based Timken, Germany's Schaeffler and Japan's NSK, with respective US market shares of 30 per cent, 8–10 per cent and 5–7 per cent. SKF comes in second with a 12–13 per cent market share. Newer low cost rivals are appearing from Eastern Europe and China. However, SKF is the most capable ball bearing manufacturer. So on the face of it, there is a fit between SKFs success factors, positioning strategy and customer demands. One client moving from one segment to another does not necessarily indicate that SKF needs to change its strategy and take part in the reverse auction. Therefore, there does not seem to be much cause for further debate.

However, there are things to consider and keep an eye on. For instance, what is the relative size of the two market segments? If the high quality segment is relatively small and primarily served by SKF, one big customer's change of mind can have a big impact. If this is just one client changing the nature of its demand or whether there is a larger trend of clients wanting to downgrade would change the conclusion entirely. This refers to possible developments going into the future and indicates the continuous need for reconsideration.

* Value Selling at SKF Service, IMD-5-0751, 2009.

made, so much has happened that it is obsolete before it has had a chance to be acted upon. Or circumstances and planning assumptions have changed since the intention was formulated, prompting all kind of improvisations and work-arounds that never were part of the plan.

Moreover, to see management work primarily as decision-making tends to separate thinking from acting. The thinkers of the firm, doing the decision-making, very often have little contact with the doers or the people who have to implement the plan. Some concluded that it is not decision-making or the decisions that are wrong but that it is strategy implementation that is seen as the enduring problem (Noble 1999; Whipp 2003). Alternatively, decision-making and planning is seen as a 'theoretical exercise' with outcomes that will never work in 'practice'. As was explained earlier, this is bitterly debated among various prominent strategy scholars (Ansoff 1991; Mintzberg 1990, 1991; Mintzberg and others 1996).

Marketing-inspired strategic thinking is not helped either by this approach's static character. The analyses this approach provides basically are snapshots, descriptions of situations at a particular moment in time (Pettigrew, Woodman and Cameron 2001). With a concept like the product life cycle, there is recognition that things change over time; that product markets and the products that are traded on them have a limited life span. Market dynamics are also present in Ansoff's (1965) matrix as firms can develop new products and go after new markets. However, the nature of the change that is incorporated into marketing-inspired strategic thinking is predictable change, including for instance with the product life cycle, or with seasonal fluctuations in demand.

There is, however, little explanation about more fundamental and unpredictable change and how this takes place. What makes that customers change their tastes? At a very basic level, people may have a number of prime needs but how these manifest themselves and translate into ever changing customer preferences, is not covered by marketing-inspired strategic thinking. Marketing-inspired strategic thinking can only start when customer wants and needs are sufficiently clear so that these customers can be asked about their preferences. Only if this is the case can firms start considering ways to satisfy them. The question remains unanswered of what to do in situations where customers are unsure about what they might need or could want. Therefore, there is little on offer with regard to firms taking their destiny into their own hands to proactively be strategic about needs and wants that might or might not develop in the future.

It is important to recognize that this way of doing strategic management comes with very specific basic assumptions about the information that is used to formulate a strategy as well as about the way in which management is supposed to work (Haselhoff 1977; Sminia 1994). The information that informs the analysis and on which strategic decisions are based is expected to correspond to an objectively knowable business reality out there. This business reality is taken to consist of product markets, positioning strategies and success factors. Gathering information is believed to be a matter of probing what is out there. Managers, analysts and consultants process information that they believe is true and right, depending on how well they have done their research.

This assumption of a knowable reality, existing independently of the observer, and about which objective knowledge can be gathered, is heavily debated in the philosophy of science and even within the realm of management and organization theory (e.g. Burreland Morgan 1979; Smircichand Stubbart 1985). This is the objectivism-subjectivism debate. On the face of it, taking an objectivist stance is nothing more than an assumption. Whether such a business reality out there actually exists can never be empirically verified, as the idea that it is verifiable is based on the assumption that there is an objective reality out there. Furthermore, top management is taken to consist of impartial information processors and decision-makers, whose judgments are unclouded by biases and personal preferences. A subjectivist position maintains that information is always biased: that whatever the information is that people work with, it is the result of a very personal and unique interpretation of the situation.

It is also assumed that realizing a strategy is simply a matter of top managers setting things in motion and possessing a definite ability to control what is going on. Is it justified to assume that (top) management ultimately are in control? Do managers always have the power to choose and implement a strategy at their will? Marketing-inspired strategic management takes up position towards the voluntarist end in the voluntarism–determinism debate. Voluntarism assumes humans have agency, i.e. that they are free to choose to do whatever they want and are therefore in control of their own destiny. Determinism assumes that outside influences determine the course of events and that human beings are at the mercy of external circumstances.

The extent to which these basic assumptions are justified should always be questioned. More fundamentally, the assumptions of objectivism and voluntarism, both in terms of an objectively knowable business reality as well as top management as impartial information processors and infallible implementers, on the one hand, are necessary for marketing-inspired strategic thinking to be feasible. On the other hand, these assumptions are just that: beliefs about the nature of business reality that can never be verified. The question can never be answered whether there is such a thing as an objectively knowable business reality out there, which allows impartial managers to make unbiased strategic decisions that are then simply implemented at their will.

Case 2.1 Sharp Electronics

Sharp Corporation forecasted a record US$3.8 billion loss for the trading year ending 31 March 2012. It blamed slumping prices on its Aquos TVs.[1] Sony and Panasonic were also expecting losses because the demand for TVs was diminishing. To Tsunenori Ohmaki, an analyst at Tachibana Securities Co., "it was a surprise Sharp announced such a big downward revision. I'm not sure whether the production cuts announced by the company until summer will be enough". The company announced that it would halve production at its two largest LCD factories. The Sakai plant has a capacity of 72,000 panels a month; the Kameyama plant has a capacity of 100,000 panels. There is some good news in that Apple will start using Sharp panels for their iPads and iPhones, whereas it used Samsung's before.

The company started negotiations with its labour union about a 2 per cent wage cut.[2] In the meantime, LG announced that it was introducing a 55inch flat screen TV in a number of European countries.[3] Steve Durose, Senior Director and Head of Asia-Pacific at Fitch Ratings was quoted in saying "(In the past) if you wanted a top quality TV you had to buy a Sharp, Panasonic or Sony. Those days are gone".

Sharp is a worldwide operating company, headquartered in Osaka, Japan, with product groups in audio-visual and communication equipment, health and environmental equipment, information equipment, LCDs, solar cells and other electronic devices.[4] The audio-visual and communication product group manufactures LCD TVs, Blu-ray disc recorders/players and mobile phones. In this area it is doing R&D in ultra-low-reflection surface treatment technology and super Hi-vision LCD. Net sales for 2012 were US$30,319,136, with a little over half of this being overseas.

In 2011 in the US,[5] competition in TV sets was bringing down price, yet sales volumes increased. Sony had the largest market share, but Samsung and LG were gaining ground. Value brands like Vizio, which is stocked by WalMart and is offered at a 20 per cent

1 *Business Week*, 3 February 2012, http://www.businessweek.com/news/2012-02-03/sharp-forecasts-record-3-8-billion-loss-on-tvs-write-off.html (accessed 17 July 2013).
2 *Market Watch/The Wall Street Journal*, 31 March 2012, http://www.marketwatch.com/story/sharp-proposes-2-wage-cut-to-help-recovery-2012-03-31 (accessed 17 July 2013).
3 Reuters India, 29 April 2012, http://in.reuters.com/article/2012/04/29/asia-tech-tv-idINDEE83S02D20120429 (accessed 17 July 2013).
4 Sharp 2012 Annual Report.
5 Current Trends Shaping the Television Industry, 20 July 2011, http://mashable.com/2011/07/20/consumer-trends-tv/ (accessed 17 July 2013).

lower price, increased their share of the market as well. Bigger screen sizes were the most popular. There is a correlation between disposable income and screen size. Also people under the age of 45 or with children tend to own larger TVs. People buy the biggest size they can afford, indicating that other features are less important. The number of TVs per household does not increase. Consumers are trading up. More and more viewers watch TV while being engaged in other media on their phone/tablet/laptop: checking Facebook, Twitter or surfing the internet. Of US consumers 21 per cent would pay US$100 more for a TV set if it was energy efficient. Almost half of US households have a TV in the bedroom and 18 per cent have a TV in the kitchen. People do not like 3D TV because they cannot be bothered to wear special glasses.[6]

The Indian TV market of 2011 saw 100 per cent growth, especially with regard to flat screens.[7] Sony, Samsung and LG have divided the market up amongst them, with each having more than 20 per cent market share. Smaller players are Videocon and Panasonic.

By 2013, only 32 per cent of US consumers were thinking of replacing their TV.[8] Samsung wants you to upgrade much more often but instead of having to buy a new set, they offer an upgradable TV that has an 'Evolution kit' that can be replaced when the consumer wants it, for less than buying a new TV.[9] These days, thanks to the internet, people do not need television sets to watch TV.[10] The other way round, 'smart' TVs connect to the internet.[11]

McKinsey published a report[12] about smart TVs and the expectation that they will follow smartphones and tablets in terms of popularity. TV manufacturers fight commoditization by introducing new technologies to entice consumers into new purchase cycles. 3D followed HD, which followed flat screens. Now it is the turn of smart TVs. However, there already exist various other devices from game consoles to set-up boxes that allow the consumer to use the TV screen as a computer monitor. Many computers offer the option to connect a TV as well. There are also problems with text input and ways in which the TV interfaces with the user. McKinsey is optimistic and urges manufacturers to develop the 'killer technology' that solves the interface problem.

6 *Business Week*, 3 February 2012, http://www.businessweek.com/news/2012-02-03/sharp-forecasts-record-3-8-billion-loss-on-tvs-write-off.html (accessed 17 July 2013).
7 *EE Herald*, 13 March 2011, http://www.eeherald.com/section/news/nws20110313b3.html (accessed 17 July 2013).
8 *The Atlantic Wire*, 8 January 2013, http://www.theatlanticwire.com/technology/2013/01/ces-2013-tv-news/60702/ (accessed 17 July 2013).
9 *New York Times*, 7 January 2013, http://bits.blogs.nytimes.com/2013/01/07/samsung-wants-to-evolve-your-tv-each-year/ (accessed 17 July 2013).
10 Current Trends Shaping the Television Industry, 20 July 2011, http://mashable.com/2011/07/20/consumer-trends-tv/ (accessed 17 July 2013).
11 *The Atlantic Wire*, 8 January 2013, http://www.theatlanticwire.com/technology/2013/01/ces-2013-tv-news/60702/ (accessed 17 July 2013).
12 McKinsey (2012), Smart TV: Too smart to win over consumers?

3   The industrial organization approach

The industrial organization way of strategic thinking directs us to the industry in which a firm competes and the value system of which it is part. It lets us consider the industry forces that are at play there to evaluate whether the firm is capable of a suitable response. It is credited as the first systematically thought-through treatment of strategy content.

The process logic of the industrial organization approach

The industrial organization approach states that firms compete in industries. "Although the relevant environment is very broad, encompassing social as well as economic forces, the key aspect of the firm's environment is the industry or industries in which it competes" (Porter 1980: 3). An industry is "a group of firms producing products that are close substitutes for each other" (ibid: 5). The core of the industrial organization approach is found in two books Michael Porter published in 1980 and in 1985 respectively. The 1980 book introduced the five forces framework and the generic strategies. The 1985 book added the value chain and the value system.

Michael Porter, very cleverly, took the industrial organization subfield in economics and made it relevant for strategic management (Porter 1981). Industrial organization economists try to find out why one industry apparently performs better than another industry. Their explanatory framework puts forward that the performance of an industry is determined by the conduct of all the firms operating in this industry. They continue to argue that the conduct of a firm, in turn, can be explained by the industry structure. Because firms are assumed to act rationally and given that the industry structure is the same for every firm that competes in an industry, these firms are all expected to arrive at the same decisions and consequently conduct themselves in the same way. This suggests that the industry structure determines industry performance. Industrial organization economists then try to explain performance differences between industries on the basis of differences in how these industries are structured. This explanatory framework became known as the Bain/Mason paradigm, named after two prominent industrial organization economists.

Because a strategy scholar is interested in explaining performance differences between firms instead of industries, Porter lifted the assumption that all firms will conduct themselves in the same manner. Instead, he argued that firms can and will act differently within a given industry structure. They will have different strategies. However, not every strategy will create the same level of performance. He put forward that there are only three generic strategies – cost leadership, differentiation, focus – that create, as he put it, "a superior return on investment for the firm" (Porter 1980: 34). Each one of these three strategies deals in a

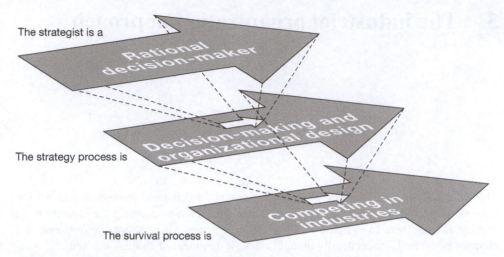

The strategist is a

The strategy process is

The survival process is

Figure 3.1 The process logic for industrial organization

particular way with the structure of the industry in which a firm has to compete. Each one of these three strategies encompasses competitive advantage in a different way. Porter understands the environmental survival process to be a process of competition in an industry (see Figure 3.1). This is where the industrial organization process logic is very different from marketing-inspired strategic thinking.

The other two process spheres are identical to marketing-inspired strategic thinking. Porter too takes it that there are only a limited number of strategists located at the top of the firm and that they are engaged in rational decision-making. And here too the organizational strategy process is one of choice and design. The difference is that the information that is being gathered and processed has to be about the industry and how best to compete within it. So the actual vocabulary and the performance logic that should be employed is different from marketing-inspired strategic thinking.

The performance logic of the industrial organization approach

The reasoning starts with the industry or, more specifically, with the industry structure. Porter (1980) defined the industry structure as consisting of five different forces: the threat of new entrants, the threat of substitutes, the bargaining power of suppliers, the bargaining power of buyers and the rivalry between competitors. The stronger a force, the more difficult it is for a focal firm to realize high performance. The reason is that each one of the forces sucks money out of the focal firm or it puts a ceiling on the price at which a product can be sold.

Intense rivalry means that a firm has to put more effort into maintaining market share and there is a downward pressure on sales prices. High bargaining power of suppliers means that they are able to negotiate high prices for their supplies. High buyer bargaining power means that the firm has to give large discounts when it tries to sell its products or services. A high threat of new entrants means that outside firms can enter easily as soon as the industry becomes more profitable. This threat puts a downward pressure on the price level. A high threat of substitutes means that there is a limit to the price at which the product can be sold, as substitutes are readily available. A substitute product is a different product that provides the same value to the customer. A rival product is the same product as what is produced by the focal firm but offered by a competitor. The strength of all five forces determines how attractive the industry is to operate in. Which of the forces is the strongest indicates what the strategist should focus on when formulating a competitive or business level strategy.

To counter these five forces, firms in an industry need to choose how they want to compete. One choice concerns the question whether they want to compete on costs or on value. The other choice concerns the question how they want to compete on value: either industry wide or targeting a segment of the industry. This part of Porter's reasoning is based on the assumption that every industry is characterized by what can be referred to as the 'standard product'. Customers are willing to spend a certain amount of money on this product, which indicates the basic sales price level for this standard product when it is offered for sale. Standard does not necessarily mean simple, as customer expectations can be quite sophisticated, depending on what they are used to and have learned to expect. Any product not fulfilling customer expectations simply will not be sold.

One strategic choice available to a firm competing in an industry is to become the most efficient producer of this standard product. This is the strategy of cost leadership. The cost leader is the firm that has the highest profit margin among those firms who supply the standard product to the market. The standard product is necessarily priced at this basic level that customers are willing to pay for it. Consequently, there can only be one cost leader (see Figure 3.2).

Competing on costs is completely different from competing on price. The cost leader does not want the price level at which the standard product is sold to erode, nor would any other firm who is competing in this industry, as it only leads to diminishing margins and consequently lower profits for everybody. Competing on costs means that you try to be the most efficient producer and maintain the price level at which the standard product is sold. Porter (1980) adamantly urges firms never to compete on price because it makes everybody worse off.

Those firms who are less efficient than the cost leader can compete on customer value. "Value is what buyers are willing to pay" (Porter 1985: 3). To increase the price buyers are

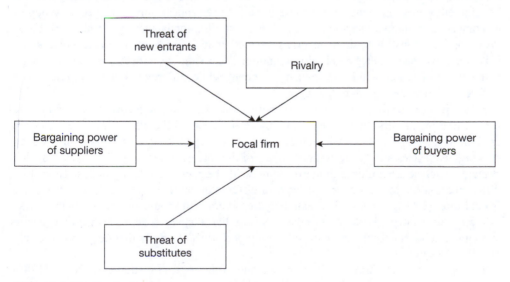

Figure 3.2 The five forces

Derived from Porter (1980)

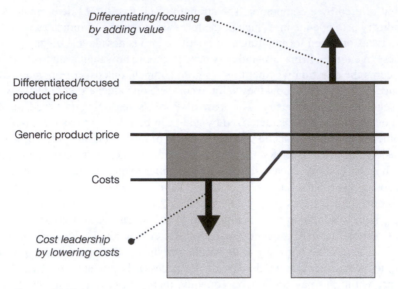

Differentiating/focusing
by adding value

Differentiated/focused
product price

Generic product price

Costs

*Cost leadership
by lowering costs*

Figure 3.3 Price, costs and value

willing to pay, you have to offer a product with extra features which, when compared to the basic product, will appeal more to customers. Not every feature will do. They have to represent enhanced value in the eyes of the people who buy the product. When this value is added at a cost lower than the extra margin that is made on the enhanced product because of the higher price customers are willing to pay for it, the firm has a higher than average performance. When these extra features have a broad appeal and are appreciated by every customer, the firm offering this product has embarked upon a differentiation strategy. It will be competing industry wide. When these extra features appeal only to a specific group of customers or an industry segment, the firm is pursuing a focus strategy. In his 1980 book, Porter presented just these three generic strategies. In his 1985 book, he made a distinction between a cost focus strategy and a differentiation focus strategy, with the cost focus strategy being the cost leader within an industry segment while differentiation focus refers to a differentiation strategy within this segment.

Every firm has to stick to one of these generic strategies to shield themselves from the five forces. Bearing in mind that there is only one cost leader, all the other firms should have a credible value proposition by which they can make enough money to withstand the 'money sucking' tendencies and 'price ceiling' effects of the forces. Essentially, the answer to what strategy to pursue is a multiple choice question, with the generic strategies of cost leadership, differentiation and focus (either cost focus or differentiation focus) as the options to choose from. Porter (1980) also described a strategy that every firm should avoid. This is the stuck-in-the-middle strategy. Porter argues that any firm that is trying to do more than one generic strategy simultaneously is outcompeted and outperformed by firms that keep to one of the generic strategies.

To assess whether a firm is able to pursue one of these generic strategies, Porter (1985) came up with the notion of the value chain. Continuing along the same lines of his 1980 book, a firm is taken to add value at a certain cost. The 1985 book adds the idea that a firm can be subdivided into separate value activities. To Porter there are nine separate value activities. The primary activities are inbound logistics, operations, outbound logistics, marketing and sales, and service. The support activities are firm infrastructure, human resource management, technology development and procurement. The primary activities are physically involved in creating the product and service and getting it to the customer. The support activities, as the term suggests, allow the primary activities to take place. There is a bit of a bias towards manufacturing firms in this model, but distinguishing between separate value activities is relevant for all kind of firms.

By elaborating on a firm as a combination of value activities, Porter makes it possible to look inside the firm and to evaluate the extent to which each activity contributes to the value proposition represented by the generic strategy the firm pursues. Given the specific added value that the firm claims to produce, the question can be asked which value activity, or specific combination of activities, is responsible for that. The additional question should be asked at what cost this value is produced. If the costs exceed the price at which the product can be sold, there is effectively no margin and no profit to be made. Hence figure 3.4 is labelled as a firm's value (and costs) chain.

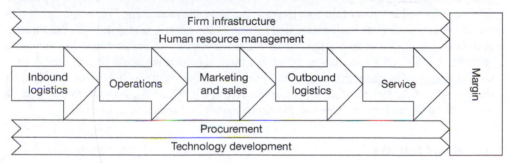

Figure 3.4 A firm's value (and costs) chain

Derived from Porter (1985)

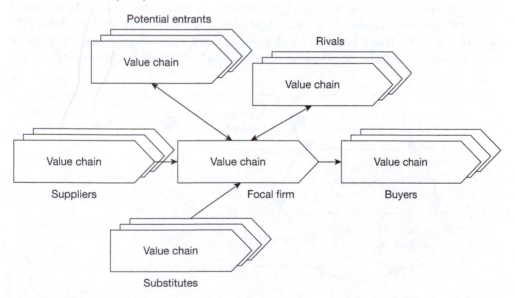

Figure 3.5 The value system

Derived from Porter (1985)

To Porter (1985), the five forces combined with the value chain make a value system. Any firm is part of this system. A firm finds itself positioned among suppliers, buyers, firms that can enter the industry, firms that offer substitutes and rival firms with which it has to compete, with each of these firms having its own specific value chain. Whether a firm performs depends on how its value chain compares with all the other value chains around it. And each value chain of these surrounding firms determines the relative strength of the force with which each surrounding firm is associated. It is up to the focal firm to position itself adequately within this system by opting for a suitable generic strategy to be able to perform and survive. One important realization to make here is that a firm not only competes for market share with direct competitors in the industry. The firm also competes with suppliers, buyers, firms that provide substitute products, and firms who can easily enter the industry. They compete with each other about how much of a margin is created and how much of this margin each firm is able to retain.

To sum up, the performance logic of the industrial organization approach, and Porter's take on it in particular, covers the three ingredients of the environment, the firm and strategy in a very specific manner (see Figure 3.6). The environment is seen as an industry that is further described in terms of the five forces and the value system. The firm is appreciated as a value chain. Strategy is further specified by way of the generic strategies, with the strategy embodying competitive advantage. Porter's framework allows the strategist to evaluate a situation because of a requirement of fit. All three ingredients should fit together. A firm should have a value chain that allows it to pursue a generic strategy that, in turn, deals with the strength of the forces, as they exist in the industry in which the firm has to compete. If any of these three elements does not contribute to this fit, the firm is in trouble.

Additional features

To further specify an industry, Porter (1980) devised the notion of strategic groups. "A strategic group is the group of firms in an industry following the same or a similar strategy along the strategic dimensions" (ibid: 129). It allows for a more fine-grained description of an industry's structure, using the value dimension in particular by which he defines the generic strategies. This is based on his observation that groups of firms behave in a similar fashion. They compete along similar lines and this can be captured in terms of the particular

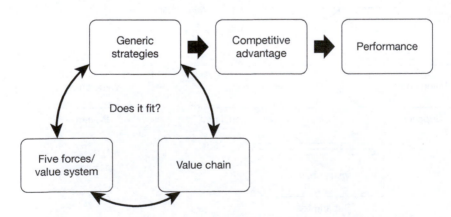

Figure 3.6 The industrial organization approach

Illustration 3.1: The automotive industry as a value system

The automotive industry has developed into a value system of global proportions (Sturgeon, Van Biesebroeck, & Gereffi, 2008). A modern car consists of many parts and sub-assemblies. Car production and sales require many suppliers and sub-contractors and together they constitute a value system. There are the major car manufacturers who are involved in the branding, engineering, design and final assembly of a range of models. Many manufacturers have a worldwide presence. However, they rely on advertising agencies and sometimes outside marketing specialists to help them with their branding. In the early stages of car design and engineering, independent specialist design and engineering firms are often involved. Car sales tend to be done by independently owned dealerships. And even car assembly is sometimes outsourced to sub-contractors who build and manage an assembly plant. When a new model has reached the stage that a decision needs to be made about where it will be produced, the car manufacturer's plant where the previous model was assembled often not only finds it has to compete with the possibility of constructing a new greenfield plant somewhere else. It also finds that it has to tender for a new contract alongside outside firms who specialize in car assembly and act as subcontractor for various different car companies.

A car consists of many different parts involving a wide range of suppliers, with companies specializing in specific sub-assemblies having their own network of suppliers as well. There are engines, transmissions, shock absorbers, car seats, electronic motor management systems, wire looms, body panels, interior trim, tires, paint etc. There are also equipment manufacturers who provide the robotics and tools with which the assembly and manufacturing plants are kitted out. Sometimes a major car manufacturer develops and builds its own engines and transmissions. Sometimes they source it from other car manufacturers or specialized firms. A more recent development is that platforms, chassis designs and drive trains are not only shared across models from the same manufacturer but also across different manufacturers. Many of the other parts and sub-assemblies are made by specialist suppliers, sometimes tied into some form of exclusivity with one car manufacturer, but often supplying many different manufacturers.

They all compete with each other for margin. Imagine that a car can be sold for a maximum of £20,000. What all these firms are competing for is how much of this £20,000 comes to them. This is determined by the value – as perceived by the customer – that their involvement or specific part adds to the final product. If it is the after sales service that nails a sale, car dealerships have the upper hand. If it is the branding, the car manufacturer will be the most powerful player, although they might depend too much on an outside advertising agency. Or is it a specific part or sub-assembly like the engine or the sound system that sets the car apart in the eyes of the customer? Is it the build quality? Depending on how crucial your role is in producing value, you will get a larger proportion of this £20,000. If you are unable to compete on value for your share of the £20,000, you will have to make your margin by lowering your costs.

value they offer to customers. Some firms that share a particular focus on an industry segment form a specific strategic group. Other firms that pursue a similar differentiation strategy form another strategic group. In this way, some industries feature a number of different strategic groups.

Strategic groups are kept apart by mobility barriers. This refers to the costs and difficulties that should be overcome to move from one strategic group to another strategic group. Competition between firms from different groups is less prevalent because of mobility barriers. Rivalry is limited to those firms within the same group. Also the supplier and buyer forces can pan out differently for different strategic groups, as can the threat of substitutes. Because of this, each strategic group is expected to have its own cost leader. Further possibilities of focus or differentiation within a group are expected to exist, but in a much more subtle fashion than the differentiation or focus that defines the strategic group in the first place.

Doing industrial organization approach strategic management

From a real time perspective, the question that continuously should be asked is whether there still is a fit between the strategy (in terms of the three generic strategies) and the industry or value system in which the firm competes and whether the firm has a value chain that allows the firm to position itself in this way. Anything that happens that disturbs this fit should be qualified as a strategic issue and action should be taken. Therefore, from an industrial organization point of view, the two questions to ask and answer are:

1   Are there any issues that jeopardize the fit between the industry in which the firm competes, which one of the generic strategies it realizes, and the firm's value chain?
2   If there are, what can you do about them?

Answering question 1: strategic analysis

Of course, if you find that the firm is 'stuck-in-the-middle' in that it has not committed to one of the generic strategies, you have already found an issue and action needs to be taken. To draw this conclusion, or any other one concerning the level of fit, you need to know about whether and which generic strategy a firm is realizing, how this compares with the value system that is the industry as a whole, and what value at which costs the firm adds in terms of its own value chain. If you do not know, you have to get 'up to speed' first.

Getting up to speed

The industrial organization approach and Porter's take on it in particular is designed to use as part of a strategic decision-making exercise (see the Introduction in Porter 1980). The 1980 book covers the external appraisal and the choice of strategy. The 1985 book adds the internal appraisal. Obviously, the external appraisal needs to be done by looking at the industry the firm competes in and the internal appraisal should assess the firm in terms of the value chain. However, the value chain allows for the industry to be further analysed as a value system.

The vocabulary and performance logic of the industrial organization approach tells us which information should be gathered and how it should be evaluated. However, before you can start, two initial questions need to be answered before any analysis can be done: one is

---

Exhibit 3.1: Industrial organization external appraisal questions

- Which industry is the firm competing in?
- Are there strategic groups in the industry and if so, which group does the firm belong to?
- Who are direct competitors of the firm?
- How many are there?
- What do their value chains look like?
  - This tells us about the strength of the rivalry force.
- Who are suppliers to the firm?
- How many are there?
- What do their value chains look like?
  - This tells us about the supplier power force.
- Who are buyers from the firm?
- How many are there?
- What do their value chains look like?
  - This tells us about the buyer power force.
- Who offer substitute products?
- How many are there?
- What does their value chain look like?
  - This tells us about the threat from substitutes.
- How easy is it to set up a similar business?
- What would their value chains look like?
  - This tells us about the threat of entry.

(Consider mobility barriers between strategic groups.)

---

about the industry definition, the other one is about customer value. The first question refers to the external appraisal, the second one to the internal appraisal.

First of all, the industry that is analysed should be defined. This is not a trivial matter for two reasons. One, if it is not clear what is actually being analysed, any result is meaningless. Two, industry definitions are not clear-cut. As was said previously, in abstract terms, Porter (1980: p.5) has defined an industry as "*a group of firms producing products that are close substitutes for each other*" (p.5). The problem is that 'close substitutes' provides little guidance on what is close and what is not. Is a chocolate bar a close substitute for an apple? If we define fruit as a very different product to confectionary, they are not. If we take them both as snacks, they are. This has its effect on the threat of substitutes and the rivalry forces. When a narrow industry definition is the basis for analysis, certain firms will be part of the substitutes threat, which with a more encompassing definition would be considered rivals or, with a very narrow definition, would not be considered at all. Who the buyers or suppliers are, would vary with the industry definition as well. If in doubt, you can always do the analysis based on a different – say a narrow and a broad – industry definition.

Secondly, it should be established what it is that the end consumer values about the product that defines the industry and what price level is attached to it. This 'value' is connected to certain attributes of the product. Only once you know what these attributes are you are able to find out who in the value system is responsible for them. It allows the strategist to evaluate the firm's value chain and to compare it with all value chains of the

---

Illustration 3.2: Industry classification

To measure economic activity, governments and their statistical offices have produced classification schemes by which they are able to slot firms into industries. The US Standard Industrial Classification (SIC) framework has been much utilized in research and has recently been replaced by the North American Industry Classification System (NICS). The UK has the United Kingdom Standard Industrial Classification of Economic Activities (UKSIC), and other countries or bodies like the UN or the EU have something similar. These schemes provide descriptions and codes of categories of business activity. Because economic data are gathered using these codes, they are being used extensively for the purpose of research but they tend to be a bit too broad to be useful for a strategic analysis of a particular firm.

---

other players in the industry. Knowing about the price level that is achieved in an industry will tell you which margins to expect and how these relate to the costs that are associated with the firm's value chain as well as all other value chains in the wider value system. So a strategist should find out what the end customer appreciates about the good or service and how much this end customer is prepared to pay for it. There are bound to be ranges of products with different value propositions and price levels, catering for specific industry segments or across the industry as a whole, offering the firm a choice to go for a cost leadership, differentiation, or focus strategy.

Once these two initial questions have been answered about industry definition and about customer value, the more specific questions in the external and internal appraisals, and what strategy the firm is realizing can be tackled (see exhibits 3.1, 3.2 and 3.3).

The information gathered as a consequence of the internal and external appraisal and the assessment of firm's strategy should be collated and evaluated. Here the performance logic

---

Exhibit 3.2: Industrial organization internal appraisal questions

- What do customers value about the product that defines the industry?
- Does any or a combination of value activities in the firm add this value to the product?
- How efficient is the firm in executing value activities in its value chain?

Exhibit 3.3: Industrial organization positioning questions

- Does the firm compete on costs or on value?
- Does the firm compete industry wide or in a specific industry segment or strategic group?
  - These two questions tell us whether the firm's strategy needs to be described as cost leadership, differentiation, cost focus, differentiation focus, or stuck-in-the-middle.

Strategy practice 3.1: An industrial organization SWOT analysis

The purpose of a SWOT analysis is to find out about threats and opportunities in the environment and about strengths and weaknesses with regard to the firm. But what makes an opportunity an opportunity, a threat a threat, a strength a strength, and a weakness a weakness? Marketing-inspired strategic thinking may be of help here.

The environment is about the industry. Opportunities are industries or strategic groups that are attractive and where the firm's value chain is particularly promising for developing a strong position. A firm's value chain that adds the value that matters for the customers obviously represents a firm's strength. If one or more of the five forces becomes stronger, this clearly is a threat and the apparent not-so-strong value chain of the focal firm becomes a weakness.

Anything can happen to a firm that has an effect with regard to the 'fit' between a firm's value chain, product value system and generic strategy, either positively or negatively, and can be described as having consequences in terms of the firm's strengths and weaknesses and opportunities and threats in the environment.

---

comes in. The strategy should fit both the industry, appreciated as a value system comprising the five forces, and the firm's value chain. One of the three generic strategies should be chosen. As was said earlier, stuck-in-the-middle is always a cause for concern. The best fit is a situation where the firm takes advantage of its value chain with the appropriate generic strategy in light of all the value chains that surround the firm in the industry in which it competes.

Going real time: debating strategy

Once the strategist knows about the industry and strategic group the firm is competing in. If the strategist knows about the firm's value chain and how it compares with the value chains in the wider value system regarding delivering the value that end consumers want. Additionally, if the strategist knows the relative efficiency of all value chains and what specific generic strategy the firm is realizing. In effect, if a comprehensive understanding of the firm's strategic position is in place, then the strategist is able to evaluate and debate anything that is happening and decide whether countermeasures are in order.

Exhibit 3.4 provides a range of questions that fuel the debate. The overall worry should be focused on the question of fit between the firm's strategy, its value chain and the wider value system that makes up the industry in which the firm competes. Whether this fit is threatened or maybe strengthened on the basis of the changes that take place should be the subject of the continuous strategy debate among top managers. These changes can happen in the value system. Firms associated with any of the forces can innovate, merge, move forward or backward in the system. In short, firms can do things that make the associated force stronger (or weaker). It could also be a change in legislation, economic up- or downturns, or natural disasters that can affect the strength of the forces. Changes can also originate from inside the firm. It can have found a way to become more efficient. It can have come across an improved value proposition. There can even be change in what customers actually value.

Exhibit 3.4: Industrial organization questions to debate

- Is there change to the strength of the rivalry force?
- Is there change to the strength of the supplier force?
- Is there change to the strength of the buyer force?
- Is there change to the threat of substitutes?
- Is there change to the threat of entry or mobility?
- Is there change to what end-consumers value about the product and the price they are prepared to pay?
- Is there change to the firm's ability to add value?
- Is there change to the firm's efficiency in adding value?

Does any of this mean that the 'fit' between the chosen generic strategy, the state of the industry, and the firm's value chain is affected?

Strategy practice 3.2: An industrial organization strategy workshop

Top management teams periodically book themselves into a nice retreat over a weekend to discuss how they or the firm are doing. This is an ideal opportunity to do some deliberate strategy debate. Quite often, an external consultant facilitates the workshop. He is asked to design a programme for the workshop and to suggest topics for discussion.

The industrial organization approach is very much suited to inform a consultant about how the workshop may be put together. He can have the management team discuss the forces in industry that the firm operates in, what the firm's value chain looks like, and whether the firm's generic strategy is still suitable. Overall, he can have the top management team spending the weekend evaluating the question of 'fit'.

Alternatively, the reason why the workshop is organized may be because something alarming has happened recently and the top management team need to put their heads together to think about how to respond. Again the industrial organization approach can inform the content and nature of the discussion. The question of 'fit' and the effect this alarming incident may have can be the focus of the debate. The response should be aimed at restoring fit if this is found to be in jeopardy.

Strategy practice 3.3: Internationalization from an industrial organization viewpoint

Porter (1986) reckons that industries vary from multi-domestic to global. In a multi-domestic industry, competition in one country is independent from competition in another country, with each country having its own five forces and value system. A firm competing internationally in a multi-domestic industry effectively is a multi-business firm. A global industry means that there is one globally organized value system in which every firm has to compete.

Answering question 2: taking action

Analysis and debate apply the performance logic of a theoretical approach. Taking action utilizes the process logic. This is about what a strategist can do so that eventually the firm remains successful. There is a 'what' to do and a 'how' to do it.

The available options with regard to 'what' to do, aim to reinstate the 'fit' between the strategy, the industry structure and the firm's value chain. The strategist can choose to work on all three of these ingredients. Switching between generic strategies, improving the value chain, or entering or leaving an industry/moving between strategic groups are all alternatives to consider. With regard to the 'how' to do it, Porter (1980) suggests that there are three courses of action that a firm can embark upon. These are vertical integration, capacity expansion and entry into new business.

Vertical integration means that the firm takes activities in house that are done by either suppliers (backward integration) or buyers (forward integration). These activities then effectively become part of the firm's value chain. This can make a firm more cost efficient – adding to the cost leadership side of the firm's strategic position. Or it can boost the ability of the firm to add value – adding to the differentiation or focus side of the firm's strategic ability. The firm has a choice to develop these additional value activities internally by investing in supplementary production facilities and know–how. The alternative is to enter into a merger or acquire a supplier or buyer firm and add the additional capability in that way.

Capacity expansion is another way of becoming a more prominent player in the industry. In an industry with a growing demand, it is an obvious choice to grow with the expanding demand and even to try to grow faster than the industry growth rate to get a bigger slice of an increasing pie. By adding capacity faster, the firm can become more efficient than the competition and improve its margin alongside growing its turnover. The experience curve from marketing-inspired strategic thinking applies here as well.

In a mature industry with limited growth, adding capacity only makes sense when it allows the firm to increase its turnover at the expense of the competition. This is very often

---

Strategy practice 3.4: Formulating a strategic business plan using the industrial organization approach

The industrial organization approach is also very well suited to formulate a strategic business plan. Again the environmental analysis comes first. Start with defining the industry the firm wants to operate in. Then find out about the strength of the forces, preferably by investigating the value chains of all the firms that can be associated with each of the forces. The next thing to do is to assess the value chain of the firm for which the plan is formulated. To be able to do this, you need to find out about what customers value about the product that defines the industry first. At this point, the analysis should look out for the existence of strategic groups as well. Once the picture is complete, on the basis of the strength of the five forces in the industry, or if applicable the five forces in the strategic group the firm wants to position itself in, and on the basis of the firm's own value chain and what value the firm actually is adding, one of the generic strategies needs to be chosen. This effectively is the formulated strategy. Finally, do the sums. Check if the expected price and cost levels allow for a positive margin. If the sums do not add up, start again or abandon the plan.

not a viable opportunity. In these kinds of situations, the industry sees a lot of consolidation activity. Firms merge with each other to create larger firms in order to dominate the industry or to prevent being dominated by such newly created combinations. This is horizontal integration. It prevents the rivalry force becoming too strong, and it warns off substitute products and new entrants into the industry.

Alternatively and especially if a firm gets crowded out, it can decide to leave the industry and start up somewhere else. Or it can move from one strategic group to another one. The firm then has to enter another industry. To do that, it has to overcome both exit barriers and entry barriers. In the case of a move between strategic groups, these are mobility barriers. Exit barriers prevent a firm from changing the nature of its business. These can be specific

---

Illustration 3.3: Positioning in the steel industry

In January 2008, the Indian company Tata acquired the Anglo-Dutch steelmaker Corus for US$12.1 billion.* Tata had beaten CSN of Brazil in a bidding war. Tata, as the 56th largest steel company in the world, combined with 8th largest Corus to create the 5th largest firm. The takeover of Acelor by Mittal had created the largest steel company in the world less than a year before. Corus in turn was the result of the 1999 merger between Dutch steel firm Hoogovens and British Steel.

The product of steel, as the label suggests, defines the steel industry. Although steel comes in grades and qualities, it is a relatively undifferentiated product. Its production requires capital-intensive plants and facilities. The demand for steel is tied into the economic tides. If the economy is up, the demand for steel goes up, and steel firms do well. If the economy goes down, over-capacity ensues and the less efficient plants suffer the most. Entry is an onerous affair. It takes 5–6 years to build a new steel plant at a cost of about US$1200/US$1300 per ton production capacity. The price at which a ton of hot rolled coil steel – an accepted reference point in the industry – was sold in 2007 was US$550, but expected to go down to US$450 in the coming year.

Buyers of raw steel tend to be big companies themselves, including for instance car manufacturers. To withstand these pressures, especially in times of over-capacity, the size of a steel company matters as well. Tata's production costs are US$150 per ton because of its access to cheap Indian coal and iron ore; the industry average is US$330. Corus makes it for US$540 per ton, mainly as a consequence of high material costs.

Corus was looking for a partner after surviving a few loss-making years and wanted to move up from a European producer to become part of a global steel company. Its management's aim was to get access to both emerging economies and to cheaper raw materials. Merging with either CSN or Tata would have solved both problems. Tata was looking to expand its production capacity without having to resort to building new facilities. Combined they think they are better equipped to pursue a low cost strategy in an industry with strong forces and in which differentiation opportunities are limited.

BBC News, 31 January 2007, http://newsvote.bbc.co.uk/mpapps/pagetools/print/news.bbc. co.uk/1/hi/business/6069492.stm (accessed 21 January 2014); Wharton, 8 February 2007, http://knowledge.wharton.upenn.edu/article/did-tata-steel-overheat-in-its-zeal-to-win-corus/ (accessed 21 January 2014); Forbes, 22 October 2006, http://www.forbes.com/2006/10/22/tata-corus-mna-biz-cx_rd_1022corus.html (accessed 21 January 2010).

assets and know-how that cannot be deployed elsewhere or a lack of knowledge about alterative business opportunities. The industry or strategic group the firm likes to move into should be attractive, i.e. the strength of the forces should be low. Yet, ironically, a high entry barrier makes an industry or strategic group attractive but also difficult to enter.

If the firm moves into another industry or strategic group whilst remaining active in the industry or group it already is part of, then this is a diversification move. This could be warranted if its existing abilities give a competitive advantage in both the new industry as well as the old one. The notion of synergy from marketing-based strategic thinking applies here too.

Illustration 3.4: SKF from an industrial organization point of view

Should SKF* compete on price and put in the lowest bid possible to retain a big US-based client, or should they step away and persist with their high-quality strategy?

The ball bearing industry is fairly global and dominated by a few big players, like SKF, Timken, Schaeffler and NSK. There appear to be two strategic groups, a low-end mostly local group consisting of Chinese and Eastern European firms and a more high-end well-established group of which SKF is a member. There are mobility barriers between the two groups. A low quality producer cannot suddenly become high quality. The other way round, SKF cannot simply abandon its more costly but sophisticated production process to become a lower priced ball bearing manufacturer. So SKF is mostly competing with the aforementioned other four, who combined serve 59 per cent of worldwide ball bearing needs. The industry is fairly mature, with total sales going up and down with world GDP and business cycles. The market is carved up between the big players with the rivalry force therefore not overwhelmingly strong as yet.

In the US, SKF sells through distributors: independent companies which act as a kind of wholesaler for end-user firms. This is a common practice in the ball bearing industry. It was through a distributor that the US-based client communicated its intention to hold a reverse auction. The distributor firms have gone through a cycle of consolidation. End-user firms have been piling pressure on distributors with ever more aggressive procurement tactics being deployed. A common expectation is that with every new contract, there will be a 5 per cent discount on the previous agreed contract price. The distributors and their suppliers, including SKF, have largely absorbed this. Some larger end-users are dispensing with distributors all together and start to negotiate directly with suppliers. The buyer force is therefore pretty strong. If distributors become less prevalent, the whole value system possibly becomes subjected to change.

SKF's value activities are strong when it comes to service, marketing and operations. This is where its reputation of high quality ball bearings is built on. In a way, SKF does not sell ball bearings. They sell solutions that make end user machinery more reliable and efficient. This has been something that end-users value and SKF solutions have always allowed for premium pricing and therefore relatively high margins. The generic strategy of differentiation best describes how SKF is positioned in the industry.

The US-based client's invitation to participate in a reverse auction is another manifestation of the strong buyer force. Ball bearing manufacturer margins are under pressure, even though SKF's are relatively high. With a number of big players being put under the same pressure, mutual rivalry might go up as well. Whether SKF is sufficiently shielded from this depends on the relative importance end-users place on low price or on high value. Obviously they are pressuring ball bearing manufacturers into accepting a lower price while retaining value. Should SKF give in and participate in the auction? Porter does say that you should never compete on price. But this looks like the price level for the whole industry is coming down. End users, distributors, and ball bearing manufacturers are competing for margin in the value system and it looks like the pressure is becoming too big to withstand it for much longer. This is not just about one end-user but more of a general trend in the industry. For SKF to remain in business, it looks like it has to accept the squeeze and to get used to offering the same solutions at a lower price. To be able to do that, it has to work on its value chain to become more efficient in offering the same product.

*Value selling at SKF Service, IMD-5-0751, 2009.

Criticisms and generating further questions

Much of the criticism that is levied against marketing-inspired strategic thinking also applies to the industrial organization approach. The emphasis on intended strategy and rational decision-making comes at the expense of actually realizing the strategy. The industrial organization approach is also essentially static, providing snap shots of industries and firm abilities. It also requires the same basic underlying assumptions regarding a real business reality out there about which objective information can be gathered to base decisions upon, and about unbiased and all powerful top management taking charge of the firm. This theoretical approach leans towards objectivism and voluntarism.

The static character of the industrial organization approach worried Porter as well (Porter, 1991). If you read his 1980 and 1985 books carefully, you find him urging strategists not to take the status quo as a given but to actively try to change industry structures and value systems to their advantage. Drawing on the product life cycle concept, he suggests that industries are subject to a life cycle too (Porter, 1980). To him, the early days of any industry are best described as 'emergent'. In an emergent industry, things are ambiguous. It is not clear yet what product defines the industry, nor who the rivals are, or any other players in the value system. Customers are unsure as well about what they value and whether they like the product at all. In such a situation it is not very meaningful to formulate a competitive strategy in terms of the generic strategies, although it is a situation of enormous potential for when the industry does settle down.

As soon as things get settled, the industry becomes 'mature'. This is a situation with a value system of vested interest, with clear definitions of products and product categories as well as clear ideas among consumers about what they expect from a product. This is the situation in which the theoretical language of the industrial organization approach tends to apply the best. The expectation is that the industry eventually winds down and becomes 'declining'. Some firms are able to hang on while others decide to opt out or are forced out by bankruptcy as a consequence of decreasing demand. Porter (1980) refers to industries that never get settled down as 'fragmented'.

While recognizing that industries change and evolve, he provides little guidance about how this happens; let alone suggests strategies of how firms can have an active role in this. His work does not deal with questions how industry structures change or how the forces become stronger or weaker. He came as far as suggesting that industries take shape within the context of particular countries (Porter, 1990) and offers this as a first step in the explanation (Porter, 1991). Yet he also recognizes that his analysis of the competitive advantage of nations is essentially static as well and that it does not deal with the process by which it actually happens.

Case 3.1 Tunnock's

Thomas Tunnock Limited is a family firm established in 1890 in Uddingston near Glasgow.[1] Since the 1950s, its main products have been caramel wafers, snowballs, caramel logs and teacakes. The firm has a production facility of 250,000 sq ft, 100 yards from the site it started from in 1890. It make its own ingredients of biscuit wafers, caramel, marshmallow and chocolate, claiming that especially the chocolate has a distinctive taste that sets the company apart. Tunnock's employs about 550 staff. Management is in the hands of the family. The founder's grandson Boyd Tunnock is at the helm, while his daughters and son-in-law also occupy management positions. The company presents its products as Scottish icons and currently exports them to over 30 countries, having the ambition to extend that to even more. The wrapper of the caramel wafer biscuit proudly boasts "more than 5,000,000 of these biscuits made and sold every week".

The caramel wafers and the teacakes in both milk and dark chocolate variants can be found in most British supermarkets in the biscuit aisle on the bottom shelf.[2] The teacakes sell for £0.95 in a pack of six while the caramel wafers can be bought for £1.59 for eight. The more prominent positions in the biscuit aisle are taken up by Nestlé's KitKats. An 8-pack of KitKats sells for £1.59. In the adjacent confectionary aisle, a shopper can pick up a 4-pack of Mars bars for £1.79.

In September 2010, the Tunnock's workforce went on strike after a 2 per cent pay rise was rejected.[3] Tunnock's production came to a standstill. The company's financial position had been mixed. Turnover grew from £31.8 million in 2008 to £35.6 million in 2009. However, the pre-tax profit went down from £1.35 million to £1.05 million. Union representative Derek Ormston said about the strike:

> There's a determination but the workers are reluctant because they value Tunnock's as a brand but feel they have no choice but to take action. The people who work there are predominantly of the locale and they are families. There are fathers and sons and mothers and daughters, so it's a big step for them to come out. If there's four people in the same family, then that's four incomes, so that

1 www.tunnock.co.uk (accessed 26 October 2012).
2 Observations made at Morrison's Supermarket, Cortonwood, South Yorkshire, UK (14 February 2013).
3 Management Today, 28 September 2010, http://www.managementtoday.co.uk/news/1031465/crumbs-tunnocks-workers-go-strike/ (accessed 26 October 2012).

shows the depth of feeling. [The company is]a proper Scottish icon that was looked upon very fondly by many, including the 550 people who work at its factory. They're well-loved and are still seen as a family business and well-respected in the community as well. Usually there's hostility between employees and employers, but there's a great affection here, although people feel the management style has changed.

In an interview in *The Times* on the occasion of the 120th anniversary of the firm in 2010, Boyd Tunnock explained:

In January we put in a £2 million robotic biscuit foil wrapping machine and we are currently putting in a £2 million robotic case packer. The girls love it because it takes away the most repetitive part of their job, which was also affecting their wrists because these boxes are $2^1/_4$ kg a case.[4]

In 2010 the company had £32 million turnover and put in £4 million of investment in its plant that year. Tunnock's operates two shifts and one shorter night shift. The company produces 350 teacakes every minute and boils 500 kg of caramel every working hour.

The products are sold all over the UK. Saudi Arabia is the largest export market. Mr Tunnock continues:

I honestly don't know why they are such popular exports other than to say that it must be the quality of the biscuits. Look, it's great making money but it's even better making money from something I like eating. We make the biscuits this way because this is the way I like them. The key to this business is to not take the general public for fools. Give them the quality they want and expect. And don't change the recipe. We source the cocoa from Ghana and coconut from the Philippines. We make our own chocolate and we make our own caramel and we make our own boiled Italian meringue — what you know as marshmallow. What we do have is a brand. And that brand is strong. It is what carries us forward. But the brand will only remain as strong as the quality of the biscuit. If the brand were to suffer it would be because the quality of the biscuit has let us down. That is why we continuously concentrate on quality.

Mr Tunnock indicates that the worries that he has are globalization and increased competition. He mentions that supermarkets tell him that they will stop stocking Tunnock's products unless he supplies them with private label biscuits as well. So far he has refused: "We remain competitive. We owe the bank no money. That is very promising at a time when the likes of Cadbury are moving to Poland. One thing that I can promise you: we have no intention of ever leaving Scotland".

Nestlé, the producer of KitKats, reported a turnover of CHF7102 million in biscuits alone.[5] They present themselves as 'The World's Leading Nutrition, Health, and Well Being Company', offering products under very well known global brand names. They

4 *The Times*, 14 April 2010, http://www.thetimes.co.uk/tto/business/industries/industrials/article2475687.ece (accessed 26 October 2012).
5 Nestlé 2011 annual report.

regularly put new products and product lines on the market and are powerful nego-tiators when it comes to safeguarding supermarket shelf space. They claim to have an "unmatched research and development capability". They are one of a few fast-moving-consumer-products multinationals, which have business interests in food and in confectionary and biscuits in particular. Others are Kraft Foods (owners of Cadbury) and Masterfoods (with brands including Mars and Snickers).

Recent market research suggest that UK consumers are prepared to pay higher prices for products that have added ingredients or are perceived as having been made from high quality ingredients.[6] British consumers are keen to try out new formats and new tastes, especially if these are products associated with health or fair-trade. The chocolate-based biscuit category has seen a fall of 6.8 per cent over the past year, as have every day treats (−5.9 per cent) and special biscuit treats (−10.5 per cent). The everyday biscuit category has gained 13.5 per cent in sales volume. This could be a trading down effect because of the economic downturn.

6 Mintel Chocolate Confectionary Report 2012.

4   The resource-based view

The resource-based view takes the firm itself as the starting point for strategic thinking. It has branched out into a static resource-based view and a dynamic resource-based view. While the static resource-based view complements marketing-inspired strategic thinking and the industrial organization approach, the dynamic resource-based view was intentionally pitted against these theoretical approaches.

The origin of the resource-based view is traced back to the economist Edith Penrose (1959). Not until a paper by Birger Wernerfelt (1984) was published, was the relevance of her work for strategy theory recognized. The resource-based view starts with the economist's definition of the firm as a production function in which the output of a firm is determined by what is put in. These inputs are described in terms of production factors like land, capital and labour. These production factors are also referred to as resources. If there are performance differences between firms, so the reasoning continues, it is due to differences between the resources available to the firm. Hence the notion of firm heterogeneity – differences between firms in terms of their resource base – became the pivot on which the resource-based view explanation why firms vary with regard to their performance turned. Furthermore, they came up with two reasons why firm heterogeneity exists (Barney 1991; Peteraf 1993; Peteraf and Barney 2003). One reason is imperfect factor markets (Barney 1986). The other reason is resource accumulation within the firm (Dierickx and Cool 1989). The factor market argument developed into a more static resource-based view and the resource accumulation argument was at the heart of a more dynamic resource-based view (Maritan and Peteraf 2011).

The process logic of the static resource-based view

Economists imagine that resources are traded on factor markets. These factor markets are purely theoretical constructs and should not be confused with procurement and the product markets where firms source their supplies. Economists like to think that firms are submitted to the market mechanism. A perfect market means that supply and demand balance out at an equilibrium price (see Figure 4.1). The reason for this is perfect information about costs and benefits among the various buyers and sellers. If the resources that a firm needs to make a product are imagined to be traded in perfect factor markets, it would be impossible for a firm to make a profit. The moment a firm makes a profit from a resource, other firms, because of perfect information, would know about this. Everybody would want to buy this resource to make a profit too. Increasing demand would make the price for this resource go up. This will go on until the price that has to be paid will equal the money that can be made from the output for which this resource is used. This is the equilibrium price and at this price nobody

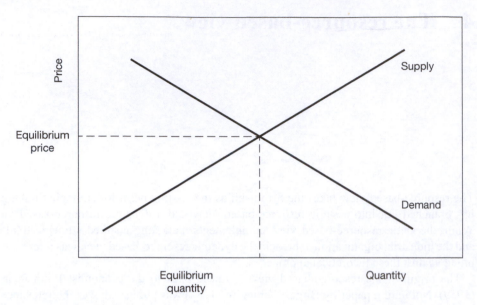

Figure 4.1 A perfect market

is able to make a profit. If a firm is able to make a profit, there should be a factor market where the market mechanism does not work (Barney 1986). This is referred to as an imperfect factor market.

So the environmental survival process that forms the basis of the static resource-based view is competition in factor markets (see Figure 4.2). The crucial question is whether a factor market for a particular resource is perfect or imperfect. Only when a factor market is imperfect, it holds the promise of sustainable competitive advantage for the firm that possesses this resource. This notion of sustainability adds to the previous theoretical approaches of marketing-inspired strategic thinking and the industrial organization approach.

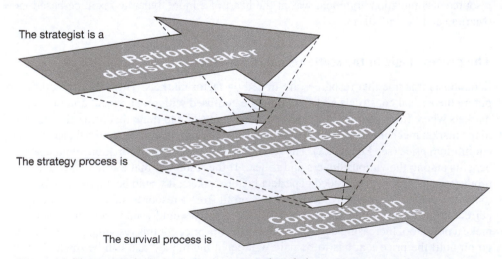

Figure 4.2 The process logic for the static resource-based view

Sustainable means that this competitive advantage will last over a certain period of time. The resource that underpins this advantage is not widely available, which makes it difficult for other firms to catch up quickly. Barney (1991) presented this insight for the benefit of doing a strategic analysis, arguing that the strategists should consider the resource base of the firm with special emphasis on finding out about the sustainability of a firm's competitive advantage. Hence the continuation of seeing the organizational strategy process as strategic planning, and the strategists' contribution in terms of rational decision-making (see Figure 4.2).

The performance logic of the static resource-based view

Barney (1991) also came up with four criteria that a resource should fulfil to allow a firm to have sustainable competitive advantage and make a profit. These are known as the VRIN criteria. A resource should be *valuable*, that is: it should be usable to implement a competitive strategy. A resource should be *rare*: it should not be so common that everybody can lay their hands on it. A resource should be *inimitable*: it should not be easy to create the same resource from scratch. Finally, a resource should be *non*-substitutable: there should not be another resource readily available with which this competitive strategy can also be implemented. If a resource fulfils these four criteria, the firm has a sustainable competitive advantage. A firm's performance is based on its competitive advantage, which it has when it possesses resources that are valuable, rare, inimitable and non-substitutable. This means that the associated factor market is imperfect.

However, there is an important caveat here, especially in light of the existence of both the static and the dynamic resource-based view. In the static resource-based view, VRIN resources only represent 'current' competitive advantage. Furthermore, the strategy that the firm pursues should exploit this particular resource in order to create performance (March 1991). This is the requirement of fit (see Figure 4.3).

The reasoning is simple enough. The difficulty lies in defining and identifying the resources that may fulfil these criteria. One problem is that as soon as this information about a resource becomes available, it makes the factor market more perfect and therefore erodes the possibility of competitive advantage (Kraaijenbrink, Spender and Groen 2010). Another problem is that the easily identifiable resources are less likely to fulfil the VRIN criteria. One rule of thumb is that if a resource is tradable, it would not be a source of competitive

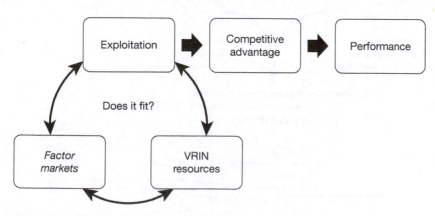

Figure 4.3 The static resource-based view

advantage (Mahoney and Pandian 1992). If a resource can be identified with a particular procurement market where a firm can source it as a supply, the rarity criterion is not fulfilled.

To get to grips with this notion of resource in the resource-based view, various strategy scholars have come up with their own extended vocabulary and associated but complicated definitions. Grant (1991) distinguished between resources as "inputs into the production process – they are the basic unit of analysis" (ibid: 118) and capabilities as "the capacity for a team of resources to perform some task or activity" (ibid: 119). To Amit and Schoemaker (1993), resources are "stocks of available factors that are owned or controlled by the firm" (ibid: 34–35). Capabilities are "a firm's capacity to deploy resources" (ibid: 35), while strategic assets are "the set of difficult to trade and imitate, scarce, appropriable and specialized resources and capabilities" (ibid: 36). Teece, Pisano and Shuen (1997: 516) distinguish between factors of production – the "'undifferentiated' inputs available in disaggregate form in factor markets", resources – the "firm-specific assets that are difficult if not impossible to imitate", organizational routines or competences – the "firm-specific assets [. . .] assembled in integrated clusters spanning individuals and groups so that they enable distinctive activities to be performed" and core competences – the "competences that define a firm's fundamental business".

A common thread can be teased out here. The term 'resource' is too coarse. If there are production factors that fulfil the VRIN criteria, they can be found among the 'capabilities' or 'competences' of a firm. These tend to be combinations of routines (Ackermann and Eden 2011), with a routine understood as an assembly of a range of resources including people's skills and motivations as well as a firm's physical, financial, knowledge, cultural, marketing and organizational resources. A 'routine' is a regular and predictable behavioural pattern in a firm (Nelson and Winter 1982), which makes particular use of a range of these more basic resources. It is rarely only one routine that fulfils the VRIN criteria. More often it is a combination of routines that is the source of competitive advantage (see Figure 4.4). The capability that these routines represent is labelled as 'core' (see Figure 4.4). Static resource-based view strategic thinking concentrates on identifying these VRIN routines by probing the existence of core capabilities.

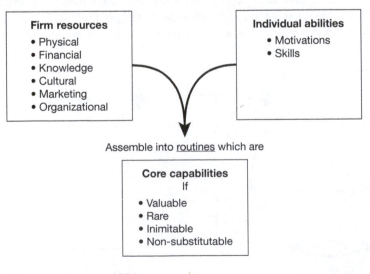

Figure 4.4 Core capabilities

Illustration 4.1: The core capability of Rolex

Rolex has a history that goes back to 1905.* It is now a premium Swiss watchmaker. Rolex watches hold their value so well that they tend to resell at a higher price than they were originally bought for. Rolex watches are made in Switzerland at sites in Bienne and Geneva. The company is fully integrated. It manufactures every one of the more than 200 bits and parts of the watches itself. Highly skilled craftsmen put each watch together by hand. The company claims to be the inventor of the wristwatch. It was the first to make the wristwatch waterproof, the first to integrate the day/date in the movement and the first to perfect a self-winding movement to become mass producible.

Both Rolex's manufacturing and marketing routines can be claimed as core capabilities. State-of-the-art facilities, a culture of Swiss watch-making and the employees' unique skills back up the daily routine of the Rolex watch-makers. Although the patent on the 'perpetual movement' ran out in 1948, new inventions such as the 'blue parachrom hairspring' take their place. Rolex marketing trades on this exclusivity and the quality of the Rolex mechanical movements, as well as the firm's history.

It is the combination of these routines, but also the assembly of the various Rolex resources and the individual abilities of Rolex employees that constitutes core capability. The high price a Rolex watch commands as part of a highly focused competitive strategy indicates its value. Relatively scarce ingredients are put together in a very rare combination of ability. A history of more than 100 years is difficult to imitate, let alone putting together an organization and facilities that produce 750,000 high quality mechanical movements as well as highly prized and carefully designed watch cases annually. There are cheaper and even more accurate substitutes available utilizing quartz technology, but that does not have the same cachet as the Rolex movement.

* www.rolex.com (accessed 27 January 2014/; What Makes Rolex Tick by David Liebeskind, http://w4.stern.nyu.edu/sternbusiness/fall_winter_2004/rolex.html (accessed 27 January 2014); RolexMagazine.com, http://rolexblog.blogspot.co.uk/2012/10/inside-rolex-rolex-manufacturing.html (accessed 27 January 2014).

The process logic of the dynamic resource-based view

The dynamic resource-based view is based on the other reason for firm heterogeneity. Firms differ because of unique trajectories of resource accumulation that occur within the confines of a firm (Dierickx and Cool 1989). The argument here is that firms develop resources from scratch, which are not offered for sale because the firm does not want to – as they are at the core of what allows the firm to out-compete the competition – or they cannot be offered for sale because they are essentially untradable. Resources by which a firm can out-compete the competition tend to be unique routines, which have developed over time. It is impossible to package such capabilities and transfer them to other settings. Quite often, the firm itself does not really know how this unique package came together in the first place and is not able purposefully to recreate it when asked. This is referred to as causal ambiguity (Reed and Defillippi 1990). In these instances, a resource is untradable and therefore unique to a particular firm.

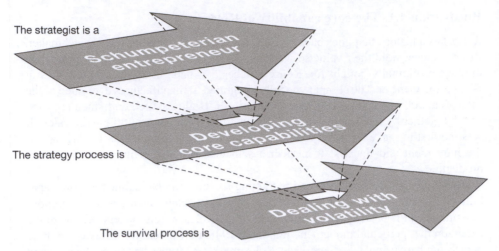

The strategist is a

The strategy process is

The survival process is

Figure 4.5 The process logic for the dynamic resource-based view

This argument of development and change is at the heart of the criticism that the dynamic resource-based view has mounted against marketing-inspired strategic thinking and against the industrial organization approach (Hamel and Prahalad 1994). These two approaches take the environment – the product market or the industry – as their starting point. The argument against this is that the environment is deemed too volatile to base a strategy on. By the time the wants and needs of the customers or the strength of the five forces are assessed, everything has changed. Furthermore, even core capabilities do not stay VRIN forever and it is only a matter of time before competitors catch up. The environment, so the reasoning goes, is characterized by hyper-competition (D'Aveni 1994), with firms engaging in quick one-upmanship to outwit each another. As a basis for strategic management, something is needed that has more of a continuous presence in such an ever-changing world. The thing having a more continuous presence is the firm's resource base.

The process logic of the dynamic resource-based view is therefore a profound departure from the previous theoretical approaches (see Figure 4.5). The environmental survival process is characterized as dealing with volatility. The way to do this is to continuously develop new routines and routine combinations, which underpin a succession of subsequent competitive advantages. The starting point here is that any competitive advantage is only temporary and that a firm has to reinvent itself over and over again. The strategist is expected to be an Schumpeterian entrepreneur (Hitt, Ireland, Camp and Sexton 2001). Joseph Schumpeter was an early Austrian economist who described economic development as creative destruction, driven by entrepreneurs who come up with "*neue Kombinationen*": new combinations of resources that allow new and previously unknown economic activity (Schumpeter 1934). Unfortunately, the dynamic resource-based view has not developed the fail-safe formula of how to be a successful entrepreneur yet, if it ever will.

The performance logic of the dynamic resource-based view

The continuity in the firm's resource base that allows dealing with environmental volatility is labelled as dynamic capability (Helfat and others 2007; Teece and others 1997). It is a process of deliberate resource accumulation (Dierickx and Cool, 1989). The identification of dynamic capability in a firm is even more difficult than locating VRIN routines and core capability in the static resource-based view. To a large extent, the jury is still out whether this actually can be done. Nevertheless, there are two schools of thought here. One school elaborates dynamic capability as an attribute of a firm. A firm either has dynamic capability or it does not have it. The other school associates dynamic capability with specific and identifiable routines that a firm has or does not have available. Dynamic capability routines are a specific subset of routines that create and change VRIN routines.

Eisenhardt and Martin (2000) proposed to understand dynamic capability as specific identifiable routines that create and change VRIN routines. They suggest that activities like R&D, business development, entering strategic alliances, or how a firm does its strategic management exemplify dynamic capability. These are examples of a whole range of activities in which a firm can engage; which purpose is to adapt to changing circumstances or to create new possibilities. It is the occurrence of these kinds of activities that indicates whether dynamic capability is present. Unfortunately, whether these activities actually create innovations and change is always an assessment after the fact. Past success is not necessarily an indicator of future performance. The degree to which a firm is actively engaged in adapting to or even creating new futures is taken as an estimate for dynamic capability. However, because the future tends to be uncertain and ambiguous, a fail-safe method to assess whether a firm's dynamic capability always gets it right still needs to be developed. The question can be asked whether that would be possible at all.

Hamel and Prahalad's (1994) 'core competence' is an example of dynamic capability seen as a firm attribute. It is a concept specifically targeted at the level of corporate strategy as they see it as a feature of a multi-business firm. Core competence refers to a basic understanding about how to combine and coordinate diverse skills and technologies. To them, a product is just a temporary manifestation as a consequence of a translation of a firm's core competences into something that fulfils customer wants and needs while these exist for a limited period of time. They picture a firm as a tree with the core competences as the roots from which core products sprout as trunks; branching out into SBUs; with the products as the leaves (see Figure 4.6). Products, like the leaves, come and go with the seasons while the roots and the trunk are more permanent fixtures that live on. A multi-business firm should have a small number of core competences and associated core products, where SBUs can tap into to remain viable in an ever-changing world. The competitive strategy at SBU level is about exploiting existing

---

Illustration 4.2: A dynamic capability routine at Cisco Systems

For a period of time, Cisco Systems acquired technology start-ups as a matter of routine (Goldblatt, 1999). Cisco makes the equipment on which the internet runs. To keep abreast of new technological developments and when it found it unable to develop a technology in-house, Cisco would look around Silicon Valley and buy the firm that was in the process of developing it. Up to 1999, Cisco had spent US$18.8 billion on acquisitions. It bought and absorbed 10 companies in 1998 alone. The company has dedicated people to look out for eligible firms, to negotiate the takeover, and subsequently to integrate the acquired firm into the Cisco organization. It has done it so many times that it can strike a deal in days and integrate the newly acquired firm in months, without much upset to the company and the acquired firm.

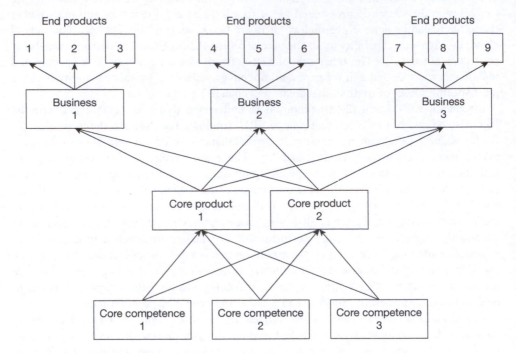

Figure 4.6 Core competence
Derived from Hamel and Prahalad (1994)

products and of finding new applications of core products, which cater for changing customer demands.

Corporate strategy for the multi-business firm is about maintaining and more importantly developing core competences through strategic intent by stretch and leverage. Strategic intent refers to an ambition about what the firm will be about in the future, not what the firm currently is. It is not based on the current resource base but on capabilities that still need to be developed. This, in the eyes of Hamel and Prahalad (1994), creates a situation of stretch, of reaching beyond the horizon to achieve something that is currently non-existent. By being ambitious and stretching out, it is possible that the firm leverages itself into the future. Hamel and Prahalad like to talk about strategic management as stretch and leverage. This requirement of stretch forms the basis of core competence as dynamic capability (see Figure 4.7).

Illustration 4.3: The core competence of Honda

Honda is showcased as a firm that is organized around core competence (Prahalad and Hamel 1990). The actual core competences that form the basis of Honda's success are combustion engineering and robotics. This translates into the combustion engine and manufacturing robots as core products. Its line of businesses ranges from cars, motorcycles and power generators to lawnmowers, outboard marine engines and snow blowers. All of these products feature a combustion engine and are manufactured to a very high standard with the aid of robots.

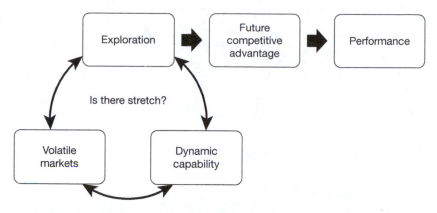

Figure 4.7 The dynamic resource-based view

The dynamic resource-based view is almost per definition a corporate strategy level type of strategic thinking. It urges a firm to constantly explore for new business. This makes it unavoidable that a firm becomes a multi-business firm, juggling the exploitation within its existing activities with the exploration to develop new business. If a firm is able to combine exploration with exploitation, it is said to be 'ambidextrous' (O'Reilly III and Tushman 2004). This is not an easy thing to do because the requirements of exploitation – doing the same thing over and over again – contradict exploration – actively looking for things to change.

Nevertheless, the reason why a particular single business is better off as part of a larger entity is found in a resource base that allows for this exploration to take place and which is only available to an SBU because it is part of a larger whole. The environment is seen as a volatile and ever changing place. Dynamic capability is expected to deal with this and fuels a deliberate strategy of exploration (March 1991). The overall strategic intent should be one of stretch: of reaching just beyond the horizon. Without stretch, so the argument goes, the firm never develops beyond what it is already doing, and eventually will wither away.

Additional features

A specific branch of the resource-based view has singled out knowledge as the key resource on which everything else hinges (Grant 1996; Kogut and Zander 1992). Their argument is based on the observation that the world economy essentially is a 'knowledge-based economy', and that economic performance is determined by what you know. There exist various types of knowledge and a common distinction is the one between explicit knowledge and tacit knowledge (Polanyi 1967). Explicit knowledge can be articulated and transferred. You find it written down, for instance, in procedures, manuals and teaching materials. Or it is materialized in equipment and machinery that can be bought and installed. Obviously explicit knowledge is transferable and cannot therefore be a basis for competitive advantage. Tacit knowledge is what people know but that they are unable to express. Transferred to the realm of the resource-based view, it is this tacit knowledge that is bound to be unique to a firm, and the quest is on to manage and develop the inexpressible.

Ironically, what you know and how you understand things cannot only propel you forward but can also hold you back. The possibility of change combined with the temporality of a firm's resource-based competitive advantage gives rise to the concept of core rigidity

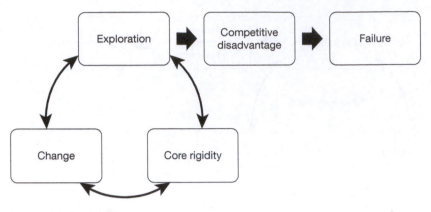

Figure 4.8 Core rigidity

(Leonard-Barton 1992). Core rigidity refers to a past core capability that a firm is geared up to exploit but whose usefulness is surpassed by changing circumstances. It is obsolete knowledge but still used by the firm and its top management and employees to make sense of the world. A core capability has a tendency to be so ingrained in the functioning of a firm that it is very difficult to get rid of. What first made the firm successful is now a reason for failure. It adds another consideration for the explanation of performance. It needs to take core rigidity as a cause for failure into account (see Figure 4.8).

Doing resource-based view strategic management

As there is a static resource-based view and a dynamic resource-based view, there are two ways to go here. The static resource-based view is more of an add-on to marketing-based strategic thinking or the industrial organization approach. It allows the strategist to assess the sustainability of a firm's competitive advantage and add that to the internal appraisal. The dynamic resource-based view departs from this and favours a way of doing strategic management that moves away from rational decision-making in favour of corporate entrepreneurship. Consequently, there are two sets of questions to answer. From a static resource-based view standpoint the two questions are:

1   Are there any issues that interfere with the firm exploiting its VRIN routines?
2   If there are, what can you do about them?

From a dynamic resource-based view standpoint, the two questions become:

1   Are there any issues that prevent the firm to stretch itself by exploring its future on the basis of its dynamic capabilities?
2   If there are, what can you do about them?

Answering question 1: strategic analysis

To be able to debate answers to these two sets of questions, the strategist should be familiar with the firm's resource base, whether there are any VRIN routines and how they are

Illustration 4.4: Core rigidity at NBL

NBL stands for North British Locomotive Company, a large Glasgow engineering firm with a proud history in producing railway steam engines (Fleming, McKinstry and Wallace 2000). The company was declared bankrupt in 1962. It could trace its history back 129 years, having produced no less than 28,000 locomotives and exporting them all over the world.

The firm and its management were fully aware of the development of new forms of traction with railway locomotives powered by diesel engines or electricity. It had reviewed its position and future in post-war Britain and concluded that there was still a market for steam locomotives for the time being, despite the inherent efficiencies that diesel and electricity hold over steam. Their analysis told them that the availability of oil is limited to a relatively small number of well developed countries. They reckoned that diesel powered locomotives would be a limited market in countries like the US, which happen to be rich in oil. The UK was an oil importing country but furnished with coal. Electric traction requires an expensive additional infrastructure of electric power supply, either through overhead catenary or a third rail. The UK would not be able to afford these investments for some time. The distances in many of their export markets were so large that electrification would not be a consideration there either. On that basis, they had set themselves up to keep on selling and producing steam locomotives while exploring the possibilities of diesel technology. In fact, NBL did have a line in small diesel-mechanical shunting engines.

Diesel-mechanical technology was not suited for the high speeds and power requirements of mainline railway locomotives. To enhance their technological abilities, NBL entered licensing agreements with German diesel engine manufacturer MAN and with the German firm Voith for hydraulic transmission systems. The British Government had nationalized the railways in the UK in 1948. By 1955, they were keen to modernize the railways and opted for dieselization. They made British Railways order small batches of diesel locomotives with various UK based suppliers. This was much earlier than NBL management had expected. However, NBL secured orders for high-powered and medium-powered diesel-hydraulic locomotives as well as medium-powered diesel-electric locomotives. This provided NBL with the opportunity to retool their production facilities for the new technologies. The diesel engines and the hydraulic equipment were going to be made by NBL by building licensed MAN and Voith designs. The electric equipment for the diesel-electrics was going to be bought in from GEC.

On completion, the diesel-hydraulic locomotives suffered from very many teething problems. The diesel-electrics fared a bit better because of the GEC equipment. As it turned out, the NBL men who were perfectly capable of designing and building high quality steam locomotives were having difficulty manufacturing diesel engines and hydraulic transmissions. The new technologies required much more precision and much tighter tolerances compared to steam. The teething problems turned out to be much more than that. British Railways stopped placing repeat orders, opting for designs from other locomotive builders instead. In the meantime, British colonies were gaining independence. These traditional markets for UK manufacturing firms took their business elsewhere. By 1962, NBL did not have any money left, was devoid of orders and decided to enter into voluntary administration.

exploited, and whether the firm has dynamic capability and is stretching itself into the future. If this familiarity is not the case, the strategist needs to get up to speed first.

Getting up to speed

The static resource-based view provides a way to probe the sustainability of a firm's competitive advantage. Marketing-inspired strategic thinking conceptualizes the firm in terms of key or critical success factors. The industrial organization approach sees the firm as a number of value activities that combine into a value chain. These success factors or value activities can be further examined to unearth the resources, or more specifically, the routines and capabilities on which these are based. Competitive advantage based on certain success factors or particular value activities is sustainable when these are based on core capabilities. Capabilities are core when they are valuable (remember these capabilities should be suitable for implementing a competitive strategy, like the ones mentioned in the marketing-derived trade-off between value and price or the generic strategies in the industrial organization approach). Furthermore, these capabilities should be rare, inimitable and non-substitutable.

To get on the tail of capabilities that are core, the strategist needs to look at the various routines that make up the firm (see Exhibit 4.1). These are the regular and predictable behavioural patterns by which the firm creates its goods or services. These routines can be broken down in terms of the firm resources and the firm members' individual abilities (see Figure 4.4). With regard to the individual abilities, skills refer to what an individual is able to do; motivation concerns whether an individual is willing to do it. On the side of the firm resources, physical resources concern the plant; equipment and materials available. Financial resources refer to the amount of money on hand. Knowledge resources concern information and shared understandings about how things can be done. Cultural resources refer to shared norms and values. Marketing resources refer to the various devices and artifacts by which a firm engages with customers. Organizational resources concern how a firm is organized to facilitate coordinated routinized activity. A common mistake to make here is to provide only an enumeration of resources; to generate a list that tells nothing more than that the firm has physical resources, financial resources, human resources or knowledge resources, without providing any indication as to how these assemble into routines and whether these routines fulfil the VRIN criteria. Obviously, when the core capabilities have been identified, there needs to be a check that these play a role in the strategy that the firm is realizing.

Exhibit 4.1: Static resource-based view internal appraisal questions

- What routines are employed within the firm?
- What physical, financial, knowledge, cultural, marketing and organizational resources are available for these routines?
- What individual abilities in terms of motivations and skills do employees and managers have to enact these routines?
- Do any or a combination of resources and individual abilities combine into *core* capabilities because they are valuable, rare, inimitable and non-substitutable?
- Are the available VRIN routines exploited by the firm's competitive strategy?

There is no need to be concerned with factor markets. By addressing capabilities in this way, the strategist automatically implies the factor markets that are imagined to exist. The question obviously is whether a particular factor market is perfect or imperfect. The answer is given as soon as a conclusion is drawn whether a capability fulfils the VRIN criteria or not. The static resource-based view does not contribute to the external appraisal.

The dynamic resource-based view leads to a completely different kind of analysis. It is not so much in aid of making rational decisions, as with marketing-inspired strategic thinking, the industrial organization approach and the static resource-based view. Instead it is an evaluation of a firm's ability to deal with changing circumstances by demonstrating corporate entrepreneurship.

In line with the view that dynamic capability is found in specific routines that indicate a firm is actively engaging with the future (Eisenhardt and Martin 2000), the strategist should try to identify these specific routines within the firm and assess their effectiveness (see Exhibit 4.2 and compare with figure 4.4). Does the firm engage in new product and business development? Does it do R&D; is it active in pursuing innovations etc? Whether a firm is engaged in acquisitions, strategic alliances and joint ventures – in effect scouting the environment and taking an interest in interesting new developments – is an activity that qualifies as a dynamic capability routine (Helfat and others 2007). Also the way in which the firm does its strategic management indicates whether there is dynamic capability. The argument can be made that if a firm develops strategy on the basis of a rigid strategic planning regime, it can be taken as an indicator of the absence of dynamic capability. Alternatively, if there is lively strategy debate going on as is advocated in this book, this can be taken as an indicator of the presence of dynamic capability.

However, anything that the firm has developed and achieved in the past does not necessarily mean that it will create something new in the future. There is only comfort in knowing that the firm is actually actively engaged with its future instead of doing nothing. Conversely, if the firm does feature specific routines that indicate dynamic capability but these do not appear to lead the firm into new territory, the question should be asked whether there is some core rigidity present. Does the firm run around in circles and continuously ends up doing the same thing?

If the view is taken that dynamic capability is a feature of the firm – like Prahalad and Hamel's (1994) core competence – the strategist should try to identify the firm's core

---

Exhibit 4.2: Dynamic resource-based view starter questions

- Is there evidence of specific routines that indicate dynamic capability like business development, innovation, R&D, etc.?
- How successful has the firm been in generating new business as a consequence of these routines?
- Are there core competences?
- Are there core products?
- Is there a succession of businesses that have come out of these core competences and core products?
- Is there activity that is aimed at maintaining and developing core competences and core products?
- Is there evidence of core rigidity?

competences and core products (see Exhibit 4.2 and compare with figure 4.6). Additionally, the strategist should try to track the succession of businesses and products that have come out of these core competences and core products, as well as the activities that go into maintaining and developing the core competences and core products.

Going real Time: debating strategy

For real time strategic management from the perspective of the static resource-based view, the strategist should start off with the same things as with the industrial organization approach or with marketing-inspired strategic thinking. Obviously a comprehensive understanding of the firm's strategic position should be in place. On the basis of that, the static resource-based view adds an additional set of questions and considerations that should be taken into account (see Exhibit 4.3). Again the continuous strategy debate should be focused on the question of fit. Adding the static resource-based view to the deliberations, this 'fit' question should consider the competitive strategy that the firm realizes and provided this

---

Strategy practice 4.1: A resource-based view SWOT analysis

The purpose of a SWOT analysis is to find out about threats and opportunities in the environment and about strengths and weaknesses with regard to the firm. But what makes an opportunity an opportunity, a threat a threat, a strength a strength, and a weakness a weakness? Marketing- inspired strategic thinking may be of help here.

The focus of the resource-based view is on the firm itself. With regard to a SWOT analysis it is mostly applicable for evaluating whether there are any strengths and weaknesses. Strengths in static resource-based view terms refer to the core capabilities: the routines that are VRIN. Weakness is a firm that does not possess any core capabilities. From a dynamic resource-based point of view, strengths are expressed as featuring dynamic capability either in terms of specific routines by which the firm actively engages with the future, combined with a successful track record, or in terms of core competences and core products. An obvious weakness is the existence of core rigidity.

Strategy practice 4.2: Internationalization from a resource-based viewpoint

There is a top-down and a bottom-up argument here. Starting from the core capabilities of country subsidiaries of a multi-national corporation (MNC), Birkinshaw, Hood and Jonsson (1998) distinguish between 'location-bound' capabilities and 'non-location-bound' capabilities. Location-bound capabilities only matter within a country and have no application elsewhere. Non-location-bound capabilities have applicability in more than one country. An MNC should seek out those capabilities and transfer and deploy them across its subsidiaries. Hamel and Prahalad's (1994) top-down core competence model implies that an MNCs core competence should be translated into core products and in turn into businesses and end products across various countries.

strategy exploits the firm's core capabilities, whether there are any developments with regard to the VRIN criteria. Although there is sustainability with regard to the firm's current competitive advantage because of the VRIN qualities, the strategists should keep an eye out for anything that undermines the firm's core capabilities. The strategy debate should be about this.

Combining the static and dynamic views, the strategy debate should also be about the tension between the continuity of exploitation and the change that exploration could create. This refers to ambidexterity (O'Reilly III and Tushman 2004) and simultaneously to be a good competitor now while developing new competitive advantage for future success.

From a dynamic resource-based point of view, one thing to debate is the firm's strategic management routine itself. As was argued earlier, having a lively real time strategy debate can be seen as dynamic capability. Taking the criticism of the dynamic resource-based view towards marketing-inspired strategic thinking or the industrial organization approach to heart, having a debate that is exclusively focused on these two approaches, because of their static nature, indicate the possible presence of core rigidity. If a firm's strategic management demonstrates an over-reliance on marketing or industrial organization vocabulary and logic, it can indicate that the firm is too much engrossed in the present with an implicit expectation

---

Exhibit 4.3: Static resource-based view questions to debate

- Is something that is happening or that is about to happen going to lose a core capability its value?
- Is something that is happening or that is about to happen going to lose a core capability its rarity?
- Is something that is happening or that is about to happen going to lose a core capability its inimitability?
- Is something that is happening or that is about to happen going to lose a core capability its non-substitutability?

Does any of this mean that the 'fit' is affected, as the chosen competitive strategy will not exploit core capabilities?

Exhibit 4.4: Dynamic resource-based view question to debate

How does the firm 'do' strategic management?

Is there change that comes with preparing for and dealing with a new future at the expense of competing successfully in the here and now?

or –

Is the firm competing successfully in the here and now at the expense of the change that comes with preparing for and dealing with a new future?

Is there 'stretch' towards an imagined future that builds on the firm's dynamic capabilities and core competences?

that what is happening now will continue very much unchanged into the future. The key subject for debate here is about where to stretch into and whether the firm is actively engaged with a future that is different from how the firm competes today (see Exhibit 4.4).

Answering question 2: taking action

The co-existence of a static and a dynamic resource-based view means that the options of what to do can be arranged in an order of increasing ambition and difficulty. From a static resource-based point of view, if there is an issue, this will concern a firm not utilizing its core capabilities. To rectify this, the firm has to change its competitive strategy. In terms of the marketing-inspired trade-off between value and price, it has to move up or down so that it is based on the VRIN routines that make up the firm's core capabilities. In terms of the industrial organization generic strategies, it has to pick the right generic strategy. This is how the static resource-based view serves as an add-on to the aforementioned other two theoretical approaches.

If the issues that a firm is facing are a matter of the core capabilities being undermined, i.e. they are losing their VRIN qualities, or if the firm is suffering from core rigidity, then the remedy is to stretch into the future by developing new core capabilities. Now we are in the realm of the dynamic resource-based view. The process logic of the dynamic resource-based view sees the firm as trying to survive in a volatile environment. There are two ways of

---

Strategy practice 4.3: A resource-based view strategy workshop

Top management teams periodically book themselves into a nice retreat over a weekend to discuss how they or the firm are doing. This is an ideal opportunity to do some deliberate strategy debate. Quite often, an external consultant is asked to design a programme for the workshop, to suggest topics for discussion and to facilitate the workshop.

The static resource-based view can add to the workshop design that the consultant puts together. He can have the management team discuss the core capabilities that the firm may have. It would be sensible to do this in addition to marketing's success factors or Porter's value chain. It provides an additional area for debate by considering the sustainability of a firm's competitive advantage because the success factors or the value adding activities in the value chain are supposed to be linked to core capabilities that are VRIN.

The dynamic resource-based view offers possibilities for debating change and possible new futures. This is a debate about 'stretch'. They can discuss the presence and effectiveness of dynamic capability routines. If this is a multi-business firm, topics to talk about include the firm's core competences, core products, whether the firm has them and how these are translated into current businesses and products. Moreover, the debate should be about how to leverage the core competences and core products to create future new businesses and products.

A grimmer topic to debate during the strategy workshop is the possibility that the firm may suffer from core rigidity. Part of this can be a management team engaging in active self-refection about how they do their strategic management and whether that closes down or facilitates change.

doing this, depending on whether you think that dynamic capability is found in specific routines by which new VRIN routines are developed, or whether you think dynamic capability is a firm attribute like core competence.

With regard to the latter, dealing with a volatile environment requires a firm to utilize its core competences to develop new core capabilities that can be exploited in new businesses (Hamel and Prahalad 1994). As was explained earlier, businesses, like leaves on a tree, come with the seasons while a firm's core competences, like the roots and the trunk, make sure that the firm survives as it develops a continuous stream of new products and businesses.

The alternative of seeing dynamic capability is the firm having specific routines like product or business development, innovation or R&D available, comes with an expectation that these routines provide a steady stream of new core capabilities that the firm can utilize. These in turn are activities that are associated with their own dedicated fields of study. Alternatively, the firm can team up with other firms in joint ventures and strategic alliances to develop new technology or business opportunities (Das and Teng 2000). Or it can acquire or merge with other firms to add to and refresh its capabilities (Schoenberg 2003).

A larger and even more severe issue that a strategist can be confronted with is a firm lacking dynamic capability. In this case, the remedy would be to start developing or acquiring dynamic capability routines or core competence if the firm can afford to do so. Change of this magnitude requires a complete metamorphosis. This is a far from easy matter.

These are all ways of how a firm utilizes, maintains and develops its resource base. From a dynamic capability perspective, the strategist should become more of an entrepreneur than a rational decision-maker. Because renewal potentially disrupts the current state of affairs, entrepreneurship is a subversive activity (Hitt and Ireland 2000). If not engaged in doing

---

Strategy practice 4.4: Formulating a strategic business plan using the resource-based view

The static resource-based view allows for an extra qualification of the success factors of marketing-inspired strategic thinking or the value chain activities of the industrial organization approach. If the routines on which these are based happen to be VRIN, that part of the business plan that deals with the firm itself can be amended. The planned strategy has gained some more credence, as the competitive advantage on which it is based is now 'sustainable' competitive advantage because of identified core capabilities.

Putting together a business plan on the basis of the dynamic resource-based view is less straightforward. There are two levels of ambition here. Firstly, the plan can entail aiming for the development of new core capabilities on the basis of the dynamic capability that the firm might have. To do this, it needs to be ascertained that the firm has dynamic capability. If this is the case, by definition, the firm knows how to go about, defying the need to write a business plan about it. Secondly, if the firm lacks dynamic capability, it sounds obvious to then write a business plan about developing it. However, the question is whether dynamic capability is something that can be developed by writing and executing a business plan. What is impossible to do is to do the sums. You cannot make an estimate of expected turnover, costs and profit margins for a business that still has to develop the dynamic capability to create new core capabilities that eventually can underpin competitive advantage.

Illustration 4.5: SKF from a resource-based view point of view

Should SKF* compete on price and put in the lowest bid possible to retain a big US-based client, or should they step away and persist with their high-quality strategy?

What is important to consider here is which one of these two alternatives involves exploiting SKF's core capabilities. This refers to those routines that are valuable, rare, inimitable and non-substitutable. The routines that need to be considered here are its manufacturing, sales and servicing routines. SKF has a production process that generates high quality reliable ball bearings for a wide range of applications. These are so reliable that they are commonly used in critical applications like jet engines and turbines, where a failure can lead to catastrophe. This has come about in the course of a firm history spanning more than 100 years. Within the SKF Service Division, this is combined with marketing and sales routines – backed up by a software tool – by which SKF sales representatives can demonstrate to a customer how much money they can save by using high quality SKF ball bearings and have more reliable machinery that requires less maintenance and lasts longer, even if the ball bearings are more expensive to buy. This supports SKF's competitive strategy of differentiation. Long term reliable manufacturing at an overall lower cost level must represent value for an end user. Therefore there is a sense that SKF has core capabilities as these routines are valuable – it underpins a competitive strategy, they are rare – SKF manufacturing and marketing is a unique combination, they are inimitable – it requires high investments to equal SKF's know-how, and they are non-substitutable – there are no immediate alternatives available to the sales software but even more so to SKF's ball bearing manufacturing process. Staying away from competition on price and continuing with the differentiation strategy exploits SKF's core capabilities. Giving in to the price competition and participating in the reverse auction does not.

* Value selling at SKF Service, IMD-5-0751, 2009.

---

new and different things themselves, strategists should facilitate innovation and change within the firm. In its extreme form, this can mean a complete reversal of the strategic planning logic, with doing things first in a trial and error fashion, and then to rationalize after the fact whether they have made any sense for future competitive advantage of the firm.

Criticisms and generating further questions

The static resource-based view comes from the same rational decision-making mould as marketing-inspired strategic thinking and the industrial organization approach. They all assume that there is a knowable business reality out there about which information can be gathered and processed to generate strategic decisions that are then implemented. They all assume top management to have the power and ability to initiate and realise a strategy at will. It also has the same issue of not being able to incorporate and explain fundamental change.

The dynamic resource-based view has been developed on the basis of the older approaches ignoring fundamental change. Instead, change is put at the heart of the argument. Dynamic capability is about dealing with change, with the implication that this fundamentally is what strategic management should be about. However, it is questionable whether the dynamic resource-based view has solved it. The ultimate answer is that a firm should have dynamic capability. Yet there is some confusion as to what this actually is, let alone how you acquire or develop it. There is also little guidance with regard to evaluating the scope or the direction of particular changes and initiatives a firm can get involved in. Thus far there are suggestions that research into dynamic capability should draw on the fields of organizational change, change management, renewal, adaptation, growth, innovation, organizational learning and knowledge management to give it more substance (Easterby-Smith, Lyles and Peteraf 2009). This still is in its early stages.

You can expect that the argument will be made that a firm has to exploit the current core capabilities as well as explore for new core capabilities on the basis of dynamic capabilities. The concept of ambidexterity makes that point (O'Reilly III and Tushman, 2004). However, this is easier said than done. March (1991) argues that exploitation and exploration are mutually exclusive. Concentrating on what the firm currently is doing and learning to become better and better at it, diminishes the capacity and inclination to experiment and try out truly new things. Besides, doing new things generates costs while the future return is uncertain because you cannot know what it will bring. The pressure to perform now adds to further postponements of investing in the future. The other way round, stepping away from becoming better at what the firm currently is doing, leaves room for competitors to catch up and overtake in the current market place. Yet, this is the consequence from devoting attention to new things.

Furthermore, dynamic capability as it stands now is just about the aptitude to acknowledge and deal with change, not about where change should lead or how to bring it about. It is a concept that appears to have the attributes of the ultimate panacea or solution for everything (Helfat and others 2007). The term is coined to capture the ultimate prize in strategic management: continued firm survival and performance in the face of fundamental change. As yet, it does not deliver in bringing us a failsafe method to deal effectively with all the threats to the future success of the firm. You can even wonder whether this is at all possible.

The dynamic resource-based view also adds subjectivity to strategic management. Top managers can get it wrong. Their field of vision can be limited and distorted. That is the implication of core rigidity. Like everybody else in the firm, top management's interpretations are informed and mediated by the knowledge they already possess: specific knowledge that is implied with particular core capabilities. This is what made the firm function and be successful in the first place. When this knowledge becomes out-dated and obsolete, there is a danger that top management becomes part of the problem. In principle, any firm's strategic management can become subject to core rigidity, as can any strategy debate that takes place within the firm. What does it mean for strategic management that the assumption of objectivity with top managers as impartial and unbiased information processors is nothing but an unattainable ideal?

Furthermore, the notion of 'stretch' as the ultimate ambition for firms to propel themselves into the future, introduces subjectivity into strategic management as well. Stretch relies on strategic intent which in turn is based on an imagined future. Nobody knows what the future will bring and any expectation has to rely on imagination. Imagination is very subjective. Imagining a future business reality – by definition – is an exercise of the mind. A future business reality does not exist out there to be measured and assessed because it has not happened yet.

Case 4.1 Starbucks

The first Starbucks coffee shop opened in Seattle in 1971.[1] Howard Schultz – still the current CEO – walked into this shop in 1981. The high quality coffee that was served had drawn him in. He started working for the shop in 1982. In 1983 on a trip to Italy, he came across the Italian coffee culture. He left Starbucks and started his own chain of Il Giornale coffeehouses in the US. In 1987, with the help of outside investment partners, he bought Starbucks. The rest is history. Starbucks now operates over 17,000 stores in 55 countries. They describe themselves as "the premier roaster and retailer of specialty coffee in the world".

The client experience is almost the same in every Starbucks store that you go into, whether it is in Denver, Taipei, Glasgow, or Sao Paulo. You walk up to the counter and order a beverage using words like 'venti', 'skinny latte', 'caramel machiatto', or 'frappuccino'. They put your name on a carton cup and then you pay. Next you move over to another part of the counter and wait. While you wait, a barista prepares your beverage, adds all the extra ingredients that you ordered and hands it over to you. You then have to go to another counter where you can add milk and sugar yourself and where you can put a lid on the cup. It is your choice to sit down and drink your coffee or walk out and have it on the go. If you like, you can also have some pre-packed food with your beverage.

The manager at Brooklyn, New York, busiest store reckons that he can get every customer served within 3 minutes; 5 minutes max when it is really busy.[2] A barista steams milk for 6–8 seconds. Latte milk is steamed for 3–5 seconds. They serve drinks an average of 165 degrees Fahrenheit but never over 180 degrees. There are four different batches of coffee to pour from all the time, with each batch rotated every 15 minutes so that coffee never gets older than 30 minutes. Before working as a barista at Starbucks, you have to undergo 30 hours of training. One of the things to master is a complex shorthand to be able to quickly communicate the vast array of different drinks that can be ordered. DCCFL stands for double chocolate chip frappuccino light. They also have to learn to operate the Swiss-made Mastreno coffee machine to make perfect espresso shots. A very few select stores have a Clover single-brew coffee machine.

---

1 http://www.starbucks.com (accessed 30 October 2012).
2 *Business Insider*, 29 July 2011, http://www.businessinsider.com/starbucks-does-better-2011-7?op=1 (accessed 29 October 2012).

In 2010 Starbucks issued new rules for serving customers to counter complaints that the company had made coffee into a mechanized process.[3] Baristas should only work on one drink at a time, they should steam milk for one drink only instead of doing a batch for several drinks, rinse out pitchers after every use, staying at the espresso bar while making a drink and not move around, and use only one machine instead of two simultaneously. When these new rules were issued, baristas feared that it would create longer lines. One commented: "While I'm blending a frappuccino, it doesn't make sense to stand there and wait for the blender to finish running, because I could be making an iced tea at the same time". Starbucks documents do acknowledge that customers probably have to wait longer but also that customers only think that Starbuck's quality is 'average' and that drinks are prepared inconsistently.

More recently Howard Schultz stated that he knows that Starbucks is losing customers because of the long lines but "the challenge for us is that we want to improve our speed, but we don't want to become a fast-food chain".[4] They even invested in Square, a company pioneering new mobile payment technologies in the expectation that this will speed up the lines.[5] Howard Schultz was appointed to the Square board of directors.

After a slump in 2009 (net revenue of US$9.8 billion down from US$10.4 billion in 2008), 2011 saw net revenue rise to US$11.7 billion.[6] Store sales growth was up 8 per cent after experiencing a decline of 6 per cent in 2009. Of total net revenue, 82 per cent came from company-operated stores. Licensed stores accounted for 9 per cent; consumer packaged goods represented 4 per cent of the net revenue and foodservice was another 4 per cent. During 2011, Starbucks spent £15 million on R&D, up from US$9 million in 2010. It was used for product testing and product and process improvements. Their stated objective was to maintain Starbucks as a global brand, to expand their store base, primarily outside of the US, and to develop new coffee products.

There is a 'Global Development Partners' design department based in Seattle, which is responsible for the design and maintenance of all Starbucks' stores all over the world.[7] Starbucks claims to have the ability to tailor their stores to every situation worldwide and to blend and adapt its design and look to local circumstances.[8] This allows them to set up shop in a variety of settings but they need to be high-traffic, high visibility locations. They also vary the product-mix in accordance with the size and location of the store

In 2008, Starbucks acquired The Coffee Equipment Company.[9] It is the firm behind the Clover coffee-making machine. Howard Schultz was intrigued by the long queue in

3 *Wall Street Journal*, 13 October 2010, http://online.wsj.com/article/SB1000142405274870416400457554840351 4060736.html, (accessed 30 October 2012).
4 *Wall Street Journal*, 29 August 2012, http://online.wsj.com/article/SB100008723963904449149045776197430 14442300.html, (accessed 30 October 2012).
5 *Wall Street Journal*, 8 August 2012, http://online.wsj.com/article/SB100008723963904444423704577575803898 185594.html (accessed 30 October 2012).
6 Starbucks 201/ annual report.
7 http://www.starbucks.com (accessed 30 October 2012).
8 Starbucks 201/ annual report.
9 *The Guardian*, / September 2008, http://www.guardian.co.uk/lifeandstyle/2008/sep/01/foodanddrink.fooddrinks, (accessed 17 February 2011).

front of an independent Café Grumpy in New York and bought a coffee. The shop operated a Clover. Schultz was so impressed that he moved almost immediately and bought the manufacturer: a small firm in Seattle, which hand-built each machine individually. "Frankly, we just don't want anyone else to have it". It is the ultimate machine for coffee aficionados. It allows the barista to vary the temperature, the brewing time, and the volume of water. It turns out one cup at a time but they sell for US$10. Daniel Kim, one of the baristas at Café Grumpy doubts whether Starbucks will be able to make much use of the Clover. "The skill of the baristas is very important, and there's just not enough great coffee beans for the volume they sell."

5 Agency theory and shareholder value

The main application of agency theory within the strategy field focuses on corporate governance and how an organization's management structure should be organized for maximum performance. For a business firm, this is further elaborated in terms of shareholder value. This means that a firm's strategic management is expected to make the interests of shareholders paramount.

The process logic of agency theory and shareholder value

Economists liken everything to markets. The market mechanism is a theoretical device that – in various forms and disguises – explains how scarce resources are allocated. This has led to what in economists' eyes is something of a conundrum. Why do organizations exist, as they are clearly not markets? It is a question first put forward by Ronald Coase (1937). One suggested answer is agency theory (Jensen and Meckling 1976). Agency theory turns an organization into a kind of a market by stating that an organization is a nexus of contracts. Jensen and Meckling continued to specify this further and came up with an explanation of why people buy shares in firms and have managers manage these firms for them. This then brings the concept of shareholder value further into focus for strategic management (Rappaport 1986).

Agency theory and corporate governance

Economists assume that people are utility maximizers. People put an effort in up to the point where the gains of this effort equal the costs that they have to endure. These gains and costs do not necessarily need to be financial but money is a handy device by which costs and gains become comparable among people. It also allows for a market to be elaborated as a conjuncture of supply and demand and to postulate that in a perfect market everything clears at an equilibrium price. Thus people involved in a firm are assumed to do so up to the point where their gains (financial or otherwise) equal their efforts (also financial or otherwise). Because of these gains people want to become involved in the first place. Such a mutual expectation, to Jensen and Meckling (1976), is a 'contract'. This can be a formal affair like an employment contract but quite often it is more informal: a kind of a common understanding of entitlements and obligations. This allows Jensen and Meckling to theorize about an organization as this nexus of contracts, of people getting involved up to a point where the gains equal the costs. These gains and costs are imagined as entitlements and obligations, which come with getting involved in the firm. They also imagine that the supply of efforts that should be put into the firm and the demand of gains that people can get out of the firm clear at a certain equilibrium price.

The specific kind of relationship every firm has to consent to is ownership. There is not much of a problem, for economists at least, when the manager is also the owner of the firm. All the efforts that the owner/manager puts in are compensated by the proceeds that the firm yields in profits, prestige or pleasure. In running the firm the manager will make decisions that maximize his utility. If ownership and management are not in the same hands, there is a problem. The manager will run the firm to maximize his utility but this is not necessarily in line with what the shareholder, as an investor, wants to get out of it. This is referred to as the agency problem (Jensen and Meckling 1976). There is an agent – the manager – who has to do something on behalf of a principal – the shareholder, but the principal cannot be sure whether his interests – in terms of the return on investment – are sufficiently taken into account by the agent.

This kind of agency problem exists throughout the whole firm. It appears at all levels of any firm where somebody has to do work for someone else. The question of how firms should be managed to maximize utility for the principals in these relationships is the question of corporate governance. It is important to note that corporate governance is not so much a top to bottom hierarchy but more of a circle, with everybody involved in the firm appearing as both agent and principal. Figure 5.1 illustrates this for a firm with dispersed ownership, where shareholders are often pension funds, banks, insurance companies or other investment vehicles, which keep money safe for their clients. These clients are very often ordinary people employed in the same firms whose shares are kept by these investors.

The same circular relationship exists with public organizations between politicians, civil servants and the general public who pay the taxes and vote politicians in or out. Non-profit organizations like charities feature a similar circle among the board of trustees, daily

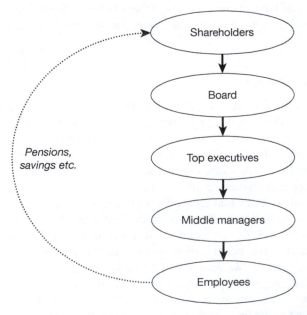

Figure 5.1 Corporate governance for a firm with dispersed ownership

management, workers, volunteers, and beneficiaries and, finally, the members who vote in the board of trustees.

However, the ramifications of the agency problem on corporate governance are mostly elaborated in the relationship between managers and shareholders. It has led to an understanding that the 'contract' between shareholders and managers should be put together in such a way that the interests are aligned. In this case, it will be a formal contract dealing with the terms of employment and remuneration of mostly top managers. Most of the time the solution is chosen to make top managers' earnings dependent on the share price. This, in turn, focuses the mind of top managers on shareholder value.

Shareholder value

There is a somewhat roundabout reasoning why top managers do focus on shareholder value. They do so because this is the way in which their terms of employment very often are set up to deal with the agency problem. It is also how their terms of employment should be set up because there is a moral obligation of firms and their managers to act in the service of shareholders. This has been most famously expressed by economist Milton Friedman (1970: 6). He stated that ". . . there is one and only one social responsibility of business - to use its resources and engage in activities designed to increase its profits so long as it stays within the rules of the game, which is to say, engages in open and free competition without deception or fraud".

Rappaport (1986) subscribes to this view and also gives two additional reasons why shareholder value, to him, is so important. The first additional reason is the market for corporate control. If a firm is underperforming, and this is indicated by a low share price, the firm becomes a target for a hostile takeover. This is because it is obvious that shaking up such an underperforming firm to substantially improve its performance, and therefore its share price, allows somebody to make money. Such a takeover involves sacking sitting top management. The second additional reason is that top managers compete for top jobs and they improve their bargaining power if they have a track record of creating high shareholder value.

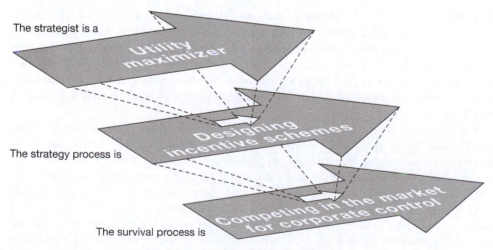

The strategist is a

The strategy process is

The survival process is

Figure 5.2 The process logic for agency theory and shareholder value

---

Illustration 5.1: The market for corporate control and Douwe Egberts

DE Master Blenders, the Dutch coffee, tea and tobacco company commonly referred to as Douwe Egberts after their best known brand, was bought and taken off the AEX Amsterdam Stock Exchange by German firm JAB, an investment vehicle for Joh. A Benckiser, in 2013.* Douwe Egberts had only been listed a year earlier, after it had demerged from Sara Lee Corp. During these few months, the company was troubled by a fraud scandal in its Brazilian subsidiary and severe differences of opinion within the executive team, leading to the resignation of the CEO. JAB had built up a minority shareholding before it offered to buy out everybody else. The share price had slumped and investors were very keen to take up JAB's offer. Their intention was to restore shareholder value for them by creating a multi-national coffee and tea firm around Douwe Egberts. They did so by taking charge of its management and combining it with future investments in this industry.

*NRC Handelsblad, 10 October 2012, http://www.nrc.nl/nieuws/2012/12/10/topman-douwe-egberts-stapt-op/; NRC Handelsblad, 28 March 2013, http://www.nrc.nl/nieuws/2013/03/28/grootaandeelhouder-komt-met-bod-op-douwe-egberts/#rel_expand=1; NRC Handelsblad, 16 August 2013, http://www.nrc.nl/handelsblad/van/2013/augustus/16/aandelen-douwe-egberts-massaal-aangemeld-1284527.

The environmental survival process thus takes place in this market for corporate control (see Figure 5.2). The strategy process is primarily a matter of solving the agency problem, of aligning the interests of the shareholders with the interest of top management. Designing incentive schemes that align top management interests with maximizing shareholder value does this. The strategist is here simply taken as a utility maximizer, as economists assume all people are.

The performance logic of agency theory and shareholder value

Firm performance here is primarily a function of shareholder value. Shareholder value, in turn, is an estimate. It is a metric that expresses what a firm is worth in terms of its earning capacity (Rappaport 1986). In its simplest form, any firm is assumed to enjoy a certain level of profitability. A firm can do two things with the money that is left over after all expenses have been paid. It can be paid out as a dividend to the shareholders. It can be added to the firm's reserves to be invested later in developing the business further to make it even more profitable.

A shareholder/investor is interested in two things. First, there is the question of how much return on an investment is expected, that is, all the dividends for the period the shareholder wants to own the shares. When profitability is expected to increase above earlier expectations, the share price rises on the back of that, creating an additional return to the investor. Second, there is the question of how much risk there is for the firm to become loss-making or go bankrupt in the period that the shareholder wants to invest in the firm. These two – risk and return – are expressed in the current share price. The share price indicates the value that a share has for an investor. There is the assumption that the financial markets are near perfect and that the price at which a share is traded reflects its value. A high risk/low

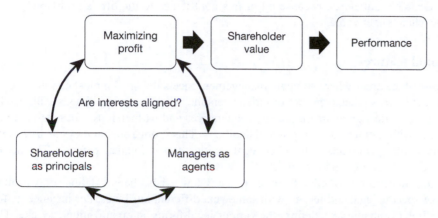

Figure 5.3 Agency theory and shareholder value

profitability firm is less in demand and therefore the share price is relatively low. A low risk/ high profitability firm is the stock market's favourite.

Maximizing shareholder value thus is the primary task of top management (see figure 5.3). The decisions they make are only judged in terms of lowering risk and increasing profits. If they are incentivised to do just that because of their terms of employment, then this adds to the shareholder value. Rappaport (1986) even argues that this benefits everybody who is involved in the firm. A financially sound and stable firm is a good place to work. The firm also pays its taxes, stays within the law and creates other

---

Illustration 5.2: CEO remuneration at Microsoft

The Microsoft 2011 Proxy Statement* prepared for the annual meeting of shareholders contained an elaborate explanation of how much CEO Steve Ballmer got paid. For 2011 he received a US$682,500 bonus on top of his US$682,500 salary.

The non-executive members of the Microsoft board of directors, acting on recommendations of the board's Compensation Committee, take the decisions on CEO pay at Microsoft. An independent compensation consultant advises the Compensation Committee. At the beginning of the fiscal year, the remuneration scheme is decided upon, as well as a set of specific targets with target incentive awards attached. At the end of the fiscal year, the CEO's performance is reviewed and decisions are made whether targets have been met, what award amount will be provided and whether the basic salary will be adjusted.

Steve Ballmer was awarded a bonus because he presided over the partnerships with Facebook and Nokia, over improvements to Windows Azure and the Bing search engine, and over a number of successful product launches like the Kinect motion-sensing controller for the Xbox and cloud-based Office. The board did not award the full amount available because of lower sales than expected of the Windows Phone 7.

Steve Ballmer also holds 3.95 per cent of Microsoft shares.

* Microsoft 2011 Proxy Statement, http://apps.shareholder.com/sec/viewerContent.aspx?comp anyid=MSFT&docid=8172917.

socially desirable outcomes, because all of this contributes to the firm's profitability and, therefore, shareholder value.

Additional features

This is one of the areas where strategic management meets the law. In most countries, civil law defines all kinds of legal entities or juristic persons, who are not individuals. This can be companies, charities, government bodies, cooperatives and partnerships. These are defined as endowed with statutory obligations and liabilities. This is done so that they can be a party in legally binding contracts with other legal entities and individual persons. The act of incorporation is a sort of contract by itself.

In almost all countries where a form of company law exists, the law defines only a small number of specific legal entities, all with somewhat different attributes. For instance, in the UK, the 2006 Companies Act defines the various legal forms an organization can take. The abbreviations of, for instance, 'Ltd' or 'Plc' indicate what form for this legal entity has been chosen. 'Ltd' stands for 'limited' and means that the shares are not publicly traded. 'Plc' stands for 'public limited company' and means that everybody can own a share in this company and you can find these companies listed on the London Stock Exchange. This distinction is made in many countries around the world and is often signalled with a particular abbreviation that is added to the company name.

When an organization is incorporated, it has to take on the form of one of these legal entities. The law prescribes specific corporate governance arrangements. For instance, the 'Plc' in the UK should have a board of directors. The chief executive and the top executive team are responsible to the board. The board appoints and dismisses the top executives and sets their remuneration. The board of directors, in turn, is responsible to the shareholders. For this, the firm is obliged to organize an annual general meeting (AGM) where the board is held to account. The firm is also obliged to publish an annual report on the accounts, which should be approved by an independent accountant.

Other forms come with different arrangements. Yet they all organize the agent–principal relationship between various parties involved in the organization in a specific and pre-set way. There are also many variations between countries. For instance, in the UK, directors can either work for the company (executive directors) or not (non-executive directors). In the Netherlands, members of the supervisory board, as it is called there, are required to be independent from the firm so all board members are non-executive.

Doing strategic management for shareholder value

To identify an issue here, there is a staggered logic. The first concern is shareholder value itself and whether the firm is actually maximizing this. The derived concern refers to the requirement of aligning the interests between the managers/agents and the shareholders/ principals. If this is the case, the expectation is that shareholder value will be maximized. Therefore the main focus is whether managers are sufficiently incentivized to maximize shareholder value. The two questions therefore are:

1　Are managers (as agents) incentivized to maximize profit (and create shareholder value) on behalf of the shareholders (principals)?
2　If this is not the case, what can you do about it?

Answering question 1: strategic analysis

In order to debate and answer these two questions, the strategist should know about the incentive or remuneration scheme. Moreover, the strategist should know about the firm's shareholder value and whether it is on par with what can be expected. The strategist needs to get up to speed first if this is not the case.

Getting up to speed

The first thing to consider is whether ownership and management are separated. If this is not the case, the corporate governance agency problem does not exist. When ownership is separated from management, the second thing to find out is under what legal framework the firm is operating. This means finding out in which country the firm is incorporated and what the legal entity is by which the firm operates. This provides a baseline for the corporate governance relationships that should be in place. Shareholder value is of particular importance to firms whose shares are freely tradable and which are listed on a stock exchange somewhere in the world. Those firms are expected to have owners/shareholders who are primarily interested in the financial gains that their investments will yield. Firms whose shares are freely tradable are exposed the most to the market for corporate control. If a firm's share price underperforms when compared with its peers, that is, firms which are in the same line of business and should have similar performance levels, then the conclusion is drawn that there is something wrong with its strategic management. For this reason, this firm is vulnerable to be taken over. A share price above average is taken as a sign of good governance and good strategic management.

The second thing to consider concerns the quality of the firm's strategy and strategic management itself and whether the firm is on track for successes and high performance, and therefore generates the profits that determine the share price. This involves estimating the future earning potential of the firm itself.

Shareholder value is a reflection of the risk/return profile of the business. It sums up the future earning potential of the firm. There are two ways to do this. One would be to look at the financial parameters of the firm and to calculate future earnings. This involves looking at future cash flows and the future cost of capital (see Rappaport 1989 for more details). The strategist should concentrate on financial performance indicators that make sense from an investor point of view.

Additional to this is the question of whether the expected future cash flows are justified. For this, the soundness of the firm's strategic management should be assessed. Rappaport (1986) relies heavily on economics-based strategy theory. He expects a firm to engage in strategic planning. If a firm's strategic management is in order, shareholders will be confident that the firm will perform in the future. The expectation is that a firm's strategic management is driven by a pursuit of competitive advantage, mostly in terms of one or more of the theoretical approaches from the previous chapters. When all of this is in place and in order, and the firm is performing well, shareholders are confident about their calculations and will project current performance levels into the future.

The strategist should bear in mind that the value of a company as an investment opportunity is relative to all other investments that can be made. Investors can put their money into government bonds, precious metals, art, property, commodities or in a savings account, to name but a few other options. These all have a risk/return profile and are valued relative to each other. So share prices also go up or down as a reaction to a price movement in any of the other investment opportunities. It is not necessarily all down to top management's decision-making. However, firms who operate in the same industry or on similar product markets are expected to be equally affected by these kinds of influences. Again this means that the firm's share price needs to be considered alongside its peers.

Whether shareholders can expect a firm to be managed in their interests depends on the remuneration schemes that are in place. For this you should look at the terms of employment. A solution often chosen is to provide top management with stock options: the guarantee to be able to buy a certain number of shares in the company at what they are worth, or sometimes even below market value, at the start of their tenure. If they are able to improve the share price while they are in office, they can exercise their options and the difference between the option price and the improved share price is their reward. Other bonus schemes that tie in with profits and share prices are found as well. On occasion, employees are incentivised in a similar manner with bonuses and share schemes tailored to their situation.

Exhibit 5.1: Agency theory and shareholder value starter questions

- How is the firm incorporated, in which country, and what are the legal requirements in terms of corporate governance?
- Who are the owners/shareholders and what are their expectations?
- What is the future earning potential of the firm? Is its strategic management in order?
- What is the current share price, what is the share price trend, is the firm considered overvalued or undervalued when compared with its peers?
- What remuneration scheme is in place for top management?
- Is there a profit-sharing arrangement for employees?

Strategy practice 5.1: Maintaining investor relations

Many listed firms actively maintain investor relations. A firm's website contains elaborate pages where they show what the current share price is. There is large PR effort explaining what a wonderful investment opportunity the firm is. This is also the place where you can download annual reports and spread sheets with quarterly results. The CEO and other top executives regularly appear in press conferences, hold presentations and organize briefings. These are predominantly aimed at 'financial analysts'. These are people working for large institutional investors who hold most of the shares in publicly traded companies throughout the world. Their opinions on the soundness of a firm's strategy can make or break a firm's reputation in the financial markets. This reputation in turn not only affects the share price but also the conditions by which these firms can access other sources of finance. CEOs and the top teams have to devote considerable time to satisfying the needs and concerns of these 'financial analysts'.

Going real time: debating strategy

For real time strategic management, the strategists should know about the incentive schemes present in the firm and what the shareholder value of the firm is. The main thing to do is to monitor the share price for upward or downward jolts and to debate what may be the cause of this. This can be something exogenous to the firm that needs consideration and that maybe has to feed into the strategy debate that is taking place in terms of any of the other theoretical

---

Exhibit 5.2: Agency theory and shareholder value questions to debate

- Is the firm's share price going up or down relative to its peers?
- Is there confidence in the firm's strategic management and the top management team, which has to carry it out?

Is there sufficient alignment of interests between shareholders and top management?

Strategy practice 5.2: A shareholder value strategy workshop

Top management teams periodically book themselves into a nice retreat over a weekend to discuss how they or the firm are doing. This is an ideal opportunity to do some deliberate strategy debate. Quite often, an external consultant is asked to design a programme for the workshop, suggest topics for discussion and facilitate the workshop.

Shareholder value can be one of the topics to be discussed. This would require some preparation by getting the share price trends of the firm itself as well as of comparable firms. Such a discussion would be very useful if the firm is underperforming. It would prompt the top management team to 'face facts' and to discuss where they apparently are going wrong.

Strategy practice 5.3: Internationalization from a shareholder value viewpoint

The tendency has been observed that capital markets become increasingly globalized (Stulz 1999). There are countries with restrictions on foreign ownership of locally registered companies. Some countries also regulate capital flows. However, this is diminishing and for a country to become a member of the World Trade Organization (WTO), these kinds of restrictions have to be lifted. Unrestricted capital flows and allowing foreign ownership has at least two effects. On the one hand, the overall cost of capital tends to come down, meaning that firms find it easier to finance their strategies. On the other hand, the market for corporate control becomes a worldwide phenomenon, meaning that firms and their top management are monitored and scrutinized by a wider range of people, with the takeover threat coming from every corner of the world.

approaches. If the jolt is traced back to the firm itself, and especially if it concerns a share price fall, top management should seriously consider taking some kind of measure. If the drop in share price is due to the shareholders/investors losing confidence in the firm's strategic management, a replacement can be considered. Overall, whatever the firm does that negatively affects the share price: it basically means that the interest alignment between management and shareholders is in disarray.

Answering question 2: taking action

When action should be taken, the question is: Who are the strategists here? All previous theoretical approaches more or less assume that the strategists of the firm are its top managers. Here a distinction is made between executives who are in charge of managing the firm on a daily basis, and directors who have a supervisory role on behalf of the shareholders. If the shareholder value goes down, it can be blamed on the firm's top managers and their strategic management. They should feel compelled to rethink what they are doing. But the actual measures they could take cannot be derived from agency theory and shareholder value as such. Their strategic management activities are supposed to be informed by the other theoretical approaches, as Rappaport (1998) suggests. Options that top managers should consider can be found there.

From an agency theory point of view, and also from a legal perspective, the supervisory board members should step in when the top managers are deemed to fail in their task to maximize shareholder value. Many countries have defined company law in such a way that the legal entities by which a firm gets incorporated have to separate out executive and supervisory roles and obligations. The supervisors/directors are then in charge of the corporate governance of the firm, which extends to the hiring and firing of top executives and making decisions on their pay.

So, strictly speaking, the strategists are the supervisory board members. One option they have in the case of a shareholder value problem is replacing the CEO or maybe the whole executive team. They can also look at the remuneration arrangements to check whether the incentive schemes do align the interests of the top executives with the shareholders. If not, a redesign is called for (see the process logic figure 5.2). Such episodes indicate that there is 'trouble at the top'.

If the existing supervisory board does not deal with the problems in an adequate manner, chances are that the 'market for corporate control' steps in. Somebody will realize that an underperforming firm with a low share price can be bought relatively easily. When such a person becomes a majority shareholder, he is in control. He is able to appoint the members of the supervisory board, who in turn control the hiring and firing of the executive board members. This creates a powerful platform from which a turnaround effort can be launched. Alternatively, if this is a multi-business firm, the new owner can decide to split the

---

Strategy practice 5.4: Formulating a strategic business plan using shareholder value

The concept of shareholder value indicates what the business plan should achieve: a sound investment opportunity. To make this point, the sums that need to be part of the plan should calculate the firm's earning potential in a way that indicates that shareholder value will increase when the business plan is implemented.

firm up and sell on the more viable parts, liquidate the less viable parts and make a profit from that.

Criticisms and generating further questions

The concept of shareholder value is probably the most contentious strategy theory in existence. Agency theory in general recognizes that people's motivations, expressed as utility gains, cover a range of things. By the time it gets more specific with the concept of shareholder value, everything is expressed in terms of money. It seems to suggest that every purpose in life is translatable into monetary value. Whether this is a useful assumption is a question that is often asked. Critics reckon that firms have many more responsibilities than merely making a profit and have obligations to live up to these responsibilities even at the expense of shareholders. This points at an underlying question of morality. Does a manager serve society best by concentrating only on making money for shareholders or does the manager have to face up to additional responsibilities that do not necessarily lead to increased shareholder value?

Agency theory also questions the impartiality of managers. In fact, it is very much part of the theory that the interests of top management do not align with the interests of the firm as a money-making entity. This is in sharp contrast with other strategy theories that assume top management to be unbiased in their information processing and decision-making. It adds another form of subjectivity to the equation by recognizing the inherent political nature of strategic management.

The concept of shareholder value is a deliberate attempt to deal with the future. It relies on estimating earnings and what the firm becomes worth during the period stretching away from the investment decision that potential shareholders make. Nevertheless, the future is unknown. Therefore, the question can be asked whether the assumption that strategy theories have predictive power is right and whether it is possible to prejudge what will happen and how much money a firm will make on the basis of applying a strategy theory, or a finance theory for that matter.

With regard to the two debates – objectivism versus subjectivism/voluntarism – determinism, the position remains on the objectivism and voluntarism sides. Agency theory assumes that there is a business reality out there – even projects it into the future – and that ultimately people are capable of impressing their intentions on the course of events. Again, the question can be asked whether that is a reasonable set of assumptions to make.

Illustration 5.3: SKF from a shareholder value point of view

Should SKF* compete on price and put in the lowest bid possible to retain a big US-based client, or should it step away and persist with its high-quality strategy?

SKF is listed on the Stockholm Stock Exchange.** Swedish shareholders own 64 per cent of the shares. Since the economic crisis, SKF shares have been on a downward trend but they have started to recover. An announcement that SKF will lose a big account would not help with maintaining shareholder confidence. However, giving in affects the profit margin and the long term earning ability of SKF.

* Value selling at SKF Service, IMD-5-0751, 2009.
** SKF 2009 Annual Report.

Case 5.1 Aviva

Aviva Plc describes itself as the UK's largest insurer and as being among Europe's leading providers of life and general insurance.[1] The company owns subsidiaries in Barbados, Canada, France, Hong Kong, Indonesia, Ireland, Italy, Lithuania, Poland, Russia, Singapore, Spain, Sri Lanka, Turkey and the United States. There are also joint ventures and minority holdings in China, India, Italy, Malaysia, the Netherlands, South Korea, Turkey and Vietnam. Yet it generates half of its profits in the UK. Aviva shares are traded on the London and New York Stock Exchanges.

Only a week after its AGM on 3 May 2012, group chief executive Andrew Moss resigned with immediate effect.[2] Of the Aviva shareholders who had attended and voted at the AGM, 54 per cent had voted against the remuneration package the board was proposing, despite Andrew Moss voluntarily turning down a salary increase of 1.5 per cent a week before the meeting, which would have taken his salary from £960,000 to well over £1 million. This was the fourth time ever that a FTSE100 company lost the vote on its remuneration package.

Aviva did not give a reason why Mr Moss resigned but analysts believe the vote was the last straw.[3] Barry Cornes of Panmure Gordon stockbrokers said: "We suspect that the latest batch of negative headlines over the remuneration report at the AGM was the last straw and Moss had to go. Few will shed any tears given his handling of the business over the last few years, which has seen the shares massively underperform the sector". Andrew Moss will be replaced by the board chairman elect John McFarlane, while they are looking for a replacement: "My first priorities are to regain the respect of our shareholders by eliminating the discount in our share price and to find the very best leader to find our future chief executive".

Before the AGM, Aviva had a 15-member board of directors, chaired by Lord Sharman of Redlynch.[4] Because he was in his final year, John McFarlane would replace him. The board has established an audit committee, a corporate responsibility committee, a nomination committee, a remuneration committee and a risk committee. There is also an 11-member executive team, headed by group chief executive Andrew Moss. Members are a chief financial officer, a group human resources director, a chief marketing and communications officer, a chief information officer, a chief risk officer

1 Aviva 2011 annual report.
2 BBC, 8 May 2012, http://www.bbc.co.uk/news/business-17987271 (accessed 29 May 2012).
3 BBC, 8 May 2012, http://www.bbc.co.uk/news/business-17987271 (accessed 29 May 2012).
4 Aviva 201/ annual report.

and the chief executives of Aviva UK, Aviva Europe, Aviva Investors, Aviva North America and Aviva Asia Pacific.

The remuneration committee had proposed a scheme in which the executive director's basic salary is going to be benchmarked against 25 FTSE companies either side of Aviva's market capitalization.[5] The maximum annual bonus would be 150 per cent of the basic salary, based on four financial key performance indicators but two-thirds would be deferred into shares for three years. There would also be a Long Term Incentive Plan, where the group chief executive would be eligible for an award in shares up to a maximum of 275 per cent of annual salary, based on three other financial performance indicators. Executive directors would be eligible for a 225 per cent standard award. There was also a requirement for executive directors to retain a minimum value of Aviva shares for the duration of their employment. The percentages in the LITP as well as the minimum share value executives need to retain would have been up compared to the scheme it intended to replace.

Shareholder profile

The categories of ordinary shareholders and the range and size of shareholdings as at 31 December 2011 are set out below:

	Number of shareholders	%	Number of shares	%
Individual	578603	96.88	270555684	9.31
Banks and nominee companies	15563	2.61	2597758882	89.40
Pension fund managers and insurance companies	241	0.04	2357297	0.08
Other corporate bodies	2838	0.47	35041075	1.21
Total	597246	100	2905712938	100
Range of shareholdings	Number of shareholders	%	Number of shares	%
1–1000	540772	90.54	150357346	5.17
1001–1500	50250	8.41	95608617	3.29
1501–10000	3389	0.57	23580910	0.81
10001–250000	2209	0.37	95497159	3.29
250001–500000	167	0.03	58280304	2.01
500001 and above	457	0.08	2466715866	84.89
ADRs	1	0.00	15672736*)	0.54
Total	597245	100	2905712938	100

Source: Aviva, http://www.aviva.com/investor-relations/institutional-investors/shareholder-profile/ (accessed 1 November 2012)

Note:
*Number of registered ordinary shares represented by American Depositary Receipts (ADRs). Each ADR represents two ordinary shares.

5 Aviva 2011 annual report.

6   Stakeholders and organizational politics

The stakeholder approach points at the wider purpose of the organization in the eyes of the various people who have some kind of stake in it. It also recognizes the organization as a political arena, where conflicts of interests need to be resolved. This is also the place where corporate social responsibility comes to the fore. Overall, the focus is on people, either individuals or collectives, and whether their interests are met.

The process logic of stakeholders and organizational politics

The stakeholder approach is formulated to recognize the many different people and organizations that are dependent on or may be affected by the actions of a focal organization. A stakeholder is defined as "[. . .] any group or individual who can affect or is affected by the achievement of an organization's purpose" (Freeman 1984: 46). The basic idea is that because an organization depends on others for its livelihood, it should take their interests into account to survive. In addition, and not unimportantly, it is often stated that every organization has a moral obligation to those who are affected by its activities. The stakeholder approach is therefore descriptive in the sense that it identifies the various types of distinguishable stakeholders, it is instrumental in the sense that it explains how stakeholders affect performance and it is managerial in the sense that it aims to tell managers how to deal with stakeholders (Donaldson and Preston 1995).

Distinguishing between the various types of stakeholders provides a list of individuals, groups and organizations all having a stake of some kind or other in a focal organization. Such a list includes the owners/shareholders, the wider financial community, customers and customer advocate groups, employees, managers and their trade unions, trade associations, competitors, suppliers, various layers of government and assorted activist and political groups (Freeman 1984). Some argue that there is a corporate social responsibility to society as a whole (Wood 1991). But it is through stakeholders that organizations are forced to face up to their accountability (Clarkson 1995).

From a stakeholder's point of view, the notion of performance becomes a somewhat troubled concept. The economist Milton Friedman (1970) notoriously suggested that the sole and only social responsibility of a business firm is to make a profit, but to do that within the confines of the law. This also underpins the concept of shareholder value (Rappaport 1986). Their argument is that businesses should not engage themselves with any other causes, however noble these might be, because this means that managers are adding costs to the operation of the firm at the expense of the firm's profit margin; effectively spending money that is not theirs to spend but should be made available as dividends to the shareholders. If money needs to be spent on good causes, it should be left to the shareholders

---

Illustration 6.1: Mutual dependence in the automotive industry supply chain

There are many firms involved in producing cars, effectively creating a network of interdependent relationships. Car manufacturers rely on suppliers not only to provide them with the various parts that assemble into a car, but also to develop new features and engineering solutions for the next generation of car models. US car manufacturers tend to be more aggressive and antagonistic, often asking one supplier to develop something for them as a one-off solution and then to change to another cheaper supplier when they incorporate the new feature in one of their models (Sturgeon and others 2008). The emphasis on costs forced suppliers to seek out savings at the expense of quality. They also felt little obligation to invest in a relationship that is always at risk of being terminated. This resulted in US carmakers producing cars with a high failure rate as a consequence of low price/low quality parts, and that were less innovative (Womack, Jones and Roos 1990). US car plants had to put considerable effort into rectifying faults before the cars were shipped out and they were still suffering from low reliability. Sales slumped. Japanese carmakers tend to be more loyal and develop enduring relationships with a range of suppliers, allowing for continuous improvements in the course of the life time of a model, but also from model to model. Consequently, cars coming out of a Japanese supply and manufacturing chain were almost faultless with higher quality parts, creating an image of reliability and quality. This was valued not only by customers; it also created a dynamic in the supply chain where firms were allowed to make a contribution and benefit from it, generating better cars, higher market share and profits.

---

to decide what they want to spend their money on. If there are unwanted side effects associated with the operations of the firm affecting other stakeholders or society as a whole, government should legislate against these. Consequently, in order to create shareholder value, a firm has to deal with only those stakeholders who negatively affect the firm's profit margin and leave any other cause or stakeholder group alone, clearly stating that the shareholders should be the prime focus of management.

This shareholder view is contested (Freeman 1984; Freeman and Reed 1983). From a stakeholder approach point of view shareholders are but one category of stakeholders. A firm has a moral obligation to take everybody's interests into account. Performance then becomes a very multifaceted phenomenon, with the firm being judged on its ability to meet the many different interests that the various stakeholders and stakeholder communities may have. Measuring performance in financial terms then becomes less relevant and other possibly more qualitative indicators are called for as well. This discussion of whether to adopt a shareholder view or a stakeholder view is obviously not important to public or third sector organizations without shareholders. Performance assessment of not-for-profit organizations has been a continuous source for debate.

To indicate what kind of demands and interests a stakeholder may have with an organization, and also to provide a more elaborate understanding of an organization's performance, we can look more closely at the requirement of legitimacy. "Legitimacy is a generalized perception or assumption that the actions of an entity are desirable, proper, or appropriate within some socially constructed system of norms, values, beliefs, and definitions" (Suchman 1995: 574). Stakeholders' interests can be described in terms of the legitimacy they demand from a focal organization. Suchman suggests that this legitimacy can be pragmatic, moral or cognitive, and is often a combination of these three.

Pragmatic legitimacy is derived from the idea of exchange. A stakeholder and a focal organization stand in some kind of mutually dependent relationship to each other. The level of legitimacy deriving from this relationship depends on the satisfaction that both parties get from the exchange that is taking place. Pragmatic legitimacy from the perspective of a stakeholder refers to the level of fulfilment the stakeholder gets from the focal organization.

Moral legitimacy concerns the norms and values to which a stakeholder subscribes. The activities of an organization are judged in accordance with what a stakeholder considers to be morally right or wrong. The interest of the stakeholder lies in upholding the formal and informal rules that the stakeholder sees as important. Moral legitimacy from the perspective of a stakeholder refers to the level of compliance the focal organization achieves regarding the stakeholder's norms and values.

The idea of cognitive legitimacy is based on the recognition that situations may be interpreted differently. The activities of an organization are judged in accordance with how the stakeholder understands what is going on. It is in the interest of a stakeholder that an organization acts at least in accordance with a mutually shared definition of the situation or preferably that the organization adapts to how the stakeholder likes to see it. Cognitive legitimacy from the perspective of a stakeholder refers to the extent to which the definition of the situation is shared.

With multiple stakeholders, it is very likely that an organization is confronted with different demands as each stakeholder may have different ideas about what makes an organization pragmatically, morally and cognitively legitimate. Stakeholders also hold power over the organization and they may exercise this power depending on how much hold they have over the organization (Frooman, 1999; Pfeffer and Salancik 1978). It is not difficult to see that the different demands that may be levied on an organization lead to different and conflicting ideas about what is considered as good and bad organizational performance. On top of that, the organization itself may have ideas and interests of its own, which do not necessarily align with the interests of the stakeholders. From a stakeholder perspective, the environmental survival process is, thus, a process of dealing with conflicting demands (see Figure 6.1).

Stakeholders are not confined to only the environment either. An organization consists of many groups and subgroups, which each have different ideas and interests. These can be

---

Strategy practice 6.1: Corporate social responsibility

Many larger organizations take their corporate social responsibility seriously enough to devote part of their website to it. There is very often a link to pages that come under the label of 'responsible business', or 'being a responsible company'. What you will find there is information on, for instance, how the firm is protecting the environment, what it does with regard to climate change, how well it is treating its employees and how ethically it sources its supplies. It is interesting to note that the contradiction between going for shareholder value and being socially responsible is dealt with by having one area of the company website devoted to investor relations and another area to corporate social responsibility.

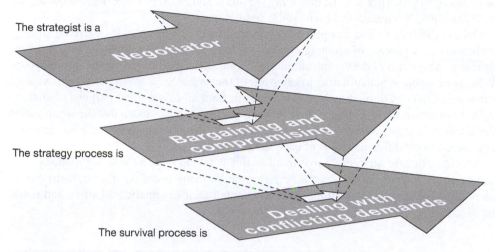

The strategist is a **Negotiator**

The strategy process is **Bargaining and compromising**

The survival process is **Dealing with conflicting demands**

Figure 6.1 The process logic for stakeholders and organizational politics

departments, subsidiaries or professionals, managers, workers or any other category an individual may identify with. Some of these subgroups can band together with external stakeholders and act as their representatives within the organization. Organizations are described as a 'negotiated order' (Fine 1984), whose functioning depends on whether inherent contradictions and conflicts of interests can be overcome (Benson 1977), and which essentially is run by a 'dominant coalition' of internal stakeholders who have found some common ground (Cyert and March 1963). The interests of internal stakeholders are also described in terms of pragmatic, normative and cognitive legitimacy.

With the recognition that stakeholders – external as well as internal – have different claims on the organization, that these claims may be contradictory and result in conflicts of interests, it can be expected that the organization becomes a battleground, where the various stakeholders exercise power to have their interests come out on top. Managing an organization then essentially is a political process. This is the conclusion drawn by many strategy scholars who studied how strategic decision-making actually takes place

---

Strategy practice 6.2: The strategy workshop and organizational politics

When a top management team retreats into a nice hotel in the country for a weekend to discuss the firm's strategy, they might appear to debate the next strategic move or discuss an issue that has come up and what to do about it. From an organizational politics point of view, what actually is taking place is that they are negotiating. They know that any decision that will be made will affect the area they are responsible for. They may get more resources out of it or maybe they will lose out. They may be arguing for their point of view (mediated by their mental map) and vigorously oppose another point of view (mediated by somebody else's metal map). Such debates can become quite heated and occasionally feature open conflict.

(e.g. Bower 1970; Hickson, Butler, Cray, Mallory and Wilson 1986; Jarzabkowski and Balogun 2009; Narayanan and Liam 1982; and Pettigrew 1973).

Quinn (1980) described this process as 'logical incrementalism'. He described strategy realization as a process of aligning conflicting demands and viewpoints arising from the different subsystems of the organization. Any organization has limited means at its disposal. What is available is not sufficient to cater for all the ambitions that may exist. The various subsystems interact through negotiation and still share an overarching purpose of sticking with the organization as a whole. Their subsequent compromises mean that the organization develops in a step-by-step incremental fashion, as the limited means are successively committed to the different causes of each subgroup.

It follows that the strategist's role in all of this is taking part in these negotiations. This can be as an arbitrator and *primus inter pares*. Or on many occasions the strategist can be identified with a specific subgroup and has adopted their pragmatic, cognitive and moral legitimacy.

Illustration 6.2: Making a decision at Toxichem

Toxichem is a pseudonym for a chemical company that had its strategic decision-making investigated (Wilson 1982). The chemical manufacturing process requires Toxichem to produce its own steam. At some point the existing low-pressure 80 psi boiler had to be replaced. Expectations were that higher pressures would be needed in the future, so Toxichem purchased a high-pressure 400 psi boiler. As it turned out, the higher pressures were not needed. However, the new boiler had to be fired up to 400 psi first before it could operate at the lower 80 psi level. This incurred an additional cost. On that basis, the works director had the idea that the spare capacity could be used by Toxichem to generate its own electricity. He calculated that this would save the company £39,000 per annum. However, an additional investment in a generator was needed – money that Toxichem did not have at the time.

A few years later, Toxichem had grown so much that it needed a second boiler. The works director saw a new opportunity for pushing the electricity idea, but the high-pressure boiler that was needed to allow for electricity generation was too expensive. Toxichem could not afford that amount of capital outlay. The purchasing director was altogether against the idea on these grounds and preferred a low-pressure boiler. While the Toxichem board was considering the options, by pure coincidence, the National Coal Board let it be known that it had large stocks of low quality coal available at a very low price. To take advantage of this and to be able to supply steam with this low quality coal, a high-pressure boiler was needed, although it would not have to operate at this higher pressure. The sums added up for Toxichem and the purchasing director now agreed with the larger investment in a high-pressure boiler. The works director did not push the electricity idea any further but was delighted that the option was still open, with two high-pressure boilers available.

Growth continued for Toxichem and a third boiler was needed to keep up with demand. The works director took this opportunity again to make the case for electricity generation. The purchasing director remained against the idea. Both produced reports with opposing arguments. The firm reached an *impasse*. Each report was based on assumptions and projections that could not be independently verified. Would the staff running the boilers also be able to run a generator? How reliable would the whole set up be? What would the future costs of coal and electricity be?

One of the key variables was the cost of standby arrangements. How much would the power company charge Toxichem if it needed to reconnect temporarily to the grid in case the generator breaks down or when it is out for maintenance? The power company was not keen on firms generating their own electricity and it refused to provide a quote. The works director then asked for quotes from two generator manufacturers and requested them to include standby charges in their tenders. For some reason the power company did provide this information to the generator manufacturers. They were told that standby charges were £5 per KVa per annum. This was too expensive and the electricity generation idea was shelved again.

Some time later, the managing director of Toxichem announced his retirement and both the works director and the purchasing director were considered to be candidates to replace him. It was known within the company that their track records were measured in terms of their success in getting their ideas implemented. The electricity idea featured heavily in this assessment. This inspired the works director to revive the plan one more time. He asked around about the £5 standby charges and found out that this was ridiculously high and some error must have been made. Investigating this further, the works director unearthed solid evidence that the actual charge would be about £1. This made the whole proposition viable again. Months of conflict ensued within Toxichem, with everybody in the firm forced to take sides. It dominated board meetings and lunch breaks. The arguments became ever more personal with the works director and the purchasing director challenging each other's competence to do their jobs. As no definitive case in favour or against could be supplied, it was put up for a vote. The majority was in favour of electricity generation. Engineers, who had more sympathy with the works director and his ideas as a fellow engineer, than with the purchasing director, dominated the board. The works director was promoted to managing director a year later.

The performance logic of stakeholders and organizational politics

As is explained above, performance is a somewhat troubled concept within the confines of the stakeholder approach. Different stakeholders have different stakes in the organization and therefore have different expectations and ideas about what performance means to them. It is the stakeholders' pragmatic, cognitive and moral legitimacy that defines beneficial outcomes for them (see Figure 6.2). Yet, the contradictions and conflicts that arise need to be dealt with. The ability of an organization to perform depends therefore on whether and how the organization achieves sufficient legitimacy among the many stakeholders to keep on functioning (see Figure 6.2).

The obvious thing for any organization to remain legitimate among all relevant stakeholders is to meet all their interests. This is very likely impossible. An organization can realistically prioritize and negotiate with stakeholders who are the most essential for an organization's performance and survival. Mitchell, Agle and Wood (1997) provide a framework by which stakeholders' relative importance can be assessed. It is based on the three variables of legitimacy, power and urgency (see Table 6.1). In this way, eight different types of stakeholders, with each type being of more or less relative importance to the organization, can be distinguished.

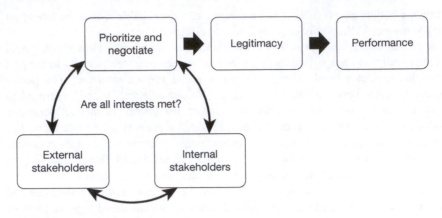

Figure 6.2 The stakeholder approach

The legitimacy variable refers to the extent to which the stakeholder's claim fits within what is considered legitimate by society as a whole (Wood 1991). Again the distinction is made between pragmatic, cognitive and moral legitimacy (Suchman 1995). Whether a stakeholder should be taken care of depends on how the stakeholder's claim and the organization's claim compare with what is considered legitimate in wider society. The party who comes closest to what is expected more generally has the upper hand here.

Emerson's (1962: 32) classic definition where "the power of actor A over actor B is the amount of resistance on the part of B which can be potentially overcome by A" indicates the usefulness of power in situations of conflict and contradiction. Mitchell and others (1997) draw on Etzioni (1964) to distinguish between three bases for power. Coercive power is based on the use of force and threat. Utilitarian power is based on the provision of (material) resources that act as an incentive. Normative power is based on the application of norms and regulations. Each stakeholder has a powerbase that extends across these three, and on which they can draw to pursue their interests. The balance of power between a stakeholder and the organization indicates the relative importance of a stakeholder with regard to this variable. If the stakeholder has a strong powerbase and the organization has little to balance it out with, this stakeholder scores high in this realm.

Finally, urgency refers to the degree to which a stakeholder needs immediate attention. When a stakeholder's claim is associated with an acute problem that should be solved instantly there is more urgency, when compared with a claim associated with an issue that has lingered on for some time and will linger on well into the future.

Depending on the scores on the three variables of legitimacy, power and urgency, a stakeholder ends up as either one of eight different types (see Table 6.1). Mitchell and others' (1997) framework also distinguishes between four layers of importance. The stakeholder type that should be prioritized is the 'definitive stakeholder'. This is a stakeholder with a legitimate claim, who is powerful, and who needs urgent attention. The next important stakeholders on the list are the dependent, dangerous and dominant stakeholders, who score on two of the three variables. The least important ones are the discretionary, demanding and dormant stakeholders, who only score on one variable. The non-stakeholder, who has no power, legitimate claim, nor needs urgent attention, can be ignored. This, of course, refers to both internal and external stakeholders.

Table 6.1 A stakeholder typology

Stakeholder type	Power	Legitimacy	Urgency
Definitive	✓	✓	✓
Dominant	✓	✓	
Dependent		✓	✓
Dangerous	✓		✓
Dormant	✓		
Discretionary		✓	
Demanding			✓
Non-stakeholder			

Derived from Mitchell et al. (1997)

Additional features

A tool to deal with stakeholders is the mission statement. Campbell (1987) tells us that an organization's mission statement has to indicate the relative attention that various stakeholders can expect to get. It should be a statement of purpose that reflects the reason why and for whom the organization exists. It should contain a vision of what the organization is destined for as well as whom the organization is trying to serve. An explicit listing of organizational values should also be part of the mission statement. An organization's existence only makes sense if it is worthwhile in the eyes of its stakeholders.

On a different note, the notion of management cognition resonates with the basic idea that different stakeholders have different points of view. The way in which the minds of strategists work has an effect on what they perceive and do not perceive, how they process information and ultimately on the strategic decisions that they take (Schwenk 1984). These effects are predominantly elaborated in terms of cognitive limitations. Herbert Simon (1957), for instance, built a theory of the organization on the basis that managers are limited with regard to their information processing abilities. He came up with the notions of 'bounded rationality' and 'satisficing' to denounce any expectation that managers will always come up with the optimal decision if all information is available. He argues that people can only consider so many alternatives and only deal with a limited amount of information. Because of that, their rationality is bounded and they pick the first alternative that solves the problem, not necessarily the best.

Cognitive limitations can also have an effect in generating all kind of biases affecting the likelihood that one alternative is preferred over another one. For instance, Tversky and Kahneman (1974) did some famous experiments in which they demonstrated that choices people make are based on all kinds of decision heuristics or mental short cuts.

The basic idea that management thought is pre-structured is derived from cognitive psychology (Sims and Gioia 1986). Things like 'schemas' (a mental structure which serves to organize knowledge), 'implicit theory' (scheme of naive, personal collections of assumptions of how things are related and how the organization works) and 'scripts' (a specific scheme about how events are supposed to organize into sequences) are already in strategists' minds and inform how they make sense of the world. Management cognition also very much feeds into cognitive legitimacy and is therefore closely intertwined with how stakeholders perceive their stake in the organization. Every individual stakeholder is seen as

Strategy practice 6.3: Mental mapping

Mental mapping is a practice where a group of people like a management team have a meeting to find out how they understand a situation. There are techniques available by which a collective cause and effect map can be generated, often with the use of a software package that allows individual participants to enter their views. During the mental mapping session, these individual views are collated and put together so that the group as a whole can discuss and settle on a shared view of the situation. This not only clarifies the mind of each individual participant but also often results in a shared action plan of how to deal with a problematic situation. Ackerman and Eden (2011) provide one of the more sophisticated examples of this kind of practice, featuring the 'Decision Explorer' software package.

equipped with a 'mental map' that informs them how they understand the world around them. It also allows them to navigate their way through the organization. These maps are profoundly individual, although there are many instances where people's individual mental maps with regard to specific areas of understanding are largely similar, especially when these people have shared the same or similar experiences.

Doing strategic management as a political process

From a stakeholder's point of view, strategic management is an opportunity for political behaviour. For instance, doing an internal and an external appraisal, picking objectives, formulating the strategic plan, everything is expected to be subjected to negotiation and bargaining. A strategic planning procedure, as Quinn (1980) observed, is a site where the various subsystems and internal stakeholders meet and arrive at compromises. Yet there are many other occasions where people interact and effectively negotiation behaviour takes place. This is referred to as micro-politics. Doing strategic management here means taking part in these negotiations. By nature, this takes place continuously and therefore requires a real time approach.

Strategy practice 6.4: Issue selling

To champion a cause or to get something on the agenda, middle management has to engage in 'issue selling' (Dutton, Ashford, O'Neill and Lawrence 2001). Issue selling is a deliberate attempt to draw attention to a situation by affecting people's understanding about it. From a cognitive and political point of view, nothing is a self-evident problem. It takes effort on the part of people who choose to champion a particular cause or issue to make people understand. Top management can expect to be approached constantly by people who perceive a particular problem and ask for guidance or support. They might even have a solution ready and only want the 'go ahead' and the resources to tackle it. In a way, there is a constant competition for attention and the best 'issue sellers' can expect to win out. It also leaves the problems that are put forward by poor 'issue sellers' unaddressed.

An organization also has to deal with the various outside stakeholders and their conflicting claims on the organization as a whole. However, a strict distinction between external and internal is not always straightforward. Some stakeholders, such as for instance the workers or employees, or a group of professionals employed by the organization can appear both as internal stakeholders and as external stakeholders and, therefore, need to be taken into account. All stakeholders can be expected to take every opportunity to put more pressure on the organization to have their interests met. Therefore there is constant dynamics of challenging, shifting and jockeying for attention in and around the organization. As the organization has to keep the most important stakeholders happy to maintain sufficient legitimacy to continue to function and perform, it has to keep track of and react to all changes that are occurring. Again, this takes place continuously and therefore requires real time strategic management. The two questions to answer here are:

1 Are there any significant changes with regard to the relative importance of any of the stakeholders?
2 If there are, what can you do about them?

Getting up to speed

To be able to track the dynamics among the various stakeholders, a strategist needs to know what stakeholders are present in and around the organization and what interests they have. The performance logic and the Mitchell and others (1997) stakeholder typology on which it is based, generates a set of basic questions by which a stakeholder analysis can be done (see Exhibit 6.1). Answering these questions provides insight into who the stakeholders are and what conflicting claims they have. What is important to learn as well is how the organization is actually dealing with these stakeholders and whether some are prioritized over others. Although the key question in the stakeholder approach is whether all interests are met, this will never be the case. What the organization has to aim for is to prioritize stakeholders in the order of importance indicated by the Mitchell and others (1997) model.

Assessing stakeholder claims is especially difficult with regard to understanding legitimacy differences. Pragmatic legitimacy may be the relatively easy one. For this the strategist should find out what is exchanged between a stakeholder and the organization. Cognitive legitimacy may be more difficult. For this the strategist should be able to understand the organization from the perspective of another stakeholder. The strategist should find out how somebody else defines the situation. This is extremely tricky because cognitive psychology tells us that a strategist's own *schemas*, implicit theory and scripts bind up any understanding of anybody else's perceptions. Finding out about a stakeholder's moral stance in comparison to one's own may be similarly difficult.

A strategist should also understand the various ways in which power is wielded, which powerbases are available, and whether various stakeholders bring them into play. Etzioni (1964) describes the use of brute force and the coercive power this generates. Utilitarian power comes with the provision and withholding of certain (material) resources in an exchange situation. He writes about rules, norms and values that allow people to sanction and to be sanctioned, effectively creating normative power. Each one of these powerbases is available in each relationship between a stakeholder and an organization. The strategist himself also has power to wield but can also appear to be relatively powerless.

Exhibit 6.1: Macro-politics starter questions

- Who are external stakeholders?
- What claims on and expectations of the organization do they have?
- In what way is the organization dependent on each external stakeholder?
  - This provides an overview of relevant external stakeholders and the interdependence between them and the focal organization.
- What is the cognitive, moral and pragmatic legitimacy of an external stakeholder's claim?
- What is the powerbase of this external stakeholder and how does this balance out against the power of the focal firm?
- How urgently should this external stakeholder be dealt with?
  - This provides the information to assess what type of external stakeholder the organization is dealing with.
- Has the organization prioritized the (external) stakeholders in accordance with the relative importance of each one?

Finally, there is the specific matter at hand for which a claim is made. From the perspective of the organization, there is a need to appreciate its relative urgency, and whether it is an issue that should be settled now or can be left to simmer in the background.

This also works the other way round from the perspective of a stakeholder. A stakeholder can evaluate his relative position in terms of power, legitimacy and urgency, among all other stakeholders. It provides the organization as well as the stakeholders insight into whether they bargain from a position of strength or a position of weakness. From the perspective of the organization, the strategist needs empathy not only to have an awareness of his own point of view but also to be able to appreciate where other stakeholders are coming from.

The macro-politics point of view assumes that a strategist can do this disinterested analysis on behalf of the organization. In effect, the interests of the organization are assumed to be the interests of the strategist.

Going real time: debating strategy

Real time strategic management from a stakeholder point of view turns almost always into micro-politics. It is individuals who have to do the negotiating, either safeguarding their own interests or representing a specific stakeholder group. The assumption of the disinterested strategist comes under pressure in this micro-political realm. Is it realistic to assume that a strategist always acts in the interest of the organization as a whole? Or does the strategist have his own interests that he will try to safeguard even at the expense of the organization?

When we assume the strategist is this disinterested party who acts on behalf of the organization, the debate he needs to enter into is about the other stakeholders. To start off with, the strategists should know who these stakeholders are, how the legitimacy of their claims differ from the organization's take on this, how urgent each claim is, and how dependent the organization is on them. The debate should then focus on any changes that might be occurring to consider whether the various different stakeholders need to be reprioritized. Exhibit 6.2 lists a range of more specific questions that should be considered.

The debate takes on a completely different dynamic if we take strategists to have their own interests to take care of, or if strategists identify more with a specific sub-group like a department, a subsidiary or an external stakeholder than with the organization as a whole. Whatever is debated becomes part of the overall struggle for power and whose viewpoints and interests will dominate the organization. The strategist is still interested in the same questions but interpreting the answers will be more geared towards whether anything that may be going on will affect the strategist's own interests rather than the organization as a whole. When there are any changes, they spark off a flurry of renegotiation. New claims gain prominence and some existing claims lose significance.

Exhibit 6.2: Macro-politics questions to debate

- Is there a new external stakeholder appearing on the scene or has an existing external stakeholder disappeared?
- Is something that is happening or that is about to happen going to affect what is considered to be legitimate?
- Is something that is happening or that is about to happen going to affect the balance of power?
- Is something that is happening or that is about to happen going to make an issue more or less urgent?

(From a disinterested position) Does any of this mean that there are new interests to be met by the organization or that existing interests need to be reprioritized?

Strategy practice 6.5: Internationalization from a stakeholder viewpoint

If there is one thing that operating internationally adds, it is that the sheer number of stakeholders multiplies. Every country an organization operates in comes with another set of stakeholders. You then have multiple governments, multiple workforces, multiple pressure groups etc. It is also not uncommon that there are differences in interests within stakeholder categories. Not every government wants the same thing. Also, within the organization there are bound to be differences of interest between internal stakeholder categories across countries. These internal conflicts of interest are often bound up with the level of centralization and decentralization within the organization. A local organization within a country would very much like to be fairly independent of the headquarters, especially if the HQ is located in another country. This would help enormously with being locally responsive. However, to be able to act as a global organization, the HQ has to coordinate across countries, limiting the degree of freedom local organizations have.

Exhibit 6.3: Micro-politics real questions to debate

- Who are the individuals who take part in the negotiations and who do they represent?
- What expectations and interests do they have in the organization and are these becoming more or less legitimate?
- What powerbase do they have and is it increasing or decreasing?
- Is an individual's claim on the organization becoming more or less urgent?
  - Answering these questions will allow a negotiator to evaluate his relative position vis-à-vis his fellow negotiators.
- How does each individual negotiator understand his position, the organization as a whole and the way it works as part of the larger environment?
- Is there any movement in how individual negotiators perceive the situation?
  - Answering these questions allows a negotiator to gain insight into a fellow negotiator's mental map.
- Whose interests and mental maps align with each other and whose interests and mental maps contradict each other?
- Is there any movement with regard to how interests and mental maps align and contradict?
  - Answering these questions will allow a negotiator to gain insight into the coalitions that may gain or lose dominance.

Strategy practice 6.6: SWOT analysis, management cognition and organizational politics

The purpose of a SWOT analysis is to find out about threats and opportunities in the environment and about strengths and weaknesses with regard to the firm. But what makes an opportunity an opportunity, a threat a threat, a strength a strength, and a weakness a weakness? When you factor in organizational politics and management cognition, the analysis takes on a different meaning.

Qualifying something about the organization as a strength or a weakness may have more to do with the political 'pecking order' inside an organization than with an attempt to assess the organization's abilities. Any part of the organization openly exposed as 'weak', or championing another part as 'strong' has an effect on whether these parts are able to defend their interests. These interests do not necessarily have to be completely selfish. A label of 'weakness' can deter investing in that part of the organization, although it may desperately need it. The manager in charge of this weak part probably has little power in the management team as well, hampering his ability to secure resources. Similar effects are created with labelling something as opportunity or threat.

From a management cognition point of view, these labels are also indicative for the mental map of each individual manager. Opportunities have a positive ring to them and threats are perceived as negative. When somebody labels issues positively or negatively, it reveals his way of thinking. Also imagine for instance a CEO qualifying something as an opportunity instead of a threat. By doing this, the boardroom discussion is primed with an initial understanding of where the CEO thinks the organization should go. Using the strength and weakness labels has similar effects.

Answering question 2: taking action

From a stakeholder approach point of view, the options of what to do are indicated by the three ingredients of strategy, organization and environment in the performance logic. With regard to strategy, the option is to reprioritize and renegotiate in accordance with the changes in legitimacy, power and urgency that have been observed. With regard to either the internal stakeholders or the external stakeholders, there is the option to alter the level of mutual dependence. By reducing dependence, a stakeholder's claim's importance is diminished and the threat to the organization's legitimacy lessened.

With regard to how to do this, we enter the realm of micro-politics. Any activity a strategist undertakes here – either from a disinterested or self-interested point of view – boils down to engaging in negotiations. It is about reaching compromises in which some stakeholders may lose out while others gain. While all these deals are struck, the stakeholder performance logic (see Figure 6.2) tells us that the organization should remain sufficiently legitimate among all the stakeholders on which the organization depends, to stay viable. This can drive the willingness of all the stakeholders with their conflicting claims eventually to compromise and also to prioritize the interests of those stakeholders whose claims are the most urgent and legitimate and who have the most power.

So, from a stakeholder point of view, a strategist should constantly be involved in building coalitions of consensus. If the strategist is taken to be primarily concerned with his own interests, this coalition and consensus building is driven by the specific stake the strategist has in the organization. When we assume that the strategist's interests are similar to those of the organization as a whole, the strategist becomes the negotiator on behalf of the organization. On the basis of this assumption, a strategist can fulfil a role in the realm of macro-politics in acting in the organization's interests; to maintain and develop the organization's legitimacy among the various stakeholders and their conflicting demands. This means giving in to those stakeholders who are very powerful and have interests that are highly legitimate and urgent. It also means that the organization and therefore the strategist has room to manoeuvre vis-à-vis stakeholders who are less powerful and whose claims are less legitimate and urgent.

Strategy practice 6.7: Implementing a strategic plan as overcoming resistance?

Implementing a strategic plan is often associated with overcoming resistance (Ford, Ford and D'Amelio 2008). This resistance, in turn, is seen as being caused by stakeholders' self-interest. From a strategy implementer point of view, resistance is often branded as irrational and emotional. So overcoming resistance then becomes a matter of 'stakeholder management'. The question can be asked whether 'stakeholder management' is a euphemism for forcing stakeholders to comply with what already has been decided. Or is it a serious attempt at compromise, based on a willingness to realize a strategy that caters for a wide range of interests? A related question is whether stakeholders are to be considered after a strategic plan has been formulated and attention has turned on how to implement it. Or are stakeholders a permanent feature or even participants in a continuous strategy debate?

Illustration 6.3: SKF from a stakeholder point of view

Should SKF* compete on price and put in the lowest bid possible to retain a big US-based client, or should they step away and persist with their high-quality strategy?

There are internal and external stakeholders who would be differently affected by what will be decided. SKF does not directly deal with the US-based client. A distributor acts as a go between. The client who wants to hold the reverse auction is the distributor's main account. The distributor also sources from the other ball bearing manufacturers and acts as the main channel by which the US-based client fulfils it ball bearing needs. That will remain so after the auction. The auction is going to determine the price at which the client will procure its ball bearings. The distributor will get paid on the basis of a fixed cost-plus arrangement. The distributor is pressuring SKF at least to take part. The distributor wants to keep representing SKF – also with other clients – because, due to premium pricing, it is one of the more profitable product lines for them. SKF not taking part would jeopardize the relationship with this distributor and could lose them all other clients the distributor deals with as well.

This dilemma translates into conflicting positions within SKF too. SKF's Global manager for customer value is opposed to taking part. He was the architect behind the software tool with which sales representatives go round to demonstrate why SKG ball bearings are expensive but worth their money. He believes in SKF's value strategy and giving in would damage SKF's brand. Furthermore, it would inspire other clients and distributors to ask for similar deals. After some time, he reckoned, this client would realize that just using price as the selection criterion would backfire and they would come back to SKF and its value proposition. The SKF account manager who deals with the distributor wants to take part because he is afraid that SKF would lose all business that is conducted through the distributor. The decision is escalated up to the SKF Service Division president. Because this is so tied in with SKF's strategy, he is charged with making the final decision. However, this problem only reached him five days before the auction will be held. So there is some urgency to this issue.

Pragmatically, this involves a considerable chunk of turnover. Morally, there is a question of loyalty. Is SKF going to stick with a distributor with which it has enjoyed a long-standing relationship? Cognitively, there is the question how the reverse auction needs to be interpreted. Will this be the exception and all other SKF clients will stick with the value proposition or will this become the rule and all other clients will start emphasizing price? All three players in this, SKF, the distributor and the client are mutually interdependent and what will happen will define who holds power over whom. As this is a dilemma, from a stakeholder point of view there is no clear indication what the right decision is. The increased urgency does indicate that both the distributor and the client move up in terms of stakeholder salience. Maybe there is a possibility to engage in direct negotiation with the client to reach a compromise.

* Value selling at SKF Service, IMD-5-0751, 2009.

Criticism and generating further questions

The stakeholder approach turns strategic management into a political process. It also makes strategy essentially subjective. The possibility of an objective benchmark to measure right or wrong against is lost, as everything is 'in the eye of the beholder'. This refers to an organization's performance as well as the strategy by which this performance is achieved. What is legitimate is subject to constant renegotiation among the stakeholders. The organization's purpose is essentially what the dominant coalition makes of it. The question about the organization's purpose is therefore an almost permanent cause for debate and the answer moves with the times.

The stakeholder approach brings a realization with it that top management is seen as another stakeholder just like anyone else. Managers have their own interests, interpretations and moral obligations. So what role do they have in the strategic management of the firm? Are they the *primus inter pares* who serve as an arbitrator among the various stakeholders, or are they a separate stakeholder group with their own interests and a particular stake in the survival and success of the organization? Or are they divided up amongst themselves because they identify individually with a specific part of the organization like a department or a subsidiary, or maybe even with an outside stakeholder? Thinking this through could lead to the conclusion that strategic management as an activity to make a firm or an organization perform and to maintain an organization's or firm's ability to perform nothing more than an *idée fixe*: an obsession in managers' and some strategy scholars' minds with little empirical grounding.

The stakeholder approach also brings into focus that the strategist's choices and activities have moral implications. The stakeholder approach is at odds with the concept of shareholder value. The stakeholder approach points out that any organization and by implication its managers, has a moral obligation to everybody who can be described as a stakeholder. Shareholder value implies – for business firms – that managers only have a moral obligation to shareholders. It is expected that there are situations where a decision in favour of a stakeholder will be at the expense of shareholders. Research by Hillman and Keim (2001) indicates that taking care of stakeholders has a negative impact on profitability because it leads to additional costs that are not always recouped by increasing sales. This is where the strategist is alone and has to decide what to do about this moral dilemma. To make matters worse, and this concerns all organizations, these kinds of situations also occur when the strategist has to take sides between stakeholders with conflicting claims, especially when these refer to issues of moral legitimacy. It is at such moments that the strategist has to decide what corporate social responsibility really means to him.

The stakeholder approach is not really decided on where it stands with regard to the philosophical debates of objectivism versus subjectivism and voluntarism versus subjectivism. It contains a subjectivist argument in that the notion of management cognition and mental maps point at the subjective world that makes up management reality. However, there are strategy scholars in this realm who implicitly or explicitly assume that there is a business reality out there whilst recognizing that that which managers work with are perceptions. They have an expectation or hope that management perception eventually is an accurate reflection of this business reality. Others stick to management perceptions as being the only relevant but inherently subjective 'reality' and do not bother with an objective business reality at all.

There is also variety with regard to voluntarism versus determinism. On the one hand, the notion of management assumes the ability to translate intentions into realization. The expectation that managers negotiate to realize their interests or the organization's interests expresses this voluntarist position. On the other hand, the many interests that need to be catered for tend to create compromises that often do not correspond to any particular interest, leaving all interested parties with outcomes that do not reflect anyone's intentions at all. When this happens, you could make the determinist argument that everybody is subjected to the circumstances that surround them.

Case 6.1 Apple

Apple has been going from strength to strength over the last couple of years, introducing the world to the iPod, the iPhone and the iPad, whilst their range of Mac computers has been gaining market share as well. Apple has been reported to be the most valuable company in the world. Some of its clients are so attached to the brand that their experience with the company resembles 'evangelical frenzy'.[1] There have also been reports that associate Apple with pollution, child labour and flouting workers' rights.

In August 2011, a group of environmental protection organizations published a report accusing 27 manufactures of Apple products – all located in China – of pollution.[2] Suzhou United Win (China) Technology Ltd allegedly uses n-hexane instead of alcohol for cleaning the iPod touchscreens they manufacture, poisoning some of their workers in 2010. Meico Electronics (Wuhan) Co Ltd, another Apple supplier, had been caught discharging hazardous waste water into the environment.

Initially Apple declined the opportunity to comment.[3] Later they sent an email to the Institute of Public and Environmental Affairs (IPE) in Beijing, an environmental protection pressure group, stating: "We would be interested in hearing more specifics on what you have discovered about these suppliers". Ma Jun, the director of IPE was cited as saying that: "the company refuses to make the identities of suppliers public and to fulfil its responsibility to disclose information about the environmental effects of the suppliers' actions. Without public supervision, suppliers are more likely to believe they can get away with releasing large amounts of hazardous waste". Apple spokesperson Huang Yuna replied that Apple is committed to "maintaining the highest standards for social responsibility throughout its supply chain. We require that our suppliers provide safe working conditions and use environmentally responsible manufacturing processes wherever Apple products are made". In April 2012, Apple and IPE agreed to conduct a joint pollution audit of Apple's China-based suppliers.

Apple's largest manufacturing partner, Foxconn Technology Group, was found to have employed underage workers at their Yantai plant.[4] Foxconn is the name under

1 *Superbrands*, broadcast on BBC THREE, 17 May 2012, short video available on http://www.bbc.co.uk/news/business-13416272.

2 *China Daily*, 9 September 2011, http://www.chinadaily.com.cn/bizchina/2011-09/01/content_13577441.htm (accessed 2 November 2012).

3 *China Daily*, 16 April 2012, http://europe.chinadaily.com.cn/business/2012-04/16/content_15061993.htm (accessed 2 November 2012).

4 *China Daily*, 17 October 2012, http://europe.chinadaily.com.cn/china/2012-10/17/content_15825651.htm (accessed 2 November 2012).

which the Hon Hai Precision Industry Co. Ltd. of Taiwan is known. When confronted with the allegations, Foxconn stated that: "an internal investigation carried out by our company found that some participants in a short-term student internship program administered at our base in Yantai are under the legal working age of 16". They also admitted that "this is not only a violation of China's Labour Law, it is also a violation of Foxconn policy and immediate steps have been taken to return the interns in question to educational institutions. We are really sorry and we apologize to the students for causing this inconvenience. Interns at Foxconn cannot be forced to work, can quit any time they want and are not allowed to work night shifts or overtime".

Yet a student of one of the colleges involved – who wanted to remain anonymous – was heard on China National Radio saying that he had worked on night shifts at the Yantai plant.[5] He was fired when he had taken leave without permission for the third time. His teacher apparently told him he would be expelled from school as well. Duan Yi, who is a lawyer at Guangdong Laowei Law Firm, said: "we've dealt with cases in which schools made profit by establishing partnerships with factories and sending students to work there". Underage labour is a common phenomenon in China according to him.

Foxconn has been in the news on more than one occasion, being scrutinized for the way it deals with its workers. 150 workers at its Wuhan plant threatened to commit suicide as part of their protest against working conditions.[6] It was reported that the production of the Apple iPhone 5 was interrupted by strikes and labour disputes, apparently because of the increased pressure as a consequence of Apple's quality demands.[7] An investigation by Reuters found workers complaining that Foxconn used all kinds of tricks to reduce its pay while there were issues with forced overtime.[8]

Foxconn, on the other hand, explains that it is constantly working to address issues and that overall working conditions in their Chinese plants are above average for the country. In their 2011 Corporate Social and Economic Responsibility annual report, they list their stakeholders as employees, customers, suppliers, community, investors and NGOs – in that order. They claim to focus on the employees' living environment, working environment, labour relations and mental health (ibid: 9):

> The goals are to ensure that voices from employees can be heard and their emotions expressed so that they feel rewarded and happy at work. In addition to the regular communication channels, Foxconn is dedicated to an effective communication procedure that provides 24-hour service to employees who need help, counselling, or other assistance to enhance employees' health and mental well-being.

5 *China Daily*, 17 October 2012, http://europe.chinadaily.com.cn/china/2012-10/17/content_15825651.htm (accessed 2 November 2012).

6 *The Daily Telegraph*, 11 January 2012, http://www.telegraph.co.uk/news/worldnews/asia/china/9006988/Mass-suicide-protest-at-Apple-manufacturer-Foxconn-factory.html (accessed 2 November 2012).

7 *The Guardian*, 5 October 2012, http://www.guardian.co.uk/technology/2012/oct/05/foxconn-apple-iphone-china-strike/print (accessed 2 November 2012).

8 *Reuters TV*, 22 October 2012, video available on http://www.youtube.com/watch?v=-X0YIE1ykjw&feature=player_embedded.

7 Institutional theory and organizational culture

Institutional theory urges us to consider the regular interaction patterns on which an organization relies to function and exist. It also brings the underlying expectations and interpretations into focus of those who are involved in these interactions. It therefore links up with social structure and organizational culture. On the whole, the focus is less on people and more on the interactions they are engaged in. The basic premise in institutional theory is that people, either as individuals or collectives, are defined by what they do and how they do it.

The process logic of institutional theory

The concepts of institution and institutionalization are key terms in sociology. Some argue that this is what sociology is about: the explanation of social order and social organization. An institution is "more or less taken-for-granted repetitive social behaviour that is underpinned by normative systems and cognitive understandings that give meaning to social exchange and thus enable self-reproducing social order" (Greenwood, Oliver, Sahlin and Suddaby 2008: 4–5). Organizations, which include business firms, operate in a society that consists of institutions. Organizations can be considered institutions themselves. But organizations also rely on this 'self-reproducing social order' to be able to function, exist and perform. Such regularities in interactions mean that organizations can be organized, that products can be sold, that public services can be delivered, that people can be employed, that investments can be made and that money can change hands. For instance, money itself is such an institution. The money economy, prevalent and self-evident as it is now all over the world, is such a 'self-reproducing social order'.

Institutions develop over time. Some take centuries to come into being and seem to persist almost indefinitely; others come and go in a relatively short time span. Institutionalization is the process by which institutions emerge and change. Institutional theory is starting to get noticed by strategy scholars (Lawrence 1999). This is happening for two reasons. One reason is that institutionalized interaction patterns impinge on the functioning and performance of any organization. Organizations thus should take notice of how they are affected to mitigate and manage their influence, or maybe make use of them to boost their performance. This is further elaborated under the header of 'isomorphism'. The other reason is that the idea has taken hold that organizations are actively involved in affecting the course of the institutionalization process and influence how institutions take shape. This is elaborated under the heading of 'institutional entrepreneurship'.

Isomorphism

The concept of isomorphism provides an answer to a question about a phenomenon that for Meyer and Rohan (1977) needs an explanation. Why do so many organizations claim that they have a formal organization structure and why do these organizations very rarely actually operate according to this formal structure? This goes back to the distinction between formal and informal organization. Anyone who goes into organizations to find out what is going on, astonishingly in a way, finds that what actually makes the organization work is not found in the formal structures and procedures. People improvise around these official arrangements, and very often have to, to get things done. Yet when asked to account for themselves, organizations maintain that everything progresses in an orderly fashion in accordance with pre-set and pre-designed standards and procedures. Meyer and Rowan (1977) suggest that formal organization is a myth. Organizations put up a front and conform to this image of formality and rationality because that is generally expected of them in society at large. People working in an organization know this. They often just 'act the part' to live up to this expectation but simultaneously deviate from it actually to get their job done.

Almost everybody who has work experience has some familiarity with what appears to be this double standard. The difference between formal and informal organization is one of those truisms in organization and management theory. Meyer and Rowan's analysis points towards a more general effect. Organizations tend to conform to outside expectations and they do so to appear legitimate. Suchman (1995: 574) defines legitimacy as "a generalized perception or assumption that the actions of an entity are desirable, proper, or appropriate within some socially constructed system of norms, values, beliefs, and definitions". Organizations need to be legitimate to maintain their reason for existence. Such 'socially constructed systems of norms, values, beliefs and definitions', to which organizations have to conform, appear and are maintained in the form of specific institutions (Scott 1995).

So, in institutional theory, legitimacy is connected with institutions. Regular interaction patterns have become institutions when they acquire a form of permanence independent of the interactions that constitute them. The norms, values, understandings and resource exchanges, which are part of these regular interactions, become so taken for granted that they prescribe how the interactions have to take place. This effect that institutions take on an existence independent of the interactions that constitute them is referred to as a 'social structure'. This social structure contains common norms, values and understandings. It stipulates how resources are supposed to be allocated. Individuals and organizations have to conform to the norms, values and interpretations that the social structure dictates to remain legitimate. Overstepping the mark contains the peril of being sanctioned or losing the ability to function altogether.

Institutions appear in all kind of shapes and sizes. Professions such as accountancy or the medical profession are institutions, as are specific types of organizations including government, charities, hospitals, universities or business firms – and within that, types of business firms such as for instance supermarkets or airlines. These are all institutions because they exist as regular interaction patterns prescribed by a social structure consisting of specific expectations and interpretations. Some of these expectations and interpretations and sometimes institutions as a whole, are part of a formal system of rules and regulations. These can vary between the legal system of a country and the rules of play in the game of football. Others are more informal but can be just as compelling.

With regard to organizations, this tendency to conform to what the social structure prescribes leads to isomorphism – the phenomenon that organizations of a certain type tend to look alike. That is why a supermarket is recognized as a supermarket or a university as a university. That is why people can tell the difference between a rugby pitch and a football pitch. It also tells people how to act in the context of a supermarket or a university, or as a member of a rugby team or a football team. Yet there is also the expectation that the supermarket or the university deals with them in a particular manner, just like a rugby player or a football player expect that their fellow teammates as well as the opponents keep to the rules of the game. The realization to make here is that football and the social structure that defines it is only seen to exist if the game is being played. Likewise, a supermarket's structural features only exist if people shop there.

There are three mechanisms of isomorphism (DiMaggio and Powell 1983). Coercive isomorphism is the result of pressure put upon the organization to conform. This can be the consequence of a dependency that forces the organization to act in a particular way. It can also be 'peer' pressure, to be accepted as part of a community or group. Conformism here is forced upon the organization. Mimetic isomorphism is voluntary. An organization can decide to mimic another organization because it cannot think of anything else to do but follow a standard model or copy a good example. This is often prompted by uncertainty about the situation and imitation then is the safe option. Normative isomorphism is a direct consequence of the limitations put upon organizations because they have to follow certain rules. For instance, legislation or professional norms and standards compel an organization to do things in a certain way.

The collection of regular institutionalized activities, and the organizations and individuals associated with them, are often collectively referred to as the organizational field. For DiMaggio and Powell (1983: 148), an organizational field consists of "those organizations that, in the aggregate, constitute a recognized area of institutional life: key suppliers, resource and product consumers, regulatory agencies, and other organizations that produce similar service or products". A field is seen as a community of activities, conforming to a social structure and in which an organization takes part. The level of legitimacy an organization maintains determines this organization's membership as well as its ability to function and perform within this community. And this in turn is a function of the meaningful interactions in which the organization is able to engage.

The organization itself is considered to be an institution as well. The activities of people working on behalf of the organization are to a large extent 'taken-for-granted repetitive social behaviours'. These regularities are reflected in particular 'normative systems and cognitive understandings'. The 'normative systems and cognitive understandings' part of an organization, in turn, is commonly referred to as the organizational culture (Fine 1984). An organizational culture is "a pattern of shared basic assumptions that the group learned as it solved its problems of external adaptation and internal integration, that has worked well enough to be considered valid, and therefore, to be taught to new members as the correct way to perceive, think, and feel in relation to those problems" (Schein, 1992: 12). Organization culture, in effect, is the organization's social structure.

However, the occurrence of conflicting demands, fuelled by differences with regard to the norms and values and how situations are to be interpreted also leads to the recognition that an organization can contain subcultures.

Meyerson and Martin (1987) thus put forward three ways to appreciate organization culture. It can be integrative when everybody in the organization shares the same norms and values and interprets situations in the same way. It can be divisive when the organization consists of various subcultures with different sets of norms, values and interpretations. It can be ambiguous when there are no clear expectations. What can be expected is that every organization has a little bit of all three. Some aspects are shared, others are disputed and a few more are not clear at all. It is also not uncommon that some subcultures within the organization share their outlook with outside institutions. For instance, medical doctors tend to identify more with the rules of their profession than the expectations of the hospital they work for. Yet what they all have in common is that they are created, maintained and changed as a consequence of people's regular interaction patterns.

The integrative effect of organization culture is manifested in what Prahalad and Bettis (1986) have labelled as the 'dominant logic'. The dominant logic is top management's preferred way of interpreting an organization's situation. It is associated with the organization's 'paradigm': "a set of beliefs held relatively commonly throughout the organization" (Johnson, 1987: 216). It sits at the centre of a 'cultural web', with the paradigm reflected in the stories that people tell, in the symbols that signify what the organization is about, in the way the organization's structure and control systems work, in the rituals and routines that people engage in and in who has power over what.

The paradigm's main effect appears when something happens and a decision has to be made to deal with it (see Figure 7.1). This event will need to be interpreted to create a response. Johnson (1987) finds that there are three ways in which this happens. The problem can be ignored and there is no reaction. Or the problem makes perfect sense because it can be and is understood in terms of the paradigm, leading to the development of a solution. Or the problem does not make sense because the paradigm does not provide a ready interpretation. Consequently, there is ambiguity. When this happens a struggle occurs about how this ambiguous situation should be interpreted. This takes on the form of politics of meaning, with the most likely outcome that the paradigm prevails and the initial ambiguity is accommodated within the belief system, with a solution developed accordingly.

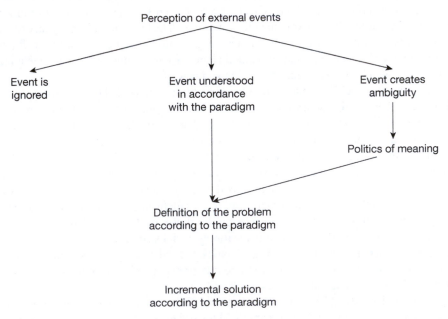

Figure 7.1 Problem solving and the paradigm

Derived from Johnson (1987)

There is one common denominator amongst these alternative ways to deal with a problem. The way people think and interpret a situation is governed by the paradigm and this subsequently drives their actions. Simultaneously, the interaction patterns that are thus created nurture the paradigm. In this way a self-preserving dynamic takes shape and the paradigm stays intact. Strategists as well as the organization as a whole maintain their organization culture and associated belief system and continue to act in the same manner. To Johnson (1988), this provides another explanatory layer to Quinn's (1980) notion of 'logical incrementalism' (see Chapter 6). The negotiation process by which a firm develops in a step-by-step manner is seen as a manifestation of 'problem-solving-according-to-the-paradigm'. Within the paradigm, there is room for conflicting interests and these are the problems that are being solved and negotiated about. There is also an overarching common understanding what the organization is about that puts the 'logical' in the 'incrementalism'. It keeps the organization together whilst the negotiations move it slowly forward.

The process logic for isomorphism sees the environmental survival process as taking place in the organizational field: this community of regular interactions that in the aggregate constitute a recognized area of institutional life (see Figure 7.2). To survive and be able to continue to interact, organizations have to yield to institutional pressure. They have to take part in the regular interaction patterns in the manner the outside world expects of them. The result is isomorphism with organizations appearing very much alike. The generalized perceptions and assumptions about the actions of the organization and their qualification as appropriate within some socially constructed system of norms, values, beliefs and definitions at field level are expected to be reflected in the organization's paradigm. Consequently, the organizational strategy process takes on the form of 'problem-solving-according-to-the-paradigm'. The strategist is a conformist: interpreting situations in accordance with the paradigm and acting in compliance, maybe without even realizing it.

Institutional entrepreneurship

Oliver (1991) suggests that organizations are able to take a more active stance when it comes to dealing with institutional pressures. An organization can opt for defiance. This is

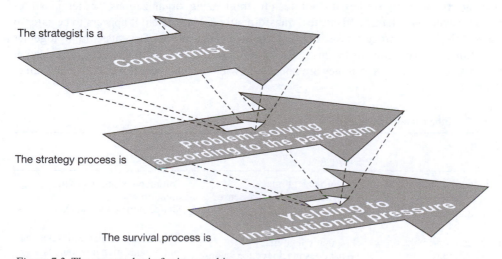

Figure 7.2 The process logic for isomorphism

an act of resistance where the organization openly demonstrates that it does not comply. One step further is the option of manipulation. This means that the organization actively attempts to change the demands that are made on it. It implies that the organization looks to achieve deliberate institutional change. Such an active involvement in shaping the institutional field is referred to as institutional entrepreneurship (DiMaggio 1988). The organization seeks to transform (part of) the organizational field and the way interactions take place in order to suit its own needs. In effect it attempts to alter (part of) the organizational field's social structure. This is referred to as fundamental change.

In both instances, a reaction from the organizational field can be expected. Either option results in a situation of open conflict with several parties joining in to try to settle the dispute in a favourable manner. Because institutional fields tend to feature contradictory and incompatible demands anyway, they often spawn conflicts and are seen as the reason why things change (Seo and Creed 2002). For instance, people who are engaged in investments and the financing of business firms expect them to make as much profit as possible and therefore expect management to keep the tax bill as low as they can within the confines of the law. They like to see the firm engage in tax avoidance schemes and consider the use of offshore tax havens as quite legitimate. Others have condemned tax avoidance activities and expect firms to pay tax on their earnings in the country where these earnings are generated.

Similarly, within organizations it is not uncommon that employees are told to provide excellent customer service and that the customer is always right. Simultaneously they are told not to incur additional costs and to stay within a limited set of instructions that they know will deter customers. Individuals, organizations and subcultures can have different ideas about what is considered to be legitimate or be at odds with the overarching social structure (see Table 7.1). Most of the time these contradictions are repaired or concealed (Lawrence and Suddaby 2006). Yet every latent contradiction can manifest itself in open conflict if somebody is inspired for some reason to take on the existing social order.

Many innovations and the rise and fall of markets and industries as a whole are found to be struggles as a consequence of institutional entrepreneurship (e.g. Garud, Jain and Kumaraswamy 2002; Hargadon and Douglas 2001; Haveman and Rao 1997; Leblebici, Salancik, Copay and King 1991; Lounsbury 2001; Munir and Phillips 2005; Sminia 2003). The course and outcome of such a struggle is difficult to predict, let alone control. Despite popular myth, these studies do not feature trailblazing organizations or heroic entrepreneurs who take charge and create a transformation from scratch. It appears to be safer to assume that such a process takes on the form of a concurrence of events coming together over time. The activities of the institutional entrepreneur and the innovating organization add events to the process but they are not able to wield so much control that they can direct the process at will.

Table 7.1 Inherent contradictions

Agents	Contested legitimacy	Social structure
Individual interpretations	Cognitive legitimacy: To whom does it make sense?	Common definitions of the situation
Individual moral obligations	Normative legitimacy: Whose rules?	Shared norms and values
Individual pragmatic considerations	Pragmatic legitimacy: What does it achieve for whom?	Distribution of material, financial and organizational resources

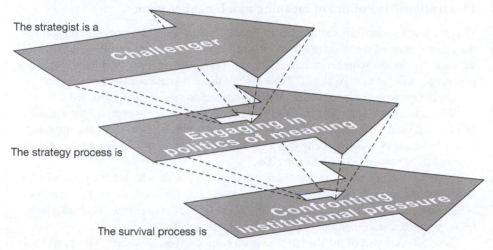

The strategist is a

Challenger

The strategy process is

Engaging in politics of meaning

The survival process is

Confronting institutional pressure

Figure 7.3 The process logic for institutional entrepreneurship

Pettigrew (1987: 659) provides a very apt description of how such a process takes shape inside an organization. He describes it as "politics as the management of meaning"; as a process in which "the content of strategic change is thus ultimately a product of a legitimation process shaped by political/cultural considerations, though often expressed in rational/ analytical terms". The top management group of an organization meets, interacts and discusses current issues all the time.

The organizational paradigm (Johnson 1987) and the dominant logic (Prahalad and Bettis 1986) play their part. Many of the encounters effectively confirm existing beliefs about the state of affairs. Yet by carefully staged but defiant behaviour, justified by different interpretations of the situation, maybe seizing the moment when difficult problems or full-blown crises manifest themselves, alternative interpretations can gain prominence. New ways of doing things are tried out and – if remotely possible – are described as successful to underline the necessity and validity of change. The actual language used features much of the vocabulary of marketing-inspired strategic thinking, the industrial organization approach, the resource-based view and shareholder value. But there is another layer to what is discussed. The 'dominant logic' is challenged, debunked and eventually replaced with a new point of view. Burgelman (1983), Johnson (1987), Greenwood and Hinings (1988), Pettigrew (1985) and Sminia (2005) have provided these kinds of accounts of the strategy process.

Many studies into institutional entrepreneurship describe a very similar process but now at the level of the organizational field (Garud and others 2002; Hargadon and Douglas 2001; Haveman and Rao 1997; Leblebici and others 1991; Lounsbury 2001; Munir and Phillips 2005; Sminia 2003). Again there is a dominant way of how things are done and many organizations subscribe to this and are able to survive and be successful. Yet, on a regular basis, initiatives are taken that aim to upset the current state of affairs and to leverage in some kind of change – described by the initiators in terms of innovation and improvement. A struggle ensues between challengers and incumbents, and sometimes a new order will replace the old one. And again this process features power, politics, ambiguity, conflict and controversy.

Illustration 7.1: Politics of meaning as a language game

Imagine that a scientific investigation has been commissioned to assess how dangerous the manufacture of the chemical compound metadioxine is. The resulting report will be used to decide whether a new chemical plant, where this compound will be processed, will get the 'go ahead'. Now look at these two alternative conclusions:

"On the existing evidence the committee can see no reason not to proceed."

"While the committee feel that there is no reason not to proceed on the existing evidence, it must be emphasized that metadioxine is a comparatively recent compound. It would be irresponsible to deny that after further research, its manufacture might be proofed to be associated with health risks."

The first conclusion means that those who have to decide whether the plant will be constructed can use the report to give it the 'go ahead'. The second conclusion allows the same people to say 'no'. Substantially, both conclusions are true. Their meaning, however, indicates something completely opposite.

These lines are part of the British television comedy 'Yes, Minister'. This particular episode was broadcast on 16 March 1981. Metadioxine is a fictional compound, and so is the chemical plant, as well as the problem. It was part of a plotline in which the minister and his chief civil servant disagreed on whether the new plant should get ministerial approval. The minister was against it. He persuaded the writer of the report to go with the second conclusion. This then allowed the minister to disapprove the plans.

Of course this is all fictional, but it does illustrate the effect the use of language has on decision-making. This is how 'management as the politics of meaning' plays out. It has been observed that many strategists play similar language games (Samra-Fredericks 2003; Sminia 2005).

So the environmental survival process for institutional entrepreneurship is very much a process of confronting the existing institutional order in an attempt to change an organizational field's social structure to benefit the challenger organization (see Figure 7.3). Within the organization, such a process takes on the form of politics of meaning. The strategist has an extremely difficult job of not only challenging the current state of affairs of how things are done and interpreted within the organization, but also simultaneously to preserve the organization as a purposeful actor, one able to take part in the struggle that takes place at the level of the organizational field (Sminia and de Rond 2012).

Illustration 7.2: Continuity and change in the US radio broadcasting industry

The Leblebici and others (1991) investigation of the US radio broadcasting industry between 1920 and 1965 found that there have been three distinct eras. Each of these eras lasted for only about 15 years. Although each era, as the industry name implies, featured the broadcasting of radio programmes, the way in which this was done was completely different between eras, with different activities and interaction patterns.

Consequently, there were specific players that dominated each era; both in terms of the kind of businesses that were successful with regard to the kind of jobs that people did working for these businesses. Whilst there was a great deal of continuity during each era, the industry was also in a continuous state of transition towards the next era.

Radio equipment manufacturers dominated the first era (1920–1934). Equipment manufacturers only made radio parts and held patents on specific components. At first, when you wanted a radio receiver or transmitter, you had to get parts from different manufacturers and put them together yourself. These manufacturers initially were competing on the basis of rival technologies, but also accusing each other of patent breaches. Creating a patent pool among these radio manufacturers solved this. Also the Radio Corporation of America (RCA) was established by the main manufactures to build and sell complete radio sets using parts supplied by its constituents. To entice people to buy radio sets, these manufacturers (but also some large retailers) started to provide radio broadcasts. This gave people something to listen to. However, at some point the market for radio sets became saturated. The manufacturers became less keen to provide radio broadcasts for free as their effectiveness for selling sets waned.

The impetus for solving this problem came from the periphery of society. A number of "sellers of questionable commodities" (Leblebici and others 1991: 345) such as hair loss remedies and fortune telling, and who were shunned by regular advertising mediums, had started to use radio broadcasts to advertise their wares. This seed of an idea developed into a mainstream business when it was picked up that advertisers could cover the costs of producing radio shows and even allow for a profit for a radio broadcasting station. This model became the basis of the second era (1935–1950), dominated by radio networks including NBC, CBS and ABC. It allowed the also emerging fast moving consumer products firms to develop their brands on a nationwide scale. Branding products on that scale was a new phenomenon at the time as well. These firms would sponsor shows and in return the broadcast would be named after them (the 'Palmolive Hour', the 'Lucky-Strike Hour'). One problem was that radio transmitters only have a limited reach. To get nationwide coverage, local radio stations were linked up and became part of these radio networks. Consequently, the networks became the key players in the industry. Alongside, an advertising industry emerged which specialized in producing the sponsored radio shows that were being broadcast by the radio networks.

The competition for listening figures and therefore value for advertisers made the radio shows ever more extravagant and increasingly expensive to make. This was another reason for radio stations to band together. It also left out stations that missed out on becoming a network member. They could not afford the costs of the mostly live shows and had only limited – local – reach. The alternative they found was to use recorded music, i.e. playing records and to broadcast commercials in between. This cheap alternative brought down their cost base and also made it affordable for local businesses to advertise their wares to local customers. Radio shows became known for their type of music, attracting specific groups of listeners, which represented particular market segments. This allowed advertisers – both national and local – to target their commercial messages to their respective customers. This also saw the emergence of the disc jockey: somebody who developed a radio personality on the basis of his music choice and who also operated the record player and mixing desk himself. This was in sharp contrast with the division of labour between radio technicians and mostly anonymous radio announcers with the radio networks. With local radio stations now outcompeting the networks, the third era (1951–1965) of the independent radio stations had come into being. It also spawned another industry and even to some extent another category of people. The music industry and the radio broadcasting industry had become entwined in producing and selling pop music to teenagers.

The performance logic of institutional theory

Looking at it from the perspective of isomorphism and the passive stance with regard to the institutional pressures an organization has to deal with, institutional theory covers the three ingredients of strategic management – strategy, environment and organization – in a very specific manner (see Figure 7.4). The environment is an organizational field of regular and institutionalized interaction patterns. The organization itself exists by way of the continuity in interaction patterns among the organization members as well as the interactions it has within the organizational field, all in accordance with the field's social structure. Isomorphism implies that the organization conforms to the institutional pressures put upon it and that it maintains its legitimacy in this way.

There are in fact three different ways or strategies how an organization can conform to institutional pressures. There is a choice between acquiescence, compromise and avoidance (Oliver 1991). The option of acquiescence means that the organization fully accedes to institutional pressures. It subscribes to the 'normative systems and cognitive understandings' as well as the associated 'taken-for-granted repetitive social behaviours', which come with these pressures, by acting accordingly. The option of compromise comes into play when fully acceding to the institutional pressures results in an unworkable situation or when there are reasons to object to the standards put upon the organization. As was said earlier, institutional pressures often conflict with each other. By compromising the organization tries to find a mutually acceptable middle ground. The option of avoidance means that the

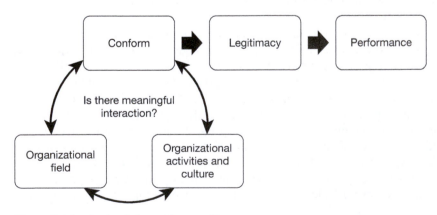

Figure 7.4 Institutional theory: isomorphism

organization conceals its non-conformity by only appearing to adhere to the standards. This is sometimes an unavoidable situation when a middle ground between conflicting expectations cannot be found. Yet it can mean that the organization enters the realm of illegality (e.g. Sminia 2011).

The overall requirement for the organization to remain viable is expressed by the question about meaningful interaction (see Figure 7.4). The institutional demands from the organizational field, the organization's activities and associated culture, the way in which the organization conforms, all three have to combine so that the organization's activities as a part of the many interaction processes that the organization relies on to continue to exist, are meaningful for all interaction partners. This refers to participants inside as well as outside the organization. As soon as this breaks down, the organization is in danger of becoming irrelevant. When the interactions the organization is involved in lose their meaning, they stop happening and, as a consequence, the viability of the organization is at stake.

The same requirement of meaningful interaction applies to the realm of institutional entrepreneurship as well. The difference is that because of the change initiative that is at the heart of this, the meaning of a range of interactions has become ambiguous. Existing patterns are put into disarray and have to institutionalize again. Part of the social structure is suspended. The organization brings this on itself as a consequence of a strategy of transformation and of willingly challenging the *status quo* (see Figure 7.5). This is the effect of Oliver's (1991) more active strategies of defiance or manipulation, described earlier.

As was said earlier, research evidence suggests that it is more or less impossible for an initiator to control the full process of institutional change and to direct it towards the most favourable outcome. Nevertheless, an organization that has initiated change should at least try to affect the course the process takes. Sminia's (2003) analysis of how such an initiative failed horribly provides a few pointers as to what an organization can do.

Organizational field

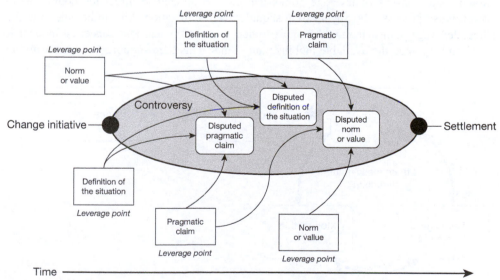

Figure 7.5 A controversy and leverage points

The first thing to realize is that most of the time a change initiative only affects a part of the organizational field. Not all interaction patterns, or the complete social structure get in disarray but only the part that is directly affected by the change initiative. When a controversy is triggered, only specific interaction patterns and associated normative systems, cognitive understandings and resource allocations are in disarray (see Figure 7.5). The meanings of the interactions affected directly by the controversy have become ambiguous and need to be resettled. There is effectively a dispute about what they achieve, how the situation is defined and what norms and values apply. Also, the resource exchange tends to be interrupted. In short, these interaction patterns have to regain meaning once more. The controversy is over when a settlement has been reached. A controversy thus only covers a limited part of the field's social structure referring to a specific range of interactions. The process from start to resolution takes shape as a sequence of events over time from initially being triggered by a change initiative to eventually being settled.

To affect the direction the controversy process will take and to shape the eventual settlement, the organization can mobilize leverage points. A leverage point is a particular norm or value, definition of the situation, a pragmatic claim, and quite often a combination of these three, which vindicates particular interactions. These leverage points are fixed points of reference respectively indicating normative, cognitive or pragmatic legitimacy (Suchman, 1995). Leverage points exist because only part of the field's social structure is disputed. Many interactions are still meaningful and supported by common norms, values, beliefs, definitions and pragmatic considerations. These meanings can be drawn on to direct the course of events and settle the dispute. Whether and how these leverage points are mobilized during the controversy process determines the eventual settlement that will be reached. The extent to which an organization is capable of coming together to muster the skill to act in a unified way – despite the politics of meaning that take place inside the organization – determines how well the organization is able to steer the course of the change process towards a favourable settlement.

This take on the process of institutional change informs the performance logic of institutional entrepreneurship (see Figure 7.6). The environment, or more specifically the organizational field, consists of leverage points that can be utilized to direct the course of the controversy process. The organization should have mobilization skills to be able to utilize these leverage points. It should be able to act in a coordinated and concerted manner to time and leverage the available mobilization points. This then supports the organization's

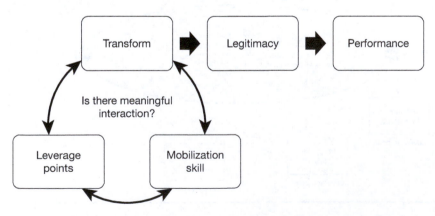

Figure 7.6 Institutional theory: institutional entrepreneurship

transformation strategy to regain new legitimacy. The question of meaningful interaction is still relevant, as this is the eventual benchmark by which a settlement of a controversy is evaluated.

Illustration 7.3: Controversies with Sport7

In 1996, the Dutch football association (KNVB) sold the broadcasting rights for domestic league games and matches involving the Dutch national team to a consortium of investors – of which it also was a member – for 900 million guilders. This consortium wanted to use these rights as a basis to establish a dedicated sports TV channel under the name of Sport7. This move created three controversies (Sminia 2003).

One of the controversies was triggered primarily between Sport7 and the Dutch public broadcaster (NOS) that had previously broadcast football matches, but it was not confined to these two. Football represents high viewing figures so there was much at stake. The NOS was outraged, as it felt cheated by the KNVB with which it had been negotiating while simultaneously and secretly the KNVB was a member of a consortium that was trying to outbid the NOS. The Dutch viewing public was unhappy as well. Sport7 was to become a cable station and wanted to charge a monthly fee of 2 guilders per cable connection. Before that, people in the Netherlands had been able to watch football for free on the public free-to-air NOS channels. Dutch football fans felt that football had been stolen from them. There were also principles of journalistic freedom at stake, with Sport7 wanting to ban filming at matches to safeguard exclusivity. TV journalists maintained that football is of national interest, which allows them to film matches and broadcast them as a news item.

A second controversy was triggered within the KNVB about the proceeds of the broadcasting rights contract. The KNVB wanted to distribute the money among the various professional and amateur leagues to boost football at every level. The top clubs in the Dutch premier league reckoned that they would get much more money by selling the broadcasting rights themselves, especially because that would mean they did not have to share with the lower league clubs.

A third controversy concerned the cable companies. Charging households for individual channels turned their business model around. Before the Sport7 deal, cable companies made their money by charging commercial TV channels a transmission fee. However, one of the larger cable companies was a member of the Sport7 consortium and was keen to transform the cable companies' business model.

All three controversies played out simultaneously. All parties involved drew on a range of leverage points to settle them in the way they wanted. The NOS went to court to challenge the deal. It also appealed to the government who became involved to safeguard the principle of journalistic freedom. The top clubs drew on the KNVB bylaws to argue that the football association did not have the right to sell broadcasting rights on their behalf. The cable companies split in favour or against changing their business model. Sport7 contested the various legal challenges and tried to win over the Dutch viewers and the cable companies by promising that football coverage on TV would be raised to unprecedented levels of quantity and quality. It also approached other minor sports and offered increased coverage to them.

When Sport7 started with its first broadcasts, it had (temporarily) withdrawn the cable companies' requirement to charge 2 guilders to boost viewing figures. With the cable companies wavering, only a minority of viewers would have been able to watch Sport7. The first broadcasts were also mired by technical glitches, putting the promise of quality under pressure. Many viewers boycotted them and this affected the keenness of advertisers, another important source of income. The legal challenges led to compromises that meant that Sport7 did not have total exclusivity in covering football on TV. Four months after the first Sport7 broadcast, the consortium pulled the plug, as the numbers did not add up anymore.

Additional features

The notion of organizational culture is closely related to the concepts of vision and visionary leadership. A vision is "a mental image of a desirable future state" (Bennis and Nanus 1985: 86). The visionary leader is the person who articulates this 'desirable future state' and who is expected to inspire others to follow him. In essence, a vision is a definition of a future situation to which the organization is supposed to aspire. It may well include statements of desirable norms and values the organization seeks to emulate. Montgomery (2008) argues that strategists should formulate a vision for the organization. The claim is that this vision and the charisma of the leader are powerful enough to initiate and effectuate the strategic change an organization might need.

Apart from organizational culture and belief systems propelling an organization into the future, it is also observed that they can hold organizations back. This is referred to in terms of 'strategic myopia' (Lorsch 1986). It leads to what Johnson (1987) labelled as 'strategic drift' (see Figure 7.7). Taking the problem solving according to the paradigm again – i.e. the strategy process as part of the process logic of isomorphism – over the long term, there have been numerous occasions that the paradigm was challenged by an initial ambiguous problem situation. Yet, most solutions will have reconfirmed the existing paradigm. In due course and in small steps, the organization's interpretations move further and further away from plausible alternative ways of looking at what is going on. Environmental change happens at a faster pace than the incremental changes the organization makes by implementing the solutions it comes up with. Eventually, the gap between the environment and the organization becomes too large and the organization finds itself out of touch. Normally when this has been going on for a while, there will be one issue too many, with an initial minor problem escalating into an existential crisis. The organization then needs a major turnaround to remain viable. Such a turnaround takes on the form of a substantial cultural upheaval or paradigm change (Baden-Fuller and Stopford 1994; Grinyer, Mayes and McKiernan 1988; Hinings and Greenwood 1988; Pettigrew 1985). This fundamental change is considered to be 'real' strategic change.

Analogous effects are observed at the level of the environment. A group of similar firms tend to adopt a common outlook on how to conduct their business. This then becomes prescriptive in order to be considered part of this business community. Spender (1989) labels this as the 'industry recipe' while Porac, Thomas and Baden-Fuller (1989) write about 'cognitive communities'. Reger and Huff (1993) suggest that a strategic group, as put forward by Porter (1980), does not come into being because of firms, independently of each other, opting for a specific competitive strategy on the basis of an analysis of the industry. They argue that it happens the other way around, i.e. that top managers of a group of firms

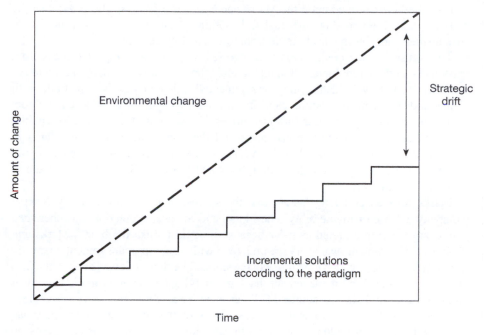

Figure 7.7 Strategic drift
Derived from Johnson (1987)

operating in the same line of business share a culture that tells them how they should operate. The ultimate effect is that a whole group of firms can find that they have become obsolete by collectively becoming the victim of strategic drift.

Illustration 7.4: Strategic drift at Marks and Spencer

Marks and Spencer is a well known chain of department stores that developed out of a trading stand on Leeds market in the 1880s. It had gained an image as one of the most successful British retailing firms ever but entered into difficulty around 2000–2002 (Mellahi, Jackson and Sparks 2002). A century of success was born out of being unorthodox. It had a strict 'buy British' policy, sourcing stock from within the UK. It only carried the one St Michael brand. It did not do marketing or advertising, relying on the trust that people had with the company. It did not accept credit cards either but had a very successful store card, which at some point was the third most used card in the UK after Visa and Mastercard. The department stores were firmly rooted in the British town and city centres. On that basis, Marks and Spencer enjoyed solid continued growth up to 1998, when it plateaued, slowly declining from 2002 onwards. Profits had plunged from 1998 onwards as well.

The late 1990s were difficult times for British retailing and Marks and Spencer responded by focusing on cost control. Simultaneously, a number of specialized competitors including Gap, Zara, Mango, Hennes & Mauritz, (all clothing retailers), Lush (soaps and cosmetics) and La Senza (lingerie) appeared, offering value at a price that rivalled or improved upon the Marks and Spencer offerings. There was also the rise of out of town shopping malls, benefiting from more efficient logistical arrangements and pulling away trade from town and city centres.

The refusal to take credit cards was reversed in 1999, after repeated pleas from customers and shareholders, although it took nine months to adapt the payment systems. The 'Buy British' policy was reluctantly abandoned. Freeing trade with China and the rising production capacity in Southeast Asia meant that competitors were able to offer higher value for lower prices. However, it turned out to be a public relations disaster with the national press and the trade unions deriding Marks & Spencer's decision to abandon Britain. Advances in IT also meant that efficient supply chains became widely available to everybody and Marks & Spencer's advantage in this area eroded away.

Marks & Spencer's long history and the success it had enjoyed had given the company a sense of invincibility. The Marks and Spencer reputation was cherished and change was interpreted as risky because it could tarnish the brand. Marks and Spencer management was very centralized, with the top management team far removed from the day-to-day realities in the stores. The focus of everybody in the firm was more on satisfying management than on satisfying customers. Middle and lower management numbers – a source of direct experience with customers – had been reduced as part of the cost cutting measures. Also the successes of the past had promoted certain individuals into powerful positions, who had a vested interest in how things had always been done. Careers were made through a string of internal promotions. By rarely appointing somebody from the outside in middle and senior management positions, new ideas and points of view were kept at bay. By 2002, the once proud company had developed a reputation as a straggler of the High Street, of being out-of-touch, and offering merchandise that had lost its appeal with the British buying public.

Strategy practice 7.1: SWOT analysis and strategic drift

The purpose of a SWOT analysis is to find out about threats and opportunities in the environment and about strengths and weaknesses with regard to the firm. But what makes an opportunity an opportunity, a threat a threat, a strength a strength, and a weakness a weakness? What does a SWOT analysis tell you about an organization in a situation of strategic drift?

When the top management team conducts a SWOT analysis, it will reflect the paradigm that characterises the organization. It does not reveal strengths, weaknesses, opportunities and threats as such. It reveals how the top team sees the organization and what it has and has not picked up with regard to environmental change. You could even argue that the analysis does not provide any information about the organization or the environment at all. It is, however, very informative about the people who have conducted the analyses. It provides an insight into their perspective on the world around them.

Doing strategic Management in an institutionalized world

Although there is less conviction that strategists are capable of safeguarding the future of an organization, the requirement of meaningful interaction in which the organization should be involved within the context of the organizational field provides a possibility to do strategic management. From an institutional theory point of view, strategy is essentially stratified (Sminia and de Rond 2012). There is a surface layer of continuity and isomorphism, kept in place by the existing institutionalized interaction patterns that conform to the social structure. Strategy at the surface level aims to conform to the current state of play. There is a deeper layer of fundamental or institutional change, brought about by institutional entrepreneurship. Strategy here aims to transform the state of play. Nevertheless, this stratified understanding of strategy generates only one set of questions. The two questions are:

1. Are there any alternative interaction patterns emerging that may create new meanings and upset the current institutionalized social structure?
2. If there are, what can you do about them?

Answering question 1: strategic analysis

Strategic analysis from an institutional theory point of view needs to be real time as a consequence of how the strategy process and the realization of performance is understood to be taking place. People and organizations interact continuously and through these interactions they conserve or alter the patterns by which institutions exist. Institutionalization is therefore taking place all the time. The organization is functioning both as and within a continuing process of ongoing interactions, which tend to conform to the social structure of the organizational field as well as the organization itself. However, there is a perpetual possibility of this social order to be challenged, with fundamental change always on the horizon. Strategic analysis is therefore something that should take place continuously and instantly, whenever alternative interactions and meanings are starting to appear. Or the organization itself might contemplate an episode of institutional entrepreneurship by trying to initiate and realize fundamental change.

Getting up to speed

A strategist should know about the institutionalized interaction patterns and associated social structure. He is supposed to know about the regular interactions inside and outside the organization on which its survival and success depends. If you do not know what the current institutionalized interaction patterns are and how well the organization conforms to them, you need to find out about them. You need to get up to speed first.

To check on conformity, the analysis should focus on whether the organization is sufficiently engaged in meaningful interactions. This requires using the isomorphism performance logic (see Figure 7.4). This logic generates specific questions about the many interactions the organization relies on (see Exhibit 7.1). At the level of the organizational field, these concern the way in which the organization provides its goods and services as well as the interactions in which these goods and services are used. Within the organization, this concerns the interactions by which the goods and services are produced and how separate but interdependent activities are coordinated. All these interactions come with expectations in terms of a social structure of normative systems and cognitive understandings

---

Exhibit 7.1: Isomorphism starter questions

- On which regular interaction patterns within the organizational field does the organization rely? This includes interactions in which the organization's goods and services are used as well as interactions by which the organization provides its goods and services to those who use them.
- On which regular interaction patterns within the organization does the organization rely to produce goods and services? This includes the actual activities by which the products and services are produced as well as how separate interdependent activities are coordinated.
- Is the organization subjected to possibly contradicting demands and expectations when engaging in all of these interactions, either internally (subcultures) or externally? Do these demands manifest themselves through coercion, mimicry or normative pressure?
- How does the organization deal with the (contradicting) demands: by acquiescence, compromise or avoidance?

These questions allow the strategist to gauge whether the organization is engaged in meaningful interaction that conforms to the prevailing social structure.

---

in which these interactions are couched. There is a good chance that some of these expectations are contradictory and this is what the strategist should know about as well. The strategist should also know whether and how these contradictions are being accommodated through acquiescence, compromise or avoidance; yet the overall effect should maintain the meaningfulness of all the interactions.

Going real time: debating strategy

As soon as the strategist is comfortable with knowing what the normal state of affairs is, a situation of continuous strategy debate needs to arise. This debate should focus on at least three different possible developments. First, there is always a possibility of the organization being confronted by a change initiative or trigger event generating a controversy and possible fundamental change. Therefore whether, when and why such a trigger could occur is something to keep an eye on. Secondly, the organization, and its management in particular, should always wonder whether they are becoming subjected to strategic drift. If this starts to creep in, the organization will have difficulty keeping an eye on changes if and when they occur. Thirdly, the organization itself should contemplate whether, when and why it could and should want to initiate fundamental change.

With regard to keeping an eye on possible fundamental change, there are bound to be problems because of the inherent contradictions among and sometimes within institutions. Expectations in one institutional sphere can be at odds with expectations in another institutional sphere. Because an organization has to deal with institutional contradictions within the organizational field, there are always latent issues that can manifest themselves as conflicts and controversies that need to be settled again. There are also issues for people inside organizations, which can flare up because they have to deal with the conflicting demands that are made on them. It is up to the strategists to keep track of these contradictions, the way

---

Exhibit 7.2: Institutional theory questions to debate

- What contradictions exist among the regular interaction patterns within the organizational field in which the organization engages as well as within the organization in which employees and managers engage?
- Which of these contradictions is increasingly creating problems and which of these contradictions is becoming less troublesome?

These questions allow the strategist to evaluate whether there are concerns with regard to maintaining 'meaningful interaction' and whether the stance toward certain contradictions should be changed.

- What is the dominant logic among top management and how does the organization understand itself, i.e. what is in the organizational paradigm?
- To what extent does the organization solve its problems in accordance with the organizational paradigm?

These questions allow the strategist to gauge whether there is any strategic drift.

---

they are dealt with and whether specific contradictions become more or less profound, and whether these inspire people or organizations to come out as an institutional entrepreneur. There is a set of more specific questions that fuels the debate here (see Exhibit 7.2).

To check on the occurrence of strategic drift, the way in which the organization deals with problematic situations that appear on its path should be scrutinized continuously. The strategist – in a way – should be able to step away from the dominant logic to get a sense for the content of the organizational paradigm. Furthermore, the strategist should investigate how problems are dealt with to find out whether the implemented solutions predominantly confirm the existing organizational paradigm or whether there is significant variability in how problems are understood and dealt with.

There is a different dynamic when it comes to institutional entrepreneurship. Instead of conforming to institutional demands, an organization has initiated, or is maybe contemplating initiating, institutional change within the organizational field. This requires the organization to re-establish interaction patterns anew and to be actively involved in a process of triggering and settling controversy. Here the strategist should focus on whether the controversy that is created as a consequence of a change initiative can be settled in a favourable manner for the organization (see Exhibit 7.3).

Exhibit 7.3: Institutional entrepreneurship questions to debate

- Which regular interaction patterns within the organizational field can be subjected to change? This includes interactions in which the organization's goods and services are used as well as interactions by which the organization provides its goods and services.
- Who in the organizational field has reason to put up resistance against the change initiative?

- What leverage points in the organizational field are available to mobilize in favour (by the change initiator) or against (by opponents) the change initiative?

These questions allow the strategist to gauge the chances of a favourable settlement of a controversy.

- Which regular interaction patterns within the organization are subject to change? This includes the actual activities by which the products and services are produced as well as how separate interdependent activities are coordinated.
- Who in the organizational field may have reason to put up resistance against the change initiative?
- What leverage points in the organization are available to mobilize in favour of the change initiative?

These questions allow the strategist to gauge whether the organization can act as a purposeful actor and strive for a favourable settlement of a controversy.

At the level of the organizational field, the main focus should be on the leverage points that can be mobilized in favour or against the change initiative. The strategist should find out which interaction patterns will become part of the controversy and which will not. Everything that remains outside of the controversy potentially provides leverage points. Depending on what they contain, these can be mobilized in favour or against the change initiative. It is also good to know who in the organizational field would be engaged in this mobilization against the initiative and whether there might be any allies who would welcome the change initiative. A similar evaluation should take place with regard to the inner workings of the organization itself. The purpose of this is to see whether the organization can act as a purposeful actor in the course of settling the controversy in a favourable manner or whether the organization will become paralyzed as a consequence of internal turmoil. By doing all of this, the strategist finds out what he is up against and whether there is a fair chance of seeing the initiative through.

Additionally, these considerations also allow the strategist to find out whether there may be any chance initiatives imminent that threaten the future existence of the organization and whether the organization will be able to resist them.

Strategy practice 7.2: A strategy workshop doing scenario planning

Strategic management from an institutional theory point of view recognizes that people can have very different interpretations of the same situation. It also recognizes that there is no way to distinguish right from wrong. The consequence of accepting that people effectively have different perceptions means that a strategist has to reconcile different points of view. He also has to recognize that he does not have a monopoly on the truth, just because he is in charge. This becomes even more of an issue when you consider that strategy has its eye on the future, and any strategic analysis is an interpretation of a possible future state.

Scenario planning as developed by van der Heijden (1996) is a method to have 'conversations' about the future that aim to bring out a range of different interpretations. Scenarios are developed as a kind of 'practice of the mind'. By questioning the 'taken for granted', alternative interpretations are generated. The purpose is not to decide which the most likely scenario is and, as it were, predict the future. It is about developing sensitivity among the participants with regard to the various ways in which the future might be interpreted so as to help their sense-making become more sophisticated while the organization moves along with the times.

Strategy practice 7.3: Internationalization and country culture

Contradictions can originate from disparities between country cultures (Trompenaars and Hampden-Turner 2004). What is considered to be pragmatically, morally and cognitively legitimate in one country will be different in another country. Organizational field social structures can therefore vary across the world. There also is an effect of country culture on organizational culture and sub-cultures.

This can be especially troublesome for corporate social responsibility. It needs to be decided which set of norms and values is going to serve as a point of reference. For a firm operating in many different countries, will the mission statement be based on a universal declaration of norms and values or will it be tailored to specific countries? If there is a universal declaration, will it be aligned with the home country culture, the country culture that is the strictest, or the country culture that is the most lenient?

Answering question 2: taking action

In analogy to strategic analysis being a real time continuous activity, taking action is real time and continuous as well. On the one hand, there is the organizational field, the regular interaction patterns and the field's social structure. At the level of the organization, there are also regular interaction patterns. But the social structure is referred to as the organization's culture. On the other hand, there are contradictions between various institutionalized arrangements and sub-cultures, continuously threatening to manifest themselves as controversies and conflicts. Taking action is about dealing with contradicting expectations.

Overall, these actions can be informed by either one of two strategic stances. One is to conform to the existing institutionalized interaction patterns and to accommodate the contradictions that come with them. The organization and its management resist attempts at institutional change. They deal with contradictions through acquiescence, compromise and avoidance (Oliver 1991). This is isomorphism. The other one is actively to try to create institutional change and to go for institutional entrepreneurship. Contradictions then are actively engaged with through defiance and manipulation (Oliver 1991) (also see under the institutional theory process logic earlier). To conform or to transform are the two basic choices of what a strategist can do.

With regard to how to do this, taking action here effectively means a choice between intervening and not intervening in the course of the organization's strategy process with the intention also to change the course of the organizational survival process. Institutionalization takes place continuously, both within the organization and in the organizational field. It is an unremitting process of continuity and change. If the strategist is happy with the course of events as a consequence of the interaction patterns by which the organization functions and exists, and if he finds that the contradictions do not create any serious problems, then the recommendation is not to intervene. The strategist basically lets the process run its course.

If the contradictions threaten to run out of hand and the survival and success of the organization is in jeopardy, the strategist should intervene in the organization's strategy process. In doing so, he also intervenes in the way the organization functions within the organizational field level survival process. The occurrence of strategic drift is an obvious indication of the need for an intervention. The strategy process takes on the form of politics of meaning with the strategists engaged in challenging existing interaction patterns. An intervention in the organizational field means that a controversy is triggered. Subsequently, leverage points need to be mobilized to direct the outcome towards a favourable settlement.

Strategy practice 7.4: Strategic planning as a cultural intervention

Strategic planning is commonly understood as a procedure by which information is processed to formulate a strategic plan. Going through a process of strategic planning is also found to have an effect on the organizational culture (Jarzabkowski and Balogun 2009). A multinational company consisting of a diverse array of business units went through a strategic planning exercise. The business units not only became more unified as a common approach to how they did their strategic management developed but the centre also learned about local concerns and anxieties and how it could serve the business units better. Initial antagonism and misunderstandings made way for a common approach, eventually leading to a more unified and integrated multi-business firm.

Illustration 7.5: SKF from an institutional theory viewpoint

Should SKF* compete on price and put in the lowest bid possible to retain a big US-based client, or should they step away and persist with their high-quality strategy?

Clearly the US-based client is engaging in some institutional entrepreneurship. The prevalent interaction patterns by which ball bearings are traded in the US involved distributors who negotiate with clients about what quality of ball bearings they want and what the best offer would be. Part of this is the common expectation that every new contract needs to come with a 5 per cent reduction in price. By initiating a reverse auction, this specific interaction pattern is now suspended and the question is whether this new way of going about with an even stronger emphasis on price will become institutionalized.

Underneath this, within many industrial firms in the US, there is another change process going on. The procurement function is gaining more prominence and has been at the heart of many cost saving drives. By centralizing practices, reducing the number of suppliers and negotiating harder, big savings are made. Company buyers are put on performance contracts to get the cheapest deals possible. Reverse auctions fit this pattern. The US based client is under pressure to reduce costs as a consequence of the economic downturn. The question is whether centralized procurement and the emphasis on price will deliver the right quality of supplies or whether it will be a matter of 'penny-wise' and 'pound-foolish'?

On the basis of these considerations, it is in SKF's interest to resist the change in procurement practices and try to have it reverted back to how it used to be done. SKF should engage in isomorphism, stick with its strategy and use the evidence produced by its marketing sales routines with the software program as a leverage point to convince the client of the merits of long-term cost savings by going for quality and durability.

* Value selling at SKF Service, IMD-5-0751, 2009.

Generating further questions

Institutional theory turns strategic management into a process where action and interpretation go hand in hand. The social structure that underpins the regular interaction patterns, and which is also maintained by them, creates a layered business reality (Sminia 2005; Sminia and de Rond 2012). An organization relies on the social structure to be able to function and exist (de Rond and Thietart 2007). This applies to both the organization culture and the organizational field social structure. A sufficient degree of shared pragmatic, moral and cognitive legitimacy is required for meaningful interaction. Without meaningful interaction, the organization ceases to exist. However, at the level of the individual and also with regard to sub-cultures, alternative understandings of what is considered to be legitimate exist. Consequently, there are layers of meaning and many local truths, which account for a myriad of multiple business realities. Given such an essentially subjective world, what basis remains for a strategist to direct an organization into the future? Which business reality forms the foundation for a feasible future?

Alongside this there is also the recognition that contradictions are commonplace and that people across the organization and the organizational field have different interests and different points of view (Meyerson and Martin 1987; Seo and Creed 2002). It is up to the strategists to navigate the organization across the differences and ambiguities, and through the controversies that will result from this and which will appear in regular succession. Change and confusion, indeed, are the only things strategists can be certain about.

But who are these strategists? If it is restricted to top management, there is a problem. Conversely, top management is expected to provide the visions and interpretations by which the organization moves forward. However, top management is a liability as these people are subjected to the organization's paradigm along with all the other organization members. To acknowledge the relevance of organizational culture implies that the ideal of impartial, unbiased information processing, with top managers arriving at clear objectives and strategies, is nothing but an *idée fixe*: an obsession that lacks solid ground. Top management can get it horribly wrong without realizing it. That is what the concept of strategic drift implies (Johnson 1988).

Fundamental change – change that involves the organizational field social structure and the organizational culture – spans both the organization itself as well as the environment. Many case studies found that the seed corn of change as well as the persistence of seeing it through originated from the periphery of the organization (e.g. Burgelman 1983; Regnér 2003) and the environment (e.g. Leblebici and others 1991). It is found to be far more the consequence of emergent strategy than the result of deliberate strategy.

Processes of fundamental change are found to be longwinded, conflict-ridden and complicated, both within the realm of the organization itself (e.g. Johnson 1987; Pettigrew 1985) as well as within the realm of the organizational field (Garud and others 2002; Hargadon and Douglas 2001; Haveman and Rao 1997; Lounsbury 2001; Munir and Phillips 2005; Sminia 2003). Yet it appears that no organization can avoid having to deal with or maybe initiating fundamental institutional change. If this process is so perilous, it poses the question of whether we expect too much of top management and their ability to lead an organization to success and survival.

Nevertheless, institutional entrepreneurship is an attempt to take the initiative. The strategist – whoever they are – takes the destiny of an organization in their own hands. A vision of the future can be sketched out. Such an initiative means that the strategist makes the organization go against the grain. The organization violates the 'existing normative systems and understandings'. Therefore, there is a question of morality here. On what basis does the strategist think that certain rules – probably mostly informal but they can be formal – can be set aside?

Summing it up, institutional theory is undecided when it comes to the objectivism versus subjectivism debate and the voluntarism versus determinism debate. Institutional entrepreneurship is a voluntarist notion but the idea of an institutionalized social structure to which organizations and people submit puts a great deal of determinism into the approach. Also, this institutionalized social structure can be taken as an objective business reality out there about which information can be gathered whilst it is simultaneously created, maintained and changed as a consequence of interactions based on interpretations and localized cultures.

Case 7.1 Google's driverless car

Chris Urmson, lead engineer on Google's driverless car project, demonstrates where the technology is at to Forbes journalist Joann Muller.[1] There are no hands on the wheel or feet on the pedals whilst they are driving down Silicon Valley's Highway 101 at 65mph in a specially equipped Lexus RX450h. There is a US$65,000 laser sensor on the roof, radar sensors in the rear and front bumpers and a high definition camera looking forward through the windscreen and another one looking inwards at the passengers. A laptop-sized computer in the boot processes all data. All in all, there is US$100,000 worth of equipment added to the car. Driving on the motorway is what the Google engineers have been perfecting.

Merging in and out of traffic is more difficult and, to do that, Chris Urmson takes the wheel again. To make the car drive itself, Google engineers have to drive the car over the route first to make it learn what to do. The data thus gathered is combined with highly detailed geographical data (think an advanced version of Google Maps). The car is then able to drive the route on its own, comparing the recorded data with what comes in through the sensors, unless there is heavy rain or snow "because the appearance and shape of the world changes. It can't figure out where to go or what to do".[2] Urmson claims that driverless car technology will reduce traffic accidents by 90 per cent; reduce commute time and energy by 90 per cent, and the number of cars on the road by 90 per cent.[3]

Stanford's Center for Automotive Research in Palo Alto, California, has put together the X1 test car to experiment with car automation.[4] "The steering is entirely drive-by-wire, it's computer controlled. It's all electronic – there's no mechanical connection so we can program it to do pretty much what we want." According to the centrey's executive director Sven Beiker, the main impetus is safety. "We're very interested in what the driver is good at, and what the computer is better at doing, and we're working on the handover between the driver and the vehicle. So what we're looking at is when the driver gets him or herself into trouble, as often happens when driving too fast, the vehicle could take over." There is also a congestion motive. "If you look at a highway, even at rush hour times, only about 20–25 per cent of the surface area is actually

1 *Forbes*, 21 March 2013, http://www.forbes.com/sites/joannmuller/2013/03/21/no-hands-no-feet-my-unnerving-ride-in-googles-driverless-car/?lc=int_mb_1001 (accessed 3 April 2013).
2 *Forbes*, 21 March 2013, http://www.forbes.com/sites/joannmuller/2013/03/21/no-hands-no-feet-my-unnerving-ride-in-googles-driverless-car/?lc=int_mb_1001 (accessed 3 April 2013).
3 *Forbes*, 22 January 2013, http://www.forbes.com/sites/chunkamui/2013/01/22/fasten-your-seatbelts-googles-driverless-car-is-worth-trillions/ (accessed 3 April 2013).
4 *BBC*, 21 March, 2013, http://www.bbc.co.uk/news/business-21804352 (accessed 3 April 2013).

occupied by vehicles. We need a lot of space around the car in order to maneuver but if you have a lot of top-notch sensors and control systems, you can probably get those vehicles much closer together."

A research team at the University of Oxford is developing driverless technology as well.[5] The goal is to produce a 'low cost system' that uses lasers and cameras to memorize regular journeys, which it can then do on its own. The research team uses a standard Nissan Leaf, to which the team added a laser pod, a camera that was acquired through eBay and a standard laptop to control it all. According to research leader professor Paul Newman:

> The car is able to gain experiences of regular routes. And the brilliance of it is that it's actually the processing power of a human driver that first makes all the decisions and allows the car to build a 3D model of its environment. So once a journey has been experienced by our software the car will be able to take control from the driver via an iPad display on the dashboard when that trip is repeated.

At the moment, the car cannot do without a driver and the technology has more of 'driver assistance' than 'driverless'. Yet it is far more affordable than the Google set up.

> The sorts of sensors that Google uses are close to £100,000 per vehicle. Whereas the hardware that powers our system is bought off the shelf. All the hardware already exists so why would we develop our own car and sensors? Essentially what we've done is create a text file to control how all that technology interacts.

Research team member Ingmar Possner adds:

> We're using sensors that cost nearer £3,000 so our project is much more affordable and our ultimate aim is to be able to fit the technology as an option on a new car – just like how you'd pick a new stereo or a reversing camera – for as little as £100. However, the public perception of a futuristic pod without a steering wheel is still a long way off or may never happen; what is very close, though, is a form of advanced driver assistance. Many drivers already use features like cruise control and that doesn't mean they happily fall asleep at the wheel. It just makes life easier.

Many car manufacturers, including BMW, Audi, Volvo and Daimler are working on and equipping cars with driver assistance systems like adaptive cruise control, lane detection, pedestrian recognition cameras, predictive emergency braking and automated parking assistance.[6] An engineer at Daimler claims that city traffic is an utterly chaotic situation and designing autonomous cars that can drive in it is not even one of their goals at this point. Autonomous driving in monotonous, steady highway

---

5 *The Independent*, 6 March 2013, http://www.independent.co.uk/life-style/motoring/features/robot-car-u...-rival-googles-driverlesscar-project-8523289.html (accessed 3 April 2013).
6 *Financial Times*, 22 March 2013, http://www.ft.com/cms/s/0/a99fee14-9238-11e2-851f-00144feabdc0.html#axzz2PPb4pMOq (accessed 3 April 2013).

traffic is a far more reasonable and feasible goal.[7] Audi is expected to offer the first fully automated car for sale. Audi spokesman Josef Schlossmacher declares that:

> [o]ur vision of a piloted driving dream follows the motto: 'When it's fun to drive, I drive myself. When I no longer want to drive, I don't drive.' Like an aircraft that can fully operate on autopilot, the Audi of the future navigates through specific situations and performs driving maneuvers on its own.[8]

German car parts supplier Continental embarked upon a joint venture with BMW to develop automated driving technology, following competitors Bosch and Denso. They believe that car automation is feasible up to speeds of 20mph. According to Continental's CEO Elmar Degenhart: "Automated systems can increase road safety many times and therefore save lives. We are familiar with this in the aviation industry. Automated driving will certainly not lead to the frequently evoked disempowerment of drivers, any more than it did for pilots".[9]

Chunka Mui claims that mass adoption of the driverless car will affect the revenue of car makers, parts suppliers, car dealers, auto insurers, medical practices, personal injury lawyers, governments, road-construction companies and oil companies massively. It is claimed that fewer cars are needed to do the same mileage because they can be used almost constantly. Cars need less safety equipment such as airbags etc because accidents will happen far less often, yet the technology allows them to move much closer together, decreasing the need for road space and expansion. For that reason, cars also can be built to be less sturdy, opening up the possibility for other materials to be used, affecting the steel industry. When accidents become a rarity, car insurance premiums will drop, leaving insurers with less income. Fewer accidents also mean less work for hospital A&E facilities as well as work for personal injury lawyers, as car related cases would largely disappear. Governments would lose income because fewer fines will need to be handed out but they could also save on traffic police. Because driverless cars are much more efficient, energy companies will lose out as well.

Glen Renwick, CEO of US insurer Progressive Insurance is not worried yet

> The technology to do an autonomous car has been around for a while. We're now seeing them; we'll see a lot of talk about them. The real issue is exactly how they are able to be part of the fleet of vehicles on the road in America, and that is probably not something that need keep anyone awake for quite some time.[10]

7 *Forbes*, 12 February 2013, http://www.forbes.com/sites/chunkamui/2013/02/12/googles-trillion-dollar-driverless-car-part-4-how-google-wins-2/2/ (accessed 3 April 2013).
8 *The Independent*, 6 March 2013, http://www.independent.co.uk/life-style/motoring/features/robot-car-u...-rival-googles-driverlesscar-project-8523289.html (accessed 3 April 2013).
9 *Financial Times*, 22 March 2013, http://www.ft.com/cms/s/0/a99fee14-9238-11e2-851f-00144feabdc0.html#axzz2PPb4pMOq (accessed 3 April 2013).
10 *Forbes*, 28 March 2013, http://www.forbes.com/sites/chunkamui/2013/03/28/will-auto-insurers-survive-their-collision-with-driverless-cars-part-6/ (accessed 3 April 2013).

Bryant Walker Smith wonders how a traffic officer can ticket a driverless car.[11] He is a fellow at the Center for Internet and Society at Stanford Law School and the Center for Automotive Research at Stanford University, California. Nevada, California and Florida are the US states that allow driverless cars on public roads. The legal system governing cars presumes that a human being is in control and ultimately liable. But what do driver licence requirements mean in the case of a car driving itself? And what about the rules of the road and product liability? If something goes wrong, is it the occupant, the owner or the manufacturer who is liable?

Nevertheless, Bruce Breslow, director of Nevada's Department of Motor Vehicles, says he believes driverless vehicles are the "cars of the future":[12]

"The vast majority of vehicle accidents are due to human error", said California state Senator Alex Padilla, when he introduced the legislation. "Through the use of computers, sensors and other systems, an autonomous vehicle is capable of analyzing the driving environment more quickly and operating the vehicle more safely."[13]

Robert Burns, who is director of the Program on Sustainability at Columbia University's Earth Institute and former head of R&D at General Motors reckons that:

[d]riverless car technology is an extraordinary opportunity to realize superior margins, especially for first movers. In cities like Ann Arbor, for example, NewCo could price its personal mobility service at US$7 per day (providing customers with a service comparable to car ownership with better utilization of their time) and still earn US$5 per day off each subscriber. In Ann Arbor alone, 100,000 residents (1/3 of Ann Arbor's population) using the service could result in a profit of US$500,000 a day. Today, 240 million Americans own a car as a means of realizing personal mobility benefits. If NewCo realizes just a 1 per cent market share (2.4 million customers) in the United States alone, its annual profit could be on the order of US$4 billion. NewCo's Business Plan explains how this idea can be realized quickly, efficiently and with effective risk management.[14]

Larry Burns, a former head of R&D and strategic planning at General Motors expects that shared-usage will become much more common.[15] To Professor Kent Larson, head of the Future Cities program at the Massachusetts Institute of Technology in Boston:

Privately owned cars are a big problem. Most cars in cities aren't being used 90 per cent of the time. The rest of the time, they're parked up and wasting valuable

11 *New Scientist*, 24 December 2012, http://www.newscientist.com/article/mg21628966.400-how-does-a-traffic-cop-ticket-a-driverless-car.html (accessed 3 April 2013).
12 *BBC*, 8 May 2012, http://www.bbc.co.uk/news/technology-17989553 (accessed 3 April 2013).
13 *BBC*, 8 May 2012, http://www.bbc.co.uk/news/technology-17989553 (accessed 3 April 2013).
14 *Forbes*, 30 January 2013, http://www.forbes.com/sites/chunkamui/2013/01/30/googles-trillion-dollar-driverless-car-part-3-sooner-than-you-think/3/ (accessed 3 April 2013).
15 *Forbes*, 1 March 2013, http://www.forbes.com/sites/chunkamui/2013/03/01/googles-trillion-dollar-driverless-car-part-5-how-automakers-can-still-win/2/ (accessed 3 April 2013).

space. But if we can move to a shared model, we can increase the use of a single vehicle by at least five times. The Holy Grail is a vehicle that can drive itself and park itself and charge itself autonomously. At that point, wherever you are in the city, you can call for a vehicle. It can come to where you are and you drive off. When you reach your destination, you get out of the car, put it into autonomy mode and the car goes back to wherever it needs to be, ready for the next trip.[16]

Will car customers give up their spot in the driver's seat though? A reader on Forbes' website commented that, for most American drivers, the car is our "iconic dream machine" and our personal freedom and status statement. Americans dream about cars, and 'no' able-bodied person 'dreams' to be 'driven' by 'robot cars,' no matter how persuasive the stats appear on paper."[17] It does not make sense to the guys at Top Gear[18] either, judging from the following conversation:

Jeremy Clarkson:	A driverless car doesn't make sense. You know Google and Oxford University are working on a driverless car that you can all buy. But I am sorry but I can't see the point.
James May:	No, neither can I. My car has arrived at work. . . . I am not in it.
	– Laughter –
Richard Hammond:	I sent the car into town to do the shopping.
	– Laughter –
Jeremy Clarkson:	The school-run perhaps. You can send the kids off while you stay in bed. But other than that, utterly pointless . . .

16 *BBC,* 21 March, 2013, http://www.bbc.co.uk/news/business-21804352 (accessed 3 April 2013).
17 *Forbes*, 30 January 2013, http://www.forbes.com/sites/chunkamui/2013/01/30/googles-trillion-dollar-driverless-car-part-3-sooner-than-you-think/2/ (accessed 3 April 2013).
18 *BBC Top Gear*, broadcast on BBC 2, 24 February 2013.

8 Similarities, differences and underlying assumptions

The six strategy theories in this book represent distinct ways to do strategic management. Nonetheless, it will probably not have gone unnoticed that there are many similarities and parallel arguments between these six theoretical approaches. There are also profound and fundamental differences.

To take the similarities and parallel arguments first, marketing-inspired strategic thinking, the industrial organization approach and the static resource-based view, all assume the strategist to be this unbiased information processor who is engaged in rational decision-making. These strategy theories have primarily been developed to assist the strategist with formulating a strategy and making strategic decisions. They presume the existence of a business reality out there, about which information can be gathered. This information can then be used to fill out these theoretical frameworks and draw conclusions. The strategy process is seen as an ordered and organized process that is the preserve of top management.

Some concepts and variables are common across these three strategy theories as well. Obviously, all three take the environment to be competitive and centre on competitive advantage as the explanation of firm performance. All three are biased toward for-profit business firms and elaborate performance mostly in financial terms. Both marketing-inspired strategic thinking and the industrial organization approach use the concept of customer value, and have put forward strategies of differentiation and focus. It is therefore possible to take, for instance, Porter's (1985) value chain and to use it to find out about a firm's success factors. The other way round can work as well. For instance, a marketing-inspired notion like the experience curve is useful for underpinning a firm's suitability for Porter's (1980) cost leadership. There are more possibilities for exchanging concepts between the two approaches.

The static resource-based view complements the industrial organization approach as well as marketing-inspired strategic thinking (Barney 1991). It provides a means to address the sustainability of a firm's competitive advantage. If the firm's capabilities underpin the value activities that add the value by which a firm differentiates or focuses itself in an industry, and if these capabilities are valuable, rare, inimitable and non-substitutable, then the firm is on more solid ground. The same holds true for core capabilities backing up the success factors for a positioning strategy in a product market. It means that the firm has a 'sustainable' competitive advantage.

Agency theory and shareholder value build on marketing-inspired strategic thinking, the industrial organization approach and the static resource-based view. The demand for shareholder value incorporates an expectation that managers – as agents for the shareholders – are incentivised through remuneration packages to be these rational decision-makers and to participate in an ordered and organized strategic planning process to realize financial performance (Rappaport 1986).

Yet there are also profound differences. One important contrast between marketing and industrial organization is the difference between competing on price and competing on costs. From a marketing point of view, being a low price/no frills supplier in a product market is a feasible strategy. Porter (1980) vehemently warns against competing on price because it ends up in a situation of cut-throat competition. It makes everybody in the industry (apart from the customers) worse off. To Porter (1980, 1985), the only feasible strategies are his generic strategies. There is no middle way, as you will get stuck-in-the-middle. In marketing-inspired strategic thinking, this is not necessarily the case. Any compromise between price and perceived customer value is feasible, as long as there is a market (segment) for it.

Another contrast between marketing and industrial organization refers back to where and for what firms compete. From a marketing point of view, competition takes place in a product market. It takes place among competitors and they compete for market share. From an industrial organization point of view, competition takes place within an industry. A focal firm not only competes with rival competitors but also with suppliers, buyers, substitutes and potential entrants in a value system. The competition is not about market share but about who ends up with most of the margin.

Although the dynamic resource-based view and the static resource-based view share the same roots in that the reasoning starts with the firm's resource base, they end up at diametrically opposed conclusions. This is not just about the tension between pursuing a strategy of exploiting the current core capabilities or exploring for future core capabilities. More fundamentally, this is a tension between a mode of strategic thinking, which presumes continuity and predictability on the one hand, and change and uncertainty on the other hand.

The static resource-based view, alongside marketing-inspired strategic thinking and the industrial organization approach are essentially static in the sense that they provide snapshots of current situations or imagined futures (Pettigrew, Thomas and Whittington 2002; Porter 1991; Whipp 1996). They do not handle fundamental change. They can cope with change that follows a regular pattern. However, they offer the strategist little understanding as to how change happens. Therefore, there is little support with regard to what to do with regard to fundamental change.

The dynamic resource-based view takes change as its point of departure. It urges the strategist to follow suit. It offers concepts such as dynamic capabilities and core competence. The recommendation is that the strategists should strive for these kinds of capabilities. Unfortunately, as it stands now, the dynamic resource-based view does not incorporate an account of how change happens either, again leaving the strategist empty handed as to how to navigate change (Arend and Bromiley 2009; Helfat and Peteraf 2009; Kraaijenbrink and others 2010). Besides, the resource-based view puts in an argument for cooperation and strategic alliances in order for a firm to work on its resource-base, indicating that strategy is not exclusively about competition (Das and Teng 2000).

Another sharp contrast can be found between shareholder value and the stakeholder approach (Freeman and Reed 1983). Agency theory and shareholder value urge the strategist to run the firm for the purpose of providing the shareholders with a maximum return on their investment. Firm performance is ultimately understood in those terms. The stakeholder approach sees the shareholder as only one among many different stakeholders, who all expect different things from the firm. It is more about striking a balance to remain legitimate, with performance being understood differently among stakeholders, depending as it does on the specific stake they have in the firm.

There are conceptual parallels between the stakeholder approach and institutional theory. They both centre on legitimacy. They both recognize issues of perception, conflict and politics.

The stakeholder approach concentrates on the people or actors – either individuals or collectives – who have a stake in a focal organization (Freeman 1984). The emphasis is put on the conflicts of interests as these may exist between the various stakeholders and the politics this generates. This is amplified by differences in perceptions as a consequence of (management) cognition and the way in which mental maps affect how people interpret the world around them differently (Schwenk 1984).

Institutional theory concentrates on the activities by which an organization exists (Greenwood and others 2008). Institutionalization takes place as a mutual reinforcing dynamic. People's understanding of the situation makes them interact in a particular way and these interactions in turn confirm the mutually shared definition of the situation. The end result is a social structure that takes on an existence of its own. Within the organization, this is normally referred to as the organizational culture. In the environment, the organizational field has a social structure as well. Yet there are contradictions within and among these institutionalized arrangements, fuelling conflict and change.

Within institutional theory, institutional entrepreneurship has been put forward as an attempt to understand how the process of fundamental change is brought about (DiMaggio 1988). In that sense, it is a step ahead of the dynamic resource-based view. Institutional entrepreneurship and fundamental change is found to be a struggle (Seo and Creed 2002). The outcome is unclear whilst the process is mired with ambiguity.

In contrast to the theoretical approaches that are centred on competitive advantage, on which predominant advice is about being different in order to outcompete competitors, isomorphism urges the strategist not to stray too far from what is expected, to maintain legitimacy. By being very similar to your competitors, your business is recognized as cognitively, morally and pragmatically legitimate.

Isomorphism as well as the stakeholder approach envisions organizations as progressing in a more regular fashion. Their starting point is continuity. Within the stakeholder approach, who the stakeholders are and what interests they have is not subject to much change. What does change is their relative importance as they juggle for attention. Isomorphism is about continuity and to conforming to the existing state of affairs.

Both in stakeholder theory and institutional theory, the strategy process and the role of the strategist are less clear-cut. Contrary to marketing-inspired strategic thinking, the industrial organization approach and the static resource-based view, this idea of the strategist/ top manager as an unbiased and impartial information processor and rational decision-maker is left behind. In the stakeholder approach, the strategist becomes a political animal engaged in negotiations. He can work just as well on behalf of his own interests as on behalf of the interests of the organization as a whole. In institutional theory the strategist becomes a manager of meaning and maybe a visionary, engaged in interpretation and sense-making. The concepts of strategic intent and stretch and leverage in the dynamic resource-based view (Hamel and Prahalad 1994) have a certain resemblance to institutional entrepreneurship (DiMaggio 1988). Moreover, the concept of core rigidity (Leonard-Barton 1992) puts a strategist's subjectivity forward as a problem and is comparable to institutional theory's strategic drift (Johnson 1987). In a way, agency theory also recognizes the political and subjective nature of management in introducing the agency problem into the shareholder-manager relationship (Jensen and Meckling 1976).

The contrast between strategists as unbiased rational decision-makers on the one hand and political animals and managers of meaning or visionary leaders on the other hand, strikes at the heart of what strategic management is about. Is strategic management – and the strategy scholarship that supports it – about top managers making the right decisions? Or is strategic management – and the scholarship that supports it – about understanding the limitations of dealing with a process over which strategists/top managers have limited control? This contrast is clearly demonstrated with very limited debate (Mintzberg, Waters, Pettigrew and Butler 1990). Mintzberg and Waters, and Pettigrew argue that to represent strategic management as a process of mere decision-making is wrong and that the full strategy process by which strategies are realized and organizations perform should be imagined as a semi-autonomous process of continuity and change. Butler argues against this and maintains that you cannot rule out the possibility that a strategy is realized as a consequence of decisions that are made by strategists.

Strategic management as continuous debate

This book puts forward the view that strategic management is essentially a continuous debate. It is a real time process during which strategists must continuously reflect and ask themselves questions about the organization they are responsible for. Depending on the theoretical approach, these are questions about 'fit', 'stretch', 'aligned interests' and 'meaningful interaction'. There is never a definitive answer and the debate moves on all the time. One reason for this is the certainty that things will change; hence the importance of real time strategic management. The other reason is strategy scholarship and the different theoretical approaches it has yielded.

The various overviews and reviews of the strategy field recognize the existence of contrasting ways of defining the field (e.g. Chaffee 1985; Eisenhardt and Zbaracki 1992; Elbanna 2006; Haselhoff 1977; Huff and Reger 1987; Hutzschenreuter and Kleindienst 2006; Johnson 1987; Mintzberg, Ahlstrand and Lampel 1998; Pettigrew and others 2002; Sminia 2009; Whipp 1996; Whittington 1993). Mintzberg and others (1998) compared strategy scholars to blind men in the poem by Godfrey Saxe (1816–1887) about the blind men and the elephant. They all approach the elephant in their own way. The one who touches the skin describes the elephant as 'like a wall'. The one who feels the tusk describes the elephant as 'like a spear'. The blind man who feels the trunk describes the animal as 'like a snake'. The elephant's knee, its ear and its tail lead to descriptions of 'like a tree', 'like a fan' and 'like a rope' respectively. The poem concludes that each man is partly in the right but they are all in the wrong. If they had the faculty of sight, would they not have seen the elephant for what it was? Can we achieve this with strategic management or are we condemned to feel our way around as these blind men?

The blindness with regard to strategic management and strategy scholarship is the result of very fundamental problems for which solutions do not readily exist. Scholarship and by implication management are bound by having to make basic assumptions about the nature of reality (objective or subjective) and about human nature (voluntarist or determinist).

It is mentioned earlier in the book that the representation of the strategist as an unbiased rational decision-maker assumes the existence of an objectively knowable business reality out there. The opposite assumption that any description of what is taken to be the business reality is but a mere interpretation and that there is no way of knowing how accurate this interpretation is, makes the strategists as subjective in his judgments and decisions as anybody else. Going one way or the other on this is making an assumption about the nature of reality, about the nature of knowledge and information, as well as about the nature of strategic management (Smircich and Stubbart 1985). It takes up a position in the philosophical debate between objectivism and subjectivism.

Another philosophical debate also has a bearing on strategic management. This is the debate between voluntarism and determinism. Are we to assume that a strategist has the power to manage and change the organization at will, or in other words has 'strategic choice' (Child 1972)? This is voluntarism. Or are we to assume that a single human being has very little control over what happens and that consequently the strategist has to accept that things happen despite and often contrary to his good intentions and management efforts (Adler and Borys 1993)? This is determinism.

If anything, this means that any way forward with regard to strategic management and strategy scholarship can only be pragmatic. The common textbook approach puts the emphasis on combining marketing-inspired strategic thinking, the industrial organization approach, the resource-based view and sometimes agency theory. It envisions strategic management as rational decision-making and as formulation followed by implementation (e.g. Johnson, Whittington and Scholes 2011; Thompson, Strickland III and Gamble 2013). It requires the strategists to do a full strategic analysis, utilizing and combining the performance logics of aforementioned theoretical approaches – maybe add a stakeholder analysis in as well – to formulate an intended strategy.

In this textbook approach, notions of organizational politics and organizational culture only come in during the implementation phase with the recognition that a newly formulated strategy may require organizational change. Realizing change then has to involve elements of negotiation to accommodate various different interests that may exist. And it has to involve elements of organization culture because people should change their understanding of their activities as part of the larger whole. This separates thinkers from doers (Lenz and Lyles 1985) and it is therefore not really surprising that the major complaint of people subjected to a strategy implementation process is a lack of clear communication (Hrebiniak 2006).

However, when politics and organizational culture are recognized as being present throughout the whole strategy process, it should not come as a surprise that communication is an issue. People have different interests, cognitions and understandings in and of the same situation. If you have not been part of the formulation phase, how should you be able to understand the strategic plan when it is communicated to you in the implementation phase? Whatever is in there will be made sense of locally, and differently from what was intended at the top of the organization (Balogun and Johnson 2005). In effect it can be argued that strategy implementation starts with formulating a plan or intention, as this already constitutes

The future is unpredictable

Dealing with a continuous succession of problems and strategy debate
Subjective interpretations
Socially constructed business reality

Independently existing business reality
Objective (inter-subjective) information
Rational decision-making and strategic planning

The future is predictable

Figure 8.1 Expectations about the future

an activity. Likewise, taking action to deal with upcoming issues and reflecting on what the effects are is part of an ongoing process of strategy formulation. This book advocates strategic management as such a real time continuous process.

Stepping back from it all, there might be a connection between how the strategist expects strategic management to take place and his ability to work with and appreciate particular strategy theories (see Figure 8.1). If a strategist expects the world to be ordered and fairly predictable, he also expects the strategy process to be ordered and predictable. This type of strategist anticipates strategy theory to provide the right answer. Strategy theory is seen to be about tools and instruments by which the situation can be analysed and assessed unequivocally. This is believed to lead to clear decisions and subsequent strictly executable courses of action. The (implicit) assumption is that there is an objective business reality out there about which information can be gathered. This strategist expects that by collecting the 'right' information and rationally presenting your case, any opposition can be overcome, as the strategist and the analysis is clearly 'right'. This type of strategist can happily work with marketing-inspired strategic thinking, the industrial organization approach, the static resource-based view, agency theory and shareholder value, and the stakeholder approach. This type of strategist would like to stick to the strategy process as a strategic planning exercise, followed by an implementation phase. Good management is seen to be about being rational.

If a strategist expects the world to be volatile and unpredictable, he also expects the strategy process to be volatile and unpredictable. This type of strategist expects strategy theory to provide alternative ways of looking at the same unfolding situation. There is a profound understanding that there is no single right answer. There are many, often conflicting viewpoints, which can quickly shift as time progresses. The (implicit) assumption is that managers have to operate in an ambiguous, uncertain and subjective world. This type of strategist is mostly attracted by the dynamic resource-based view and institutional theory, and especially institutional entrepreneurship. Marketing-inspired strategic thinking, the industrial organization approach, the static resource-based view, agency theory and shareholder value, and the stakeholder approach have their use in making a snap analysis, but they only provide partial and temporary insight. This type of strategist expects that a realized strategy is largely emergent (see Figure 1.1 in Chapter 1) and the consequence of a never-ending succession of problems that need to be solved. Good management is seen to be about being sensible and to go with the flow.

Illustration 8.1: Debating SKF

Should SKF compete on price and put in the lowest bid possible to retain a big US-based client, or should it step away and persist with its high-quality strategy?

This issue has now been analysed on the basis of all six theoretical approaches. Utilizing marketing-inspired strategic thinking, if there is a change in customer wants and needs, SKF should adapt. The industrial organization approach arrives at a similar conclusion. The buyer force appears to be on the increase and SKF's value proposition appears to be not powerful enough to withstand it. The resource-based view arrives at the opposite conclusion by arguing that SKF should continue to exploit its core capabilities. Giving in would mean that SKF would not be utilizing its competitive advantage. Shareholder value is fragile. From a stakeholder perspective, there is no clear conclusion. Institutional theory indicates SKF should resist the possible change in the organizational field. Where does this leave SKF? How do you weigh it all up?

There is no formula that combines and calculates what the preferred option should be. This is where the strategy debate comes in. What is the relative merit of each approach in this particular situation?

"I know what I would go for. Just now I would not give in. SKF has built this strong position as a quality supplier of ball bearings and I would not be willing to give this up that easily. I also prefer to go with the theoretical approach that deals with change the best. There still is a chance that the US-based client sees sense and eventually comes back to preferring quality to price. SKF should go on the offensive and make the client see sense. But that is my judgement call."

Debating options and acting upon them

Notwithstanding the continuous debate, there are moments that decisions and recommendations need to be made and acted upon. Every strategy theory generates a range of options that can be considered on the basis of information that is currently available to be interpreted. In the case of marketing-inspired strategic management, options include moving up and down the trade-off between value and price to pick a different strategy, aiming for different product markets or market segments, working on the key success factors and, in the case of a multi-business firm, improving synergy and the balance in the portfolio. The industrial organization approach offers a choice between three generic strategies, moving in and out of industries or strategic groups, improving the value chain, or covering more or less of the value system. The static resource-based view offers the option of exploiting the firm's core capabilities better. The dynamic resource-based view urges firms to become change orientated by embarking upon innovation, R&D and business development etc., preferably by building upon core competences. Agency theory and shareholder value has options in terms of (re)designing incentive schemes, replacing top management, and/or changing the firm's strategic management. Options in the stakeholder approach include reprioritizing stakeholders, or making the firm more or less dependent on specific stakeholders. Institutional theory offers a choice between isomorphism and institutional entrepreneurship by intervening in the ongoing process inside and outside the organization.

These are the options that can be debated and decided upon within each of these strategy theories. They also need to be made concrete within the specific circumstances of the firm. It is with regard to linking concrete activity and current information and questioning what it indicates within the realm of a theoretical approach that choices need to be made to arrive at a recommendation and associated actions.

It is not uncommon that the preferred option based on one strategy theory is at odds with the preferred option on the basis of another strategy theory. Again, this offers opportunities for debate, but this time it is effectively about the relative merits of a theoretical approach. If an argument can be put together why one approach might be preferred over another approach, then automatically the recommendation based on the preferred approach becomes the best option under the circumstances. This level of debate should consider the basic assumptions on which a specific theoretical approach is based to see which assumptions are the most reasonable given the current situation.

Another important debate to have is to discuss a recommendation that comes out of applying one theoretical approach in the context of another theoretical approach. It is especially useful to see what an option that improves a firm's competitive advantage does to the firm's legitimacy, or the other way round. Ideally firms strive for both but often find that competitive advantage and legitimacy are at odds with each other and a trade-off needs to be made.

This book starts with the statement that strategic management is about making a firm or an organization perform and about maintaining the organization's or the firm's ability to perform (Sminia and de Rond 2012). It explains how strategy theory is to be used to evaluate whether the firm or organization will be performing, whether the firm or organization will maintain the ability to perform and what a strategist can do about it. It does so by introducing process logics and performance logics for six different theoretical approaches. Every one of the strategy theories has its role within this as fuel for the continuous strategy debate. They all contain an albeit partial truth. The utilization of a range of strategy theories enhances the quality of this debate. And helping to improve the quality of the debate is the ultimate purpose of this book.

Case 8.1 BlackBerry

Canadian firm BlackBerry is thought of as the instigator of the smartphone. In January 2013, BlackBerry introduced the BlackBerry Z10, a completely new smartphone, running on the newly developed BB10 operating system.[1] This was also the occasion for the company to change its name from Research In Motion (RIM) to BlackBerry. It did not go without a hitch as the product launch had been postponed several times. Alongside, the BlackBerry World store was revamped, offering 70,000 apps and movies, TV shows and music from the major studios. This phone was a major departure from the company's previous offerings by not incorporating the typical BlackBerry keyboard but by relying on a touch screen.

Nomura Securities analyst Stuart Jeffrey reckons that: "there is strong pent-up demand from BlackBerry fans and corporate users for a BlackBerry with a competitive multimedia experience. BB10 promises to drive strong initial sales of RIM's first compatible products, supporting its share price".[2] However, he sees two major problems:

> While most handset vendors try to compete on one or two layers of the smart-phone value chain RIM is vertically integrated – like Apple. This means that if RIM is to succeed the company must somehow offset the greater component purchasing power of its larger rivals, match Apple and Samsung on design, attract application developers away from iPhone, Android and Windows Phone – all while pushing a compelling marketing message on a relatively limited budget. If RIM fails in any of these tasks – which we consider likely – then sales may end up being restricted to the relatively small corporate market. The second problem concerns the new operating system. RIM's move to BB10 is likely to erode a significant profit stream: BB7 subscribers pay RIM, through their carriers, a monthly fee for RIM's unique services. We estimate that consumers pay around US$2 to US$3 per month and corporate users US$7 to US$8. With BB10 this monthly fee drops away for consumers and for smaller companies. We estimate that this may cut RIM's gross profit by over US$1 billion (£635m) over the next two years. To replace this profit stream RIM needs to raise device sales by approximately 15 million units, or a 50 per cent increase. Only if sales exceed this level can RIM's profits start to rise.

1 *BBC*, 30 January 2013, http://www.bbc.co.uk/news/technology-21242606 (accessed 14 February 2014).
2 *BBC*, 30 January 2013, http://www.bbc.co.uk/news/technology-21242606 (accessed 14 February 2014).

CCS Insight consultant Ben Wood thinks that: "RIM will be going after three main groups with its new BlackBerry 10-powered devices".[3] The first group consists of older current BlackBerry owners

> . . . who initially had one for business and have continued to tough it out in recent years. Many of them feel they've fallen behind friends and colleagues when it comes to having an all-singing, all-dancing smartphone, but the allure of the full keyboard, a great e-mail experience and other things like the BlackBerry Messaging (BBM) service have kept them loyal. If RIM can't hold onto these people, the new platform and devices face a very uncertain future. If they decide to stay, these users will be evangelists for the updated products and could help kick start RIM's recovery.

The second group is former BlackBerry owners:

> There are plenty of them out there who have been seduced away by an iPhone or an Android device – usually a Samsung. RIM hasn't had a good reason for these former customers to return, but it now has something to tempt them back. The challenge with this group is that many of them will be locked into a contract. This means it's likely to be the second half of the year before they start thinking about switching back to a Blackberry.

The third group is

> . . .the teenagers and 20-somethings who got a Blackberry primarily because of BBM and Facebook. These are the customers that made the Blackberry the third best-selling smartphone in the UK at the end of 2012. This group probably won't be able to afford the flagship products RIM is unveiling today, but I expect we'll see lower-cost products later in the year. RIM must ensure that BB10 pushes the right buttons for the youth segment that was once its powerhouse for growth.

Announcing the 2013 first quarter results, BlackBerry was back in profit, after having incurred heavy losses last year.[4] In early May 2013, BlackBerry announces that its Messenger System (BBM) is to become available for Google's Android and Apple's iOS, opening it up for users of rival smartphones. Before that, BBM only worked on BlackBerry devices and 60 million BlackBerry owners already use it. According to CEO Thorsten Heins: "It's a statement of confidence. The BlackBerry 10 platform is so strong and the response has been so good that we are confident the time is right for BlackBerry Messenger to become an independent multiplatform messaging solution".[5] Alternatives such as Whatsapp and Facebook are already multi-platform. They also announce an addition to their BB10 product line up. The low price Q5, with a physical 'qwerty' keyboard, is targeted at emerging markets including Eastern Europe, Asia, Africa and Latin America. However, these are markets that are already well served by Android phones.

---

3 *BBC*, 30 January 2013, http://www.bbc.co.uk/news/technology-21242606 (accessed 14 February 2014).

4 *BBC*, 28 March 2013, http://www.bbc.co.uk/news/business-21966363 (accessed 14 February 2014).

5 *BBC*, 14 May 2013, http://www.bbc.co.uk/news/technology-22529074 (accessed 14 February 2014).

In early August 2013, rumours are going round that BlackBerry is considering going private with a leveraged buyout.[6] This means that BlackBerry will be delisted. This is based on an assessment that BlackBerry is undervalued and that borrowing the money to buy up all the shares and to service this debt allows for higher profits than BlackBerry is making now as a listed company under its current management. BlackBerry shares jump on the news.[7] BlackBerry manufactures its own phones.[8] The handset division can be closed, as it has 'negative value', with the hardware being made elsewhere. BlackBerry is valued at about US$5 billion on the basis of its cash reserves, patents and software. However, some argue that the BB10 operating system is losing out against Android, Apple's iOS and Windows Phone.

In September 2013, BlackBerry introduces the new Z30 smartphone: featuring a large 5 inch screen and large battery to compete with similar Sony and Samsung handsets.[9] These 'phablets' fit between a smartphone and a tablet. Market research company IDC reports that BlackBerry has 9.3 per cent market share in the UK, 1.7 per cent in the US and 0.1 per cent in China. China is the biggest market for smartphones. Simultaneously, the firm announces 4500 job cuts, 40 per cent of its workforce.[10] This is done as a reaction to an anticipated US$995 million loss over the 2013 second quarter. CEO Thorsten Heins says:

> We are implementing the difficult, but necessary operational changes announced today to address our position in a maturing and more competitive industry, and to drive the company toward profitability. Going forward, we plan to refocus our offering on our end-to-end solution of hardware, software and services for enterprises and the productive, professional end user.

The losses are attribute to disappointing sales of its Z10 model. Other measures that are being taken include cutting its number of smartphone models from six to four and lowering the price of the Z10 model.[11] The actual second quarter loss is later reported as US$965 million.[12]

BlackBerry relies on what is labelled as its 'enterprise business'. Its hardware and software is linked with a high security messenger service that is appreciated by corporate clients who value high security communications, such as banks, governments and law firms. BlackBerry used to be the only one offering this but the market has seen the rise of dedicated companies such as Citrix, which offers similar secure messenger services that are independent of specific operating systems or hardware platforms.

Bob Egan, a commentator writing for *Forbes*, reports that he has sat in meetings where retail bank CIO/IT people told BlackBerry sales executives that they prefer to go

6 *BBC*, 18 September 2013, http://www.bbc.co.uk/news/technology-24148641 (accessed 14 February 2014).
7 *BBC*, 9 August, 2013, http://www.bbc.co.uk/news/business-23642189 (accessed 14 February 2014).
8 Reuters, 10 August 2013, http://www.reuters.com/article/2013/08/10/us-blackberry-private-idUSBRE97805C20130810 (accessed 18 February 2014).
9 *BBC*, 18 September 2013, http://www.bbc.co.uk/news/technology-24148641 (accessed 14 February 2014).
10 *BBC*, 20 September 2013, http://www.bbc.co.uk/news/business-24182038 (accessed 14 February 2014).
11 *Forbes*, 20 September 2013, http://www.forbes.com/sites/bobegan/2013/09/20/requiem-for-blackberry/ (accessed 14 February 2014).
12 *BBC*, 27 September 2013, http://www.bbc.co.uk/news/business-24302139 (accessed 14 February 2014).

with alternative providers[13]. It used to be the case that firms could tell their employees what computers, phones, software and apps to use. In those days, BlackBerrys were often the preferred option of IT managers. This has waned. People started to bring their own devices into work, frustrated by company hardware and software that was outdated and less sophisticated. Many companies were forced to adapt and now have a BYOD policy (Bring Your Own Device).

In 2007, then RIM co-CEO and co-founder Mike Lazaridis was quoted saying about the threat of the Apple iPhone: "How much presence does Apple have in business? It's vanishingly small".[14] He was also dismissive about the idea that anyone would want to buy a phone that does not have a keyboard. BlackBerry management is accused of being over-confident.[15] Despite the emergence of the iPhone and other smartphones, they expected that what they saw as a superior offering of security features would mean that their existing customer base would stick with them. The iPhone was dismissed as just a consumer device, not fit for purpose for professional users.

On 23 September 2013, Fairfax announces a deal by which it will acquire Black-Berry for US$4.7 billion. Fairfax is controlled by Canadian billionaire Prem Watsa. He says:

> We believe this transaction will open an exciting new private chapter for Blackberry, its customers, carriers and employees. We can deliver immediate value to shareholders, while we continue the execution of a long-term strategy in a private company with a focus on delivering superior and secure enterprise solutions to BlackBerry customers around the world.[16]

The turbulence around the company makes BlackBerry publish an open letter to its customers reassuring them that the company will be around in the future.[17] Lenovo from China is reported to be interested in buying BlackBerry and has opened talks.[18] Lenovo not only makes PCs but is also the biggest seller of smartphones in China. They are interested in the brand and the patent base.

On 4 November 2013, the announced takeover by Fairfax is called off. BlackBerry shares plummet. CEO Thorsten Heins resigns and will be replaced by John Chen. On accepting his new position he states: "BlackBerry is an iconic brand with enormous potential – but it's going to take time, discipline and tough decisions to reclaim our success".[19] However, according to the 'Brand Keys Loyalty and Engagement Indices', customers' answers to the question how well the brand is seen as meeting the expectations for the ideal smartphone are worrying. Apple scores 92 per cent, Samsung

13 *Forbes*, 20 September 2013, http://www.forbes.com/sites/bobegan/2013/09/20/requiem-for-blackberry/ (accessed 14 February 2014).
14 *BBC News*, 24 September 2013, http://www.bbc.co.uk/news/technology-24218339 (accessed 14 February 2014).
15 *Forbes*, 7 November 2013, http://www.forbes.com/sites/hershshefrin/2013/11/07/psychological-traps-snare-blackberry-decision-makers/ (accessed 14 February 2014).
16 *BBC News*, 23 September 2013, http://www.bbc.co.uk/news/business-24223727 (accessed 14 February 2014).
17 *BBC*, 15 October 2013, http://www.bbc.co.uk/news/business-24529990 (accessed 14 February 2014).
18 *China Daily*, 2 November 2013, http://usa.chinadaily.com.cn/business/2013-11/02/content_17075702.htm (accessed 14 February 2014).
19 *BBC News*, 4 November 2013, http://www.bbc.co.uk/news/business-24808012 (accessed 14 February 2014).

89 per cent, LG 84 per cent, Nokia 82 per cent, Motorola/HTC 80 per cent and BlackBerry 54 per cent.[20] John Chen has previously turned ailing Sybase around. Doing that he said in 2009 that: "CEOs find win-win situations, thread the needle and move on. There will be ups and downs and choppiness. It is never smooth sailing".[21]

John Chen quickly dismisses BlackBerry's chief financial officer, chief marketing officer and chief operating officer. On this occasion he says these changes are aimed at refining BlackBerry's strategy "to ensure we deliver the best devices, mobile security and device management. I look forward to working more directly with the talented teams of engineers, and the sales and marketing teams around the world to facilitate the BlackBerry turnaround and to drive innovation".[22] In an open letter[23] to BlackBerry's enterprise customers, published on their own website, John Chen insists that their investments in BlackBerry infrastructure and technology is safe, as he plans for BlackBerry to be around in the future. He states that the BB10 operating system and BlackBerry Messenger is ideally suited for BYOD policies, that they still have the most secure messenger system and the firm has enough cash to survive. Meanwhile, recent download data reveals that the BlackBerry Messenger app for iOS and Android is the most downloaded app of its kind in Asia.[24]

John Chen also announces a strategic alliance with Foxconn, with the latter going to take care of BlackBerry's manufacturing needs, initially for Asian markets. As he says:

> This partnership demonstrates BlackBerry's commitment to the device market for the long-term and our determination to remain the innovation leader in secure end-to-end mobile solutions. Partnering with Foxconn allows BlackBerry to focus on what we do best – iconic design, world-class security, software development and enterprise mobility management – while simultaneously addressing fast-growing markets leveraging Foxconn's scale and efficiency that will allow us to compete more effectively.[25]

BlackBerry simultaneously announces that the third quarter has generated an operational loss of US$354 million, with revenue going down from US$2.73 billion to US$1.19 billion. BlackBerry shares go up on the announcement of the Foxconn deal. One commentator asserts that: "The bet here is that BlackBerry can transition to what is essentially an enterprise software company, focused on providing messaging and communications services to corporate customers that prioritize reliability and security".[26]

20 *Forbes*, 7 November 2013, http://www.forbes.com/sites/robertpassikoff/2013/11/05/blackberry-brand-re-boot-boots-ceo/ (accessed 14 February 2014).

21 *Forbes*, 11 November 2013, http://www.forbes.com/sites/bobegan/2013/11/04/blackberry-has-a-new-chief-whats-next/ (accessed 14 February 2014).

22 *BBC News*, 26 November 2013, http://www.bbc.co.uk/news/business-25098970 (accessed 14 February 2014).

23 Open Letter to our Enterprise Customers, 2 December 2013, http://bizblog.blackberry.com/2013/12/john-chen-open-letter/ (accessed 14 February 2014).

24 *Forbes*, 4 December 2013, http://www.forbes.com/sites/terokuittinen/2013/12/04/blackberrys-november-triumph-exclusive-new-bbm-download-data/ (accessed 14 February 2014).

25 *BBC News*, 20 December 2013, http://www.bbc.co.uk/search/news/?q=blackberry%20and%20foxconn (accessed 14 February 2014).

26 *Forbes*, 26 December 2013, http://www.forbes.com/sites/panosmourdoukoutas/2013/12/26/will-an-old-strategy-turn-blackberry-business-around/ (accessed 14 February 2014).

However, there is also some speculation that BlackBerry will move away from mobile phones to concentrate on a new piece of software.[27] The company's QNX software is a new operating system for use in cars, communication hardware and industrial goods, opening the company up to many more applications than simply mobile phones.

At the beginning of 2014, BlackBerry confirms that it now sees itself as serving a niche market with smartphones for business users, with keyboards and security as its distinguishable features.[28] BlackBerry shares rise 26 per cent on this news, whilst competitor shares remain flat. This is an acknowledgement that last year's Z10 touchscreen phone was a mistake. BlackBerry even sues Typo, which is selling an iPhone case with an in-built keyboard, for infringing BlackBerry's design rights. John Chen says: "[The] keyboard is our identity. If you copy our keyboard, of course we need to assert that right. If somebody wants to license it they're welcome to do that, but they can't just take it".[29]

In an interview, John Chen explains about his plans for the company.[30] As he sees it:

> In the short term there are enough users of serious computing – meaning this is what they do for their living, this is how they operate – that want a keyboard. You have CEOs of major companies who whip out their BlackBerrys because of the keyboard. They don't care about apps. And, by the way, from a security point of view I'm starting to worry about where these apps are actually coming from. There's a huge market segment out there for any regulated industry. Governments, financial services, health care. I think we can go capture those and become a winner. I have two companies in Europe now that have reversed their policies on letting people bring their own devices to work. It presents too much of a security risk. After Angela Merkel was hacked she moved straight to a BlackBerry.

In the long term he sees that: "The devices will change, but the need for security, productivity and communication will continue to grow. These are the three building blocks of all things internet".

27 *Forbes*, 20 December 2013, http://www.forbes.com/sites/sarahcohen/2013/12/20/blackberry-gives-glimpses-of-turnaround-strategy/ (accessed 14 February 2014).
28 *Forbes*, 22 January 2014, http://www.forbes.com/sites/briansolomon/2014/01/22/blackberry-continues-surprising-surge-as-it-refocuses-on-keyboards-business/ (accessed 14 February 2014).
29 *Forbes*, 9 January 2014, http://www.forbes.com/sites/parmyolson/2014/01/09/ceo-says-blackberry-sued-typo-because-the-keyboard-is-our-identity/ (accessed 14 February 2014).
30 *Forbes*, 12 February 2014, http://www.forbes.com/sites/richkarlgaard/2014/02/12/john-chen-speaks-on-saving-blackberry/ (accessed 14 February 2014).

References

Abell, D. F. (1980). *Defining the Business: The Starting Point of Strategic Planning*. Englewood Cliffs, NJ: Prentice Hall.

Ackermann, F. and Eden, C. (2011). *Making Strategy: Mapping Out Strategic Success* (2nd ed.). London: Sage.

Adler, P. S. and Borys, B. (1993). Meterialism and idealism in organizational research. *Organization Studies*, 14(5), 657–79.

Amit, R. and Schoemaker, P. J. H. (1993). Strategic assets and organizational rent. *Strategic Management Journal*, 14, 33–46.

Ansoff, H. I. (1965). *Corporate Strategy*. New York: McGraw Hill.

Ansoff, H. I. (1991). Critique of Henry Mintzberg's 'the design school': reconsidering the basic premises of strategic management. *Strategic Management Journal*, 12, 449–61.

Ansoff, H. I. (1994). Comment on Henry Mintzberg's rethinking strategic planning. *Long Range Planning*, 27(3), 31–32.

Arend, R. J. and Bromiley, P. (2009). Assessing the dynamic capabilities view: Spare change, everyone? *Strategic Organization*, 7(1), 75–90.

Baden-Fuller, C. and Stopford, J. M. (1994). *Rejuvenating the Mature Business*. Cambridge, MA: Harvard Business School Press.

Bagwell, P. S. (1955). The rivalry and working union of the South Eastern and London, Chatham and Dover Railways. *Journal of Transport History*, 2(2), 33–45.

Balogun, J. and Johnson, G. (2005). From intended strategies to unintended outcomes: The impact of change recipient sensemaking. *Organization Studies*, 26(11), 1573–1601.

Barney, J. (1986). Strategic factor markets: Expectations, luck, and business strategy. *Management Science*, 32(10).

Barney, J. (1991). Firm resoures and sustained competitive advantage. *Journal of Management*, 17(1), 99–120.

Bartlett, C. A. and Ghoshal, S. (1992). *Transnational Management: Text, Cases and Readings in Cross-Border Management*. Homewood, IL: Irwin.

Bennis, W. and Nanus, B. (1985). *Leaders: The Strategies for Taking Charge*. New York: Harper & Row.

Benson, J. K. (1977). Organizations: A dialectical view. *Administrative Science Quarterly*, 22, 1–21.

Biggadike, E. R. (1981). The contributions of marketing to strategic management. *Academy of Management Review*, 6(4), 621–32.

Birkinshaw, J., Hood, N. and Jonsson, S. (1998). Building firm-specific advantages in multinational corporations: The role of subsidiary initiative. *Strategic Management Journal*, 19, 221–41.

Bower, J. L. (1970). *Managing the Resource Allocation Process*. Cambridge, MA: Harvard University Press.

Burgelman, R. A. (1983). A process model on internal corporate venturing in the diversified major firm. *Administrative Science Quarterly*, 28, 223–44.

Burrell, G. and Morgan, G. (1979). *Sociological Paradigms and Organizational Analysis*. London: Heinemann.

Burt, S., Johansson, U. and Thelander, Å. (2011). Standardized marketing strategies in retailing? IKEA's marketing strategies in Sweden, the UK and China. *Journal of Retailing and Consumer Services*, 18, 183–93.

Campbell, A. (1987). Mission statements. *Long Range Planning*, 30(6), 931–32.

Chaffee, E. E. (1985). Three models of strategy. *Academy of Management Review*, 10(1), 89–98.

Child, J. (1972). Organisational structure, environment and performance: The role of strategic choice. *Sociology*, 6(1), 1–22.

Christensen, C. R., Andrews, K. R. and Bower, J. L. (1973). *Business Policy: Text and Cases* (3rd ed.). Homewood, IL: Richard D Irwin.

Clarkson, M. B. E. (1995). A stakeholder framework for analyzing and evaluating corporate social performance. *Academy of Management Review*, 20(1), 92–117.

Coase, R. H. (1937). The nature of the firm. *Economica*, 4(16), 386–405.

Cyert, R. L. and March, J. G. (1963). *A Behavioral Theory of the Firm*. Englewood Cliffs, NJ: Prentice Hall.

D'Aveni, R. (1994). *Hypercompetition: Managing the Dynamics of Strategic Maneuvering*. New York: Free Press.

Das, T. K. and Teng, B.-S. (2000). A resource-based theory of strategic alliances. *Journal of Management*, 26(1), 31–61.

Day, G. S. (1981). Strategic market analysis and definition: An integrated approach. *Strategic Management Journal*, 2, 281–99.

Day, G. S. (1994). The capabilities of market-driven organizations. *Journal of Marketing*, 58, 37–52.

de Rond, M. and Thietart, R.-A. (2007). Choice, chance, and inevitability in strategy. *Strategic Management Journal*, 28, 535–51.

Dierickx, I. and Cool, K. (1989). Asset stock accumulation and sustainability of competitive advantage. *Management Science*, 35(12), 1504–11.

DiMaggio, P. J. (1988). Interest and agency in institutional theory. In L. Zucker (ed.), *Institutional Patterns and Organizations* (pp. 3–32). Cambridge, MA: Ballinger.

DiMaggio, P. J. and Powell, W. W. (1983). The iron cage revisited: Institutional isomorphism and collective rationality in organizational fields. *American Sociological Review*, 48(2), 147–60.

Donaldson, T. and Preston, L. E. (1995). The stakeholder theory of the corporation: Concepts, evidence, and implications. *Academy of Management Review*, 20(1), 65–91.

Dutton, J. E., Ashford, S. J., O'Neill, R. M. and Lawrence, K. A. (2001). Moves that matter: Issue selling and organizational change. *Academy of Management Journal*, 44(4), 716–36.

Easterby-Smith, M., Lyles, M. and Peteraf, M. A. (2009). Dynamic capability: Current debates and future directions. *British Journal of Management*, 20, S1–S8.

Eisenhardt, K. M. and Martin, J. A. (2000). Dynamic capabilities: What are they? *Strategic Management Journal*, 21, 1105–21.

Eisenhardt, K. M. and Zbaracki, M. J. (1992). Strategic decision making. *Strategic Management Journal*, 13, 17–37.

Elbanna, S. (2006). Strategic decision-making: Process perspectives. *International Journal of Management Reviews*, 8(1), 1–20.

Emerson, R. M. (1962). Power-dependence relations. *American Journal of Sociology*, 27(1), 31–41.

Etzioni, A. (1964). *Modern Organizations*. Englewood Cliffs, NJ: Prentice Hall.

Faulkner, D. and Bowman, C. (1992). Generic strategies and congruent organizational structures: Some suggestions. *European Management Journal*, 10(4), 494–9.

Fine, G. A. (1984). Negotiated orders and organizational cultures. *Annual Review of Sociology*, 10, 239–62.

Fleming, A. I. M., McKinstry, S. and Wallace, K. (2000). The decline and fall of the North British Locomotive Company, 1940–62: Mismanagement or institutional failure? *Business History*, 42(4), 67–90.

Ford, J. D., Ford, L. W. and D'Amelio, A. (2008). Resistence to change: The rest of the story. *Academy of Management Review*, 33(2), 377–382.

Freeman, R. E. (1984). *Strategic Management: A Stakeholder Approach*. Boston, MA: Pitman.

Freeman, R. E. and Reed, D. L. (1983). Stockholders and stakeholders: A new perspective on corporate governance. *California Management Review*, 25(3), 88–106.

Friedman, M. (1970, December 13). The social responsibility of business is to increase its profits. *New York Times Magazine*.

Frooman, J. (1999). Stakeholder influence strategies. *Academy of Management Review*, 24(2), 191–205.

Garud, R., Jain, S. and Kumaraswamy, A. (2002). Institutional entrepreneurship in the sponsorship of common technological standards: The case of Sun Microsystems and Java. *Academy of Management Journal*, 45(1), 196–214.

Goldblatt, H. (1999, November 8). Cisco's secrets. *Fortune*, 177–84.

Grant, R. M. (1991). The Resource-based theory of competitive advantage: Implications for strategy formulation. *California Management Review*, 33(3), 114–35.

Grant, R. M. (1996). Toward a knowledge-based theory of the firm. *Strategic Management Journal*, 17, 109–22.

Greenwood, R. and Hinings, C. R. (1988). Orgnizational design types, tracks and the dynamics of strategic change. *Organization Studies*, 9(3), 293–316.

Greenwood, R., Oliver, C., Sahlin, K. and Suddaby, R. (2008). Introduction. In R. Greenwood, C. Oliver, K. Sahlin and R. Suddaby (eds.), *The SAGE Handbook of Organizational Institutionalism* (pp. 1–46). Los Angeles, CA: Sage.

Grinyer, P. H., Mayes, D. and McKiernan, P. (1988). *Sharpbenders: The Secrets of Unleashing Corporate Potential*. Oxford: Basil Blackwell.

Hamel, G. and Prahalad, C. K. (1994). *Competing for the Future*. Boston, MA: Harvard Business School Press.

Hargadon, A. B. and Douglas, Y. (2001). When innovations meet institutions: Edison and the design of the electric light. *Administrative Science Quarterly*, 46, 476–501.

Haselhoff, F. (1977). *Ondernemingsstrategie, een dilemma: de moderne ondernemingsorganisatie in het spanningsveld van doelmatigheid, overleving en zingeving*. Alphen aan de Rijn: Samson.

Haveman, H. A. and Rao, H. (1997). Structuring a theory of moral sentiments: Institutional and organizational coevolution in the early thrift industry. *American Journal of Sociology*, 102(6), 1606–51.

Helfat, C. E., Finkelstein, S., Mitchell, W., Peteraf, M. A., Singh, H., Teece, D. J. and Winter, S. G. (2007). *Dynamic Capabilities: Understanding Strategic Change in Organizations*. Malden, MA: Blackwell.

Helfat, C. E. and Peteraf, M. A. (2009). Understanding dynamic capabilities: Progress along a developmental path. *Strategic Organization*, 7(1), 91–102.

Henderson, B. (1984). *The Logic of Business Strategy*. Cambridge, MA: Ballinger.

Hickson, D. J., Butler, R. J., Cray, D., Mallory, G. R. and Wilson, D. C. (1986). *Top Decisions: Strategic Decision-Making in Organizations*. Oxford: Basil Blackwell.

Hillman, A. J. and Keim, G. D. (2001). Shareholder value, stakeholder management, and social issues: What's the bottom line? *Strategic Management Journal*, 22, 125–39.

Hinings, C. R. and Greenwood, R. (1988). *The Dynamics of Strategic Change*. Oxford: Basil Blackwell.

Hitt, M. A. and Ireland, R. D. (2000). The intersection of entrepreneurship and strategic management research. In D. L. Sexton and H. A. Landstrom (eds.), *Handbook of Entrepreneurship* (pp. 45–63). Oxford: Basil Blackwell.

Hitt, M. A., Ireland, R. D., Camp, S. M. and Sexton, D. L. (2001). Guest editor's introduction to the special issue strategic entrepreneurship: Entrepreneurial strategies for wealth creation. *Strategic Management Journal*, 22, 479–91.

Hodgkinson, G. P., Whittington, R., Johnson, G. and Schwarz, M. (2006). The role of strategy workshops in strategy development processes: Formality, communication, co-ordination and inclusion. *Long Range Planning*, 39, 479–96.

Hofer, C. W. (1975). Toward a contingency theory of business strategy. *Academy of Management Review*, 18(4), 784–810.

Hofer, C. W. and Schendel, D. E. (1978). *Strategy Formulation: Analytical Concepts*. Minneapolis / St Paul, MN: West Publishing.

Hrebiniak, L. G. (2006). Obstacles to effective strategy implementation. *Organizational Dynamics*, 35(1), 12–31.

Huff, A. S. and Reger, R. K. (1987). A review of strategic process research. *Journal of Management*, 13(2), 211–36.

Hunt, S. D. and Lambe, C. J. (2000). Marketing's contribution to business strategy: Market orientation, relationship marketing and resource-advantage theory. *International Journal of Management Reviews*, 2(1), 17–43.

Hutzschenreuter, T. and Kleindienst, I. (2006). Strategy-process research: What have we learned and what is still to be explored. *Journal of Management*, 32(5), 673–720.

Jarzabkowski, P. A. and Balogun, J. (2009). The practice and process of delivering integration through strategic planning. *Journal of Management Studies*, 46(8), 1255–88.

Jensen, M. C. and Meckling, W. H. (1976). Theory of the firm: Managerial behavior, agency costs and ownership structure. *Journal of Financial Economics*, 3, 305–60.

Johnson, G. (1987). *Strategic Change and the Management Process*. Oxford: Basil Blackwell.

Johnson, G. (1988). Rethinking incrementalism. *Strategic Management Journal*, 9, 75–91.

Johnson, G., Whittington, R. and Scholes, K. (2011). *Exploring Strategy: Text & Cases* (9th ed.). Harlow: Prentice Hall.

Kiechel III, W. (1982, December 27). Corporate strategist under fire. *Fortune*, 34–39.

Kiechel III, W. (1984). Sniping at strategic planning. *Planning Review* (May), 8–11.

Kogut, B. and Zander, U. (1992). Knowledge of the firm, combinative capabilities, and the replication of technology. *Organization Science*, 3(3), 383–97.

Kotler, P. (1976). *Marketing Management*. Englewood Cliffs, NJ: Prentice Hall.

Kraaijenbrink, J., Spender, J.-C. and Groen, A. J. (2010). The resource-based view: A review and assessment of its critiques. *Journal of Management*, 36(1), 349–72.

Lawrence, T. B. (1999). Institutional strategy. *Journal of Management*, 25(2), 161–88.

Lawrence, T. B. and Suddaby, R. (2006). Institutions and institutional work. In S. R. Clegg, C. Hardy and T. Lawrence (eds.), *Handbook of Organization Studies* (2nd ed., pp. 215–55). London: Sage.

Learned, E. P., Christensen, C. R., Andrews, K. and Guth, W. D. (1965). *Business Policy: Text and Cases*. Homewood, IL: Richard D Irwin.

Leblebici, H., Salancik, G. R., Copay, A. and King, T. (1991). Institutional change and the transformation of interorganizational fields: An organizational history of the US radio broadcasting industry. *Administrative Science Quarterly*, 36, 333–63.

Lenz, R. T. and Lyles, M. (1985). Paralysis by analysis: Is your planning system becoming too rational? *Long Range Planning*, 18, 28–36.

Leonard-Barton, D. (1992). Core capabilities and core rigidities: A paradox in managing new product development. *Strategic Management Journal*, 13, 111–25.

Levitt, T. (1960). Marketing myopia. *Harvard Business Review* (July/August), 45–56.

Levitt, T. (1965). Exploit the product life cycle. *Harvard Business Review* (November/December), 81–94.

Levitt, T. (1983). The globalization of markets. *Harvard Business Review* (May/June), 92–102.

Lewin, K. (1945). The research center for group dynamics at Massachusetts Institute of Technology. *Sociometry*, 8, 126–35.

Lorsch, J. W. (1986). Strategic myopia: Culture as an invisible barrier to change. *California Management Review*, 28, 95–109.

Lounsbury, M. (2001). Institutional sources of practice variation: Staffing college and university recycling programs. *Administrative Science Quarterly*, 46, 29–56.

Mahoney, J. T. and Pandian, J. R. (1992). The resource-based view within the conversation of strategic management. *Strategic Management Journal*, 13, 363–80.

Mair, A. (1999). Learning from Honda. *Journal of Management Studies*, 36(1), 25–44.

March, J. G. (1991). Exploration and exploitation in organizational learning. *Organization Science*, 2(2), 71–87.

Maritan, C. A. and Peteraf, M. A. (2011). Building a bridge between resource acquisition and resource accumulation. *Journal of Management*, 37(5), 1374–89.

Mellahi, K., Jackson, P. and Sparks, L. (2002). An exploratory study into failure in successful organizations: The case of Marks & Spencer. *British Journal of Management*, 13, 15–29.

Meyer, J. W. and Rowan, B. (1977). Institutionalized organizations: Formal structure as myth and ceremony. *American Journal of Sociology*, 83(2).

Meyerson, D. and Martin, J. (1987). Cultural change: An integration of three different views. *Journal of Management Studies*, 24(6), 623–47.

Mintzberg, H. (1973). *The Nature of Managerial Work*. Englewood Cliffs, NJ: Prentice Hall.

Mintzberg, H. (1987). The strategy concept I: Five Ps for strategy. *California Management Review*, 30(1), 11–24.

Mintzberg, H. (1990). The design school: Reconsidering the basic premises of strategic management. *Strategic Management Journal*, 11, 171–95.

Mintzberg, H. (1991). Learning 1, Planning 0: Reply to Igor Ansoff. *Strategic Management Journal*, 12, 463–66.

Mintzberg, H. (1994a). Rethinking strategic planning part I: Pitfalls and fallacies. *Long Range Planning*, 27(3), 12–21.

Mintzberg, H. (1994b). Rethinking strategic planning part II: New roles for planners. *Long Range Planning*, 27(3), 22–30.

Mintzberg, H., Ahlstrand, B. and Lampel, J. (1998). *Strategy Safari: A Guided Tour Through the Wilds of Strategic Management*. London: Prentice Hall.

Mintzberg, H., Pascale, R. T., Goold, M. and Rumelt, R. P. (1996). The "Honda effect" revisited. *California Management Review*, 38(4), 78–117.

Mintzberg, H., Raisinghani, D. and Théorêt, A. (1976). The structure of "unstructured" decision processes. *Administrative Science Quarterly*, 21, 246–75.

Mintzberg, H. and Waters, J. A. (1985). Of strategies, deliberate and emergent. *Strategic Management Journal*, 6, 257–72.

Mintzberg, H., Waters, J. A., Pettigrew, A. M. and Butler, R. J. (1990). Studying deciding: An exchange of views between Mintzberg and Waters, Pettigrew, and Butler. *Organization Studies*, 11(1), 1–16.

Mitchell, R. K., Agle, B. R. and Wood, D. J. (1997). Towards a theory of stakeholder identification and salience: Defining the principle of who and what really counts. *Academy of Management Review*, 22(4), 853–86.

Montgomery, C. A. (2008). Putting leadership back into strategy. *Harvard Business Review* (January), 54–60.

Morgan, G. (1980). Paradigms, metaphors, and puzzle solving in organization theory. *Administrative Science Quarterly*, 25, 605–22.

Munir, K. A. and Phillips, N. (2005). The birth of the 'Kodak moment': Institutional entrepreneurship and the adoption of new technologies. *Organization Studies*, 26(11), 1665–87.

Narayanan, V. K. and Liam, F. (1982). The micro-politics of strategy formulation. *Academy of Management Review*, 7(1), 25–34.

Nelson, R. R. and Winter, S. G. (1982). *An Evolutionary Theory of Economic Change*. Cambridge, MA: Harvard University Press.

Noble, C. (1999). The eclectic roots of strategy implementation research. *Journal of Business Research*, 45, 119–34.

O'Reilly III, C. A. and Tushman, M. L. (2004). The ambidextrous organization. *Harvard Business Review* (April), 74–81.

Oliver, C. (1991). Strategic responses to institutional processes. *Academy of Management Review*, 16(1), 145–79.

Pascale, R. T. (1984). The real story behind Honda's success. *California Management Review*, 26(3), 47–72.

Penrose, E. (1959). *The Theory of the Growth of the Firm*. New York: Wiley.

Peteraf, M. A. (1993). The cornerstones of competitive advantage: A resource-based view. *Strategic Management Journal*, 14, 179–91.

Peteraf, M. A. and Barney, J. (2003). Unraveling the resource-based tangle. *Managerial and Decision Economics*, 24, 309–23.

Pettigrew, A. M. (1973). *The Politics of Organizational Decision Making*. London/Assen: Tavistock/Van Gorcum.

Pettigrew, A. M. (1985). *The Awakening Giant: Continuity and Change in ICI*. Oxford: Basil Blackwell.

Pettigrew, A. M. (1987). Context and action in the transformation of the firm. *Journal of Management Studies*, 24(6), 649–70.

Pettigrew, A. M. (1990). Longitudinal field research on change: Theory and practice. *Organization Science*, 1(3), 267–92.

Pettigrew, A. M., Thomas, H. and Whittington, R. (2002). Strategic management: The strengths and limitations of a field. In A. M. Pettigrew, H. Thomas and R. Whittington (eds.), *Handbook of Strategic Management* (pp. 3–29). London: Sage.

Pettigrew, A. M. and Whipp, R. (1991). *Managing Change for Competitive Success*. Oxford: Basil Blackwell.

Pettigrew, A. M., Woodman, R. W. and Cameron, K. S. (2001). Studying organizational change and development: Challenges for future research. *Academy of Management Journal*, 44(4), 697–713.

Pfeffer, J. and Salancik, G. R. (1978). *The External Control of Organizations: A Resource Dependence Perspective*. New York: Harper & Row.

Polanyi, M. (1967). *The Tacit Dimension*. Garden City, NY: Anchor Books.

Porac, J. F., Thomas, H. and Baden-Fuller, C. (1989). Competitive groups as cognitive communities: The case of Scottish knitwear manufacturers. *Journal of Management Studies*, 26(4), 397–416.

Porter, M. E. (1980). *Competitive Strategy: Techniques for Analyzing Industries and Competitors*. New York: Free Press.

Porter, M. E. (1981). The contributions of industrial organization to strategic management. *Academy of Management Review*, 6(4), 609–20.

Porter, M. E. (1985). *Competitive Advantage: Creating and Sustaining Superior Performance*. New York: Free Press.

Porter, M. E. (1990). *The Competitive Advantage of Nations*. New York: Free Press.

Porter, M. E. (1991). Towards a dynamic theory of strategy. *Strategic Management Journal*, 12, 95–117.

Porter, M. E. (ed.). (1986). *Competition in Global Industries*. Boston, MA: Harvard Business School Press.

Prahalad, C. K. and Bettis, R. A. (1986). The dominant logic: A new linkage between diversity and performance. *Strategic Management Journal*, 7, 485–501.

Prahalad, C. K. and Hamel, G. (1990). The core competence of the corporation. *Harvard Business Review* (May/June), 79–91.

Quinn, J. B. (1980). *Strategies for Change: Logical Incrementalism*. Homewood, IL: Richard D Irwin.

Rappaport, A. (1986). *Creating Shareholder Value: The New Standard of Business Performance*. New York: Free Press.

Reed, R. and Defillippi, R. J. (1990). Causal ambiguity, barriers to imitation, and sustainable competitive advantage. *Academy of Management Review*, 15(1), 88–102.

Reger, R. K. and Huff, A. S. (1993). Strategic groups: A cognitive perspective. *Strategic Management Journal*, 14, 103–24.

Regnér, P. (2003). Strategy creation in the periphery: Inductive versus deductive strategy making. *Journal of Management Studies*, 40(1), 57–82.

Rockart, J. F. (1979). Chief executives define their own data needs. *Harvard Business Review* (March/April), 81–93.

Rumelt, R. P., Schendel, D. E. and Teece, D. J. (eds.). (1994). *Fundamental Issues in Strategy: A Research Agenda.* Boston, MA: Harvard Business School Press.

Samra-Fredericks, D. (2003). Strategizing as lived experience and strategists' everyday efforts to shape strategic direction. *Journal of Management Studies*, 40(1), 141–74.

Schein, E. H. (1992). *Organizational Culture and Leadership* (2nd ed.). San Francisco, CA: Jossey-Bass.

Schoenberg, R. (2003). Mergers and acquisitions: Motives, value creation, and implementation. In D. Faulkner and A. Campbell (eds.), *The Oxford Handbook of Strategy* (Vol. 2, pp. 95–117). Oxford: Oxford University Press.

Schumpeter, J. A. (1934). *The Theory of Economic Development.* Cambridge, MA: Harvard University Press.

Schwenk, C. R. (1984). Cognitive simplification processes in strategic decision-making. *Strategic Management Journal*, 5, 111–28.

Scott, W. R. (1995). *Institutions and Organizations.* Thousand Oaks, CA: Sage.

Seo, M.-G. and Creed, W. E. D. (2002). Institutional contradictions, praxis, and institutional change: A dialectical perspective. *Academy of Management Review*, 27(2), 222–47.

Simon, H. A. (1957). *Models of Man: Social and Rational.* New York: John Wiley & Sons.

Sims, H. P. and Gioia, D. A. (eds.). (1986). *The Thinking Organization.* San Francisco, CA: Jossey Bass.

Sminia, H. (1994). *Turning the Wheels of Change.* Groningen: Wolters-Noordhoff.

Sminia, H. (2003). The failure of the Sport7 TV-channel: Controversies in a business network. *Journal of Management Studies*, 40(7), 1621–49.

Sminia, H. (2005). Strategy formation as layered discussion. *Scandinavian Journal of Management*, 21, 267–91.

Sminia, H. (2009). Process research in strategy formation: Theory, methodology and relevance. *International Journal of Management Reviews*, 11(1), 97–125.

Sminia, H. (2011). Institutional continuity and the Dutch construction industry fiddle. *Organization Studies*, 32(11), 1559–85.

Sminia, H. and de Rond, M. (2012). Context and action in the transformation of strategy scholarship. *Journal of Management Studies*, 49(7), 1329–49.

Smircich, L. and Stubbart, C. (1985). Strategic management in an enacted world. *Academy of Management Review*, 10(4), 724–36.

Spender, J.-C. (1989). *Industry Recipes: An Enquiry into the Nature and Sources of Managerial Judgement.* Oxford: Basil Blackwell.

Stulz, R. M. (1999). Globalization, corporate finance, and the cost of capital. *Journal of Applied Corporate Finance*, 12(3), 8–25.

Sturgeon, T., Van Biesebroeck, J. and Gereffi, G. (2008). Value chains, networks and clusters: Reframing the global automotive industry. *Journal of Economic Geography*, 8, 297–321.

Suchman, M. C. (1995). Managing legitimacy: Strategic and institutional approaches. *Academy of Management Review*, 20(3), 571–610.

Teece, D. J., Pisano, G. and Shuen, A. (1997). Dynamic capabilities and strategic management. *Strategic Management Journal*, 18, 509–33.

Thompson, A., Strickland III, A. J. and Gamble, J. (2013). *Crafting & Executing Strategy: Concepts and Readings* (19th ed.). New York: McGraw Hill.

Trompenaars, F. and Hampden-Turner, C. (2004). *Managing People Across Cultures.* Oxford: Capstone.

Tversky, A. and Kahneman, D. (1974). Judgement under uncertainty: Heuristics and biases. *Science*, 185, 1124–31.

Van de Ven, A. H. (1989). Nothing is quite so practical as a good theory. *Academy of Management Review*, 14(4), 486–89.

Van de Ven, A. H. and Poole, M. S. (1995). Explaining development and change in organizations. *Academy of Management Review*, 20(3), 510–40.

Van de Ven, A. H. and Sminia, H. (2012). Aligning process questions, perspectives, and explanations. In M. Schultz, S. Maguire, A. Langley and H. Tsoukas (eds.), *Constructing Identity In and Around Organizations* (pp. 306–19). Oxford: Oxford University Press.

van der Heijden, K. (1996). *Scenarios: The Art of Strategic Conversation.* Chichester: Wiley.

Watson, T. J. (1994). *In Search of Management: Culture, Chaos & Control in Managerial Work.* London: Routledge.

Weick, K. E. (1989). Theory construction as disciplined imagination. *Academy of Management Review*, 14(4), 516–31.

Wernerfelt, B. (1984). A resource-based view of the firm. *Strategic Management Journal*, 5(2), 171–80.

Whipp, R. (1996). Creative deconstruction: Strategy and organizations. In S. R. Clegg, C. Hardy and W. R. Nord (eds.), *Handbook of Organization Studies* (pp. 261–75). London: Sage.

Whipp, R. (2003). Managing strategic change. In D. Faulkner and A. Campbell (eds.), *The Oxford Handbook of Strategy* (pp. 729–58). Oxford: Oxford University Press.

Whittington, R. (1993). *What Is Strategy – and Does It Matter?* London: Routledge.

Whittington, R. (2006). Completing the practice turn in strategy research. *Organization Studies*, 27(5), 613–34.

Wilson, D. C. (1982). Electricity and resistance: A case study of innovation and politics. *Organization Studies*, 3(2), 119–40.

Womack, J. P., Jones, D. T. and Roos, D. (1990). *The Machine That Changed The World.* New York: Rawson.

Wood, D. J. (1991). Corporate social performance revisited. *Academy of Management Review*, 16(4), 691–718.

Index